Microsoft Certified
Azure Fundamentals
Study Guide

Microsoft Certified
Azure Fundamentals

Study Guide

Exam AZ-900

Jim Boyce

A Wiley Brand

Acknowledgments

I've written more than 60 books over the past 30+ years, and each has been a unique experience. With every book, however, success comes from a team approach. Once again, I need to thank the members of the team who helped bring this book together.

First, thanks to Kenyon Brown for bringing me this opportunity and helping to get it off the ground. Thanks also to my agent, Carole Jelen, for all she has done through the years and for this project. Many thanks also to John Sleeva, the book's project editor, and to Rob Tidrow, the technical editor for this project and a partner in crime throughout most of my writing career. Special thanks to Victoria Hester, one of my peers at Microsoft, for taking the time out of her busy schedule to also review the content. Finally, thanks go to Liz Welch, the book's copyeditor, to Louise Watson, the proofreader, and to Saravanan Dakshinamurthy for helping polish the rough content. Thanks also to all of the people who push the buttons and move the levers to turn words on virtual paper into a finished product.

About the Author

Jim Boyce has been involved in IT since the late 1970s in a wide range of roles. He has been a structural steel designer, CAD operator and trainer, college instructor, consultant, ISP owner, and freelance author. He was a director at Xerox, where he managed globally distributed teams providing managed services for Windows Server and collaboration platforms, including SharePoint and Documentum. Over the past 10 years, Jim has held multiple roles as an individual contributor and people manager at Microsoft, including Technical Account Manager, Delivery Management Manager, and now Customer Success Account Manager. In a writing career spanning over 30 years, Jim has written more than 60 books and upwards of a thousand articles for many print and online publications, including *InfoWorld*, TechRepublic.com, *WINDOWS Magazine*, and Microsoft.com. He has also created video training content for WatchIT and Lynda.com. In his spare time, he is a building inspector for his small town; works on construction and woodworking projects; flies model aircraft, drones, and full-sized aircraft; and participates as a coach and unified player for Special Olympics.

About the Technical Editor

Rob Tidrow works as an information technology consultant in the education field. He has been working with technologies professionally for more than 25 years, including operating systems, cloud-based technologies, databases, mobile devices, networking, security, and more. He has written over 15 books and contributed to over 30 books. His focus is on Microsoft Windows, Microsoft Azure, Microsoft 365, and SharePoint. He resides in Richmond, Indiana, IN and can be reached at robtidrow@yahoo.com.

Contents at a Glance

Introduction   *xix*

Assessment Test   *xxxii*

Chapter 1   Cloud Concepts   1

Chapter 2   Azure Core Services   25

Chapter 3   Azure Core Networking Services   59

Chapter 4   Security, Compliance, Privacy, and Trust   75

Chapter 5   Azure Solutions   123

Chapter 6   Azure Pricing, Service Levels, and Lifecycle   137

Chapter 7   Creating and Managing Azure Resources   157

Appendix   Answers to Review Questions   179

Index   *193*

Contents

Introduction   *xix*

Assessment Test   *xxxii*

Chapter   1   Cloud Concepts   **1**

Understanding Cloud Computing   2
Benefits of Cloud Computing   4
    Economic Benefits   4
    Scalability and Elasticity   5
    High Availability   7
    Fault Tolerance   7
    Disaster Recovery   8
    Human Resources   9
Financial Models   9
Cloud Computing Models and Responsibilities   10
    Software-as-a-Service   10
    Infrastructure-as-a-Service   12
    Platform-as-a-Service   13
    Shared Responsibility   15
Public, Private, and Hybrid Cloud Models   16
    Public Cloud   16
    Private Cloud   17
    Hybrid Cloud   17
Summary   18
Exam Essentials   18
Review Questions   21

Chapter   2   Azure Core Services   **25**

Core Azure Architectural Components   26
    Geographies and Regions   26
    Availability Zones   28
    Bringing It All Together   30
    Resources and Resource Groups   31
    Azure Resource Manager   33
Azure Subscriptions and Billing Scope   33
    Azure Subscriptions   33
    Azure Billing Accounts   34
    Billing Scope   35
    Azure Tenants   37
Core Azure Services   37
    Virtual Machines   38

Virtual Machine Scale Sets	39
Availability Sets	40
Azure App Service	42
Azure Container Instances	42
Azure Kubernetes Service	43
Windows Virtual Desktop	44
Core Azure Storage	44
Blob Storage	44
Blob Storage Tiers	45
Disk Storage	45
File Storage	46
Storage Accounts	46
Core Data Services	47
Structured and Unstructured Data	47
Azure SQL Database	47
SQL Managed Instance	48
Cosmos DB	48
Azure Database for MySQL	49
Azure Database for PostgreSQL	49
Azure Database Migration Service	49
Microsoft Marketplace	50
Summary	50
Exam Essentials	51
Review Questions	53

Chapter 3	**Azure Core Networking Services**	**59**

Networking Concepts	60
Client-Server and Serverless Computing	60
Network Addressing	61
Domain Name System	61
Routing	63
Virtual Networks	63
Load Balancers	64
VPN Gateway	66
Azure VPN Gateway	67
ExpressRoute	68
Content Delivery Networks	69
Summary	70
Exam Essentials	71
Review Questions	72

Chapter 4	**Security, Compliance, Privacy, and Trust**	**75**

Network Security	77
Defense in Depth	77

Azure Firewall 78
Web Application Firewall 80
Network Security Groups 81
Application Security Groups 83
User-Defined Routes 83
Azure DDoS Protection 84
Authentication and Authorization 84
Azure Active Directory 84
Authentication and Authorization 86
Azure Multifactor Authentication 87
Conditional Access 87
Single Sign-On (SSO) 88
Security Tools and Features 88
Azure Security Center 88
Azure Key Vault 90
Azure Information Protection 91
Azure Advanced Threat Protection 91
Azure Sentinel 92
Azure Dedicated Hosts 92
Azure Governance Methodologies 93
Azure Policies 93
Azure Initiatives 94
Role-Based Access Control 94
Resource Locks 97
Azure Blueprints 97
Microsoft Cloud Adoption Framework for Azure 99
Azure Monitoring and Reporting Options 100
Azure Monitor 100
Azure Service Health 102
Azure Advisor 103
Compliance and Data Protection
Standards 105
Industry Compliance Standards and Terms 105
Microsoft Privacy Statement 106
Online Service Terms 107
Data Protection Addendum 107
Trust Center 107
Service Trust Portal 107
Compliance Manager 108
Azure Government 109
Azure China 109
Summary 110
Exam Essentials 111
Review Questions 114

Chapter	**5**	**Azure Solutions**	**123**
		Internet of Things (IoT)	124
		Azure IoT Hub	124
		Azure IoT Central	125
		Azure Sphere	126
		Artificial Intelligence	126
		Azure Machine Learning	127
		Azure Cognitive Services	128
		Azure Bot Service	128
		Serverless Computing	128
		Azure Functions	129
		Azure Logic Apps	129
		DevOps	130
		Azure DevOps Services	130
		GitHub and GitHub Actions	130
		Azure DevTest Labs	131
		Summary	131
		Exam Essentials	131
		Review Questions	133
Chapter	**6**	**Azure Pricing, Service Levels, and Lifecycle**	**137**
		Purchasing Azure Services	138
		Azure Subscriptions	138
		Purchasing Services	139
		Factors Affecting Cost	139
		Billing Zones	141
		Planning and Managing Azure Costs	141
		TCO Calculator	141
		Pricing Calculator	143
		Managing and Minimizing Azure Cost	144
		Azure Cost Management + Billing	148
		Service Level Agreements	149
		Composite SLAs	150
		Availability Zones	150
		Service Lifecycles	151
		Preview	151
		General Availability	151
		Summary	152
		Exam Essentials	152
		Review Questions	154
Chapter	**7**	**Creating and Managing Azure Resources**	**157**
		Azure Management Tools	158
		Azure Portal	158

Azure PowerShell   160
Azure CLI   161
Azure Cloud Shell   161
Azure Mobile App   162
Using ARM Templates   163
Bringing It All Together   163
Creating and Managing Resources   163
Creating a Free Subscription   164
Creating Resource Groups   165
Creating Azure Resources and Services   166
Deleting Resources and Services   174
Summary   175
Exam Essentials   175
Review Questions   177

Appendix   **Answers to Review Questions**   **179**

Chapter 1: Cloud Concepts   180
Chapter 2: Azure Core Services   181
Chapter 3: Azure Core Networking Services   184
Chapter 4: Security, Compliance, Privacy, and Trust   185
Chapter 5: Azure Solutions   189
Chapter 6: Azure Pricing, Service Levels, and Lifecycle   190
Chapter 7: Creating and Managing Azure Resources   192

Index   *193*

Introduction

I currently manage the support and proactive services experience for a portfolio of Microsoft customers, many of whom have either already made a significant transition from on-premises to Azure or are in the process of evaluating a move to Azure. I field questions daily about Azure services, deployment strategies, and proactive services designed to not only educate our customers on Azure and Microsoft 365, but also assist them in planning, deploying, and supporting their Azure and M365 workloads.

Continuing technical training is one of the commitments that most Microsoft employees make in addition to the core responsibilities of their roles. As part of that commitment, I completed the AZ-900 Microsoft Azure Fundamentals Certification. The certification helped broaden my background across the entire Azure service portfolio. It also reinforced my understanding that not only highly technical roles benefit from the training and certification—less technical roles benefit from the certification as well.

That's the approach we've taken for this book. The content is intended to help you understand the requirements of the AZ-900 Fundamentals exam and prepare to successfully pass the exam. The book does not go deep into Azure but rather focuses on core concepts, services, and resources in Azure that are covered by the exam objectives. The goal of the AZ-900 exam is not to give you a technical depth in Azure, but rather to give you a broad understanding that will enable you to understand the benefits that Azure offers and begin to integrate Azure into your role, whether technical or not.

Microsoft AZ-900 Certification Exam

Microsoft currently offers 17 certifications at many levels across the Azure cloud offering, ranging from fundamental to very technical. The AZ-900 exam and certification should be the first certification step in your Azure certification path if you do not yet have a fundamental understanding of cloud offerings and Azure in particular. So, whether you are interested in certification in Azure solutions, data, AI, or other areas, your certification path often begins with AZ-900.

The following section explores the certification paths and process in more detail.

How Do You Become Certified in Azure?

As explained earlier, Microsoft currently offers 17 certifications for Azure. Obviously, fundamentals is one certification area, but there are multiple certification paths for Azure administration, app development, data, AI, security, DevOps, IoT, and Azure Stack. These certifications are currently supported by 39 exams. Even if you plan to pursue certification in, for example, Azure IoT development, you should consider AZ-900 Fundamentals to give you a broader understanding of Azure; the knowledge you gain will supplement your understanding of your selected certification. It will also help you leverage and integrate additional Azure workloads in your area of specialization.

Becoming certified in Azure is relatively simple. Choose the certification you want to achieve, work through the prescribed learning path for the certification, prepare for the exam, and pass it. Preparation can take many forms, and this book is intended to be your primary one. People have different learning styles, varying backgrounds and experiences, differing amounts of time to study, and so on. So, this book might be one of a handful of resources you use to prepare for the exam.

To begin, work through the chapters of this book and develop a strong understanding of the questions and answers offered in each one. Practice does make perfect, so consider working through additional practice test options before taking the exam. Microsoft offers some knowledge checks online within the content at the following URL:

`docs.microsoft.com/en-us/learn/certifications/azure-fundamentals`

You will also find other sample test options online, some for free and some for a fee. All of them provide good additional preparation for the exam. The more questions you work through before taking the exam, the more likely you are to be successful on your first attempt.

Types of Exam Questions

We have tried to model the sample questions in this book on the types of questions you will see in the official AZ-900 exam. Because the test is online, however, some types of questions are difficult to model in print. The following sections explore the types of questions you will experience in the official, online AZ-900 exam.

Multiple Choice

These are generally straightforward and come in two variants. The first is a simple question followed by a selection of possible answers. The test question indicates whether there is a single answer or multiple correct answers. Each correct response counts toward your point total. Example (you would choose one answer):

1. Which one of the following provides container orchestration services for containers in Azure?

    A. Azure Container Instances (ACI)

    B. Azure Kubernetes

    C. Azure Logic Apps

    D. Azure Container Orchestration Services

Many multiple-choice questions are scenario based, describing a planning, deployment, or management scenario, followed by a question about the scenario. Example:

2. You are the IT director for Contoso Corporation. Your CIO has asked you to recommend a solution that will enable the development team to quickly deploy VMs for testing applications. The solution must provide flexibility but also result in the lowest cost. Which of the following solutions meets these requirements? (You would choose one or more correct solutions.)

Drag-and-Drop and Select Questions

Drag-and-drop questions provide a list of answers that you must match with a corresponding description. For example, the answers might include Disaster Recovery, Fault Tolerance, Low Latency, and Dynamic Scalability. You would drag each of these answers into a box beside the correct description of each.

Select questions describe a scenario and you must choose the correct answer from a drop-down list that typically offers three possible answers. Example:

3. Which cloud deployment model is used for Azure VMs and Azure SQL Database instances? (You would choose Infrastructure-as-a-Service from a drop-down list beside Azure VMs and choose Platform-as-a-Service from the drop-down list beside Azure SQL Database.)

Yes/No Questions

These questions typically include three questions related to a specific topic. You answer by selecting either Yes or No beside each one. Example (for each you would select either Yes or No):

4. Azure resources can access other resources only in the resource group in which they reside. Yes No

Deleting a resource group also deletes all resources in the group.   Yes No

A resource group can include resources from multiple Azure regions.   Yes No

Text Replacement Questions

These questions offer a statement with part of the statement underlined. The statements sometimes include leading sentences providing additional information. The question offers four options, A through D. Three offer alternative text that you would use in place of the underlined text to make it correct. Or, you choose the answer *No change is needed* if the underlined text is correct. Example:

5. Azure Data Lake Analytics <u>is a PaaS solution that enables you to query data in a data lake and build visualizations without deploying hardware or supporting services.</u>

   A. is built on SQL Managed Service to provide analytics for large SQL implementations.

   B. is a component of Azure IoT Central that provides deep analysis of IoT telemetry.

   C. integrates with Azure DevTest Labs to provide code analysis capabilities.

   D. No change is needed.

In this example, the underlined text makes the statement correct, so the appropriate answer is D (no change is needed). But, if Azure Data Lake Analytics were instead a component of Azure IoT that provided deep analysis of IoT telemetry (it is not), then you would choose B.

Achieving AZ-900 Fundamentals Certification

The previous sections have explored the concepts surrounding AZ-900 certification. The following sections offer guidance on preparing and registering for the exam, and for taking the exam.

Preparing for the Exam

Each person has a unique learning style, and one preparation method is not necessarily the best for everyone. However, the following list of preparation methods will help anyone be successful if used as a whole:

- **Studying:** This book obviously provides a great set of resources for learning about Azure fundamentals, but you might prefer a deeper discussion of some topics to help you better understand them. Many online sources are available, but Microsoft's website is perhaps the best, most authoritative source. When I need to go deeper into a particular topic, I usually open Bing in a browser and use a search similar to the following, specifying where to confine the search and the search terms (replace *Service Health* with the topic you need to find): site:docs.microsoft.com Azure Service Health.

- **Hands-on experience:** You can create a free Azure subscription that provides a monthly credit that you can use to deploy and experiment with Azure resources and services. Although you can't feasibly experience all of Azure this way (you're unlikely to deploy Azure Data Lake and begin mining data), but you can at least explore basic concepts and resources such as VMs, virtual networking, and so on. Equally important, you can gain understanding of and experience with the Azure portal and other management tools covered by the AZ-900 exam.

- **Sample tests:** The test questions in this book are designed to cover the exam objectives outlined by Microsoft for the AZ-900 exam. However, it's a good idea to use additional sample test resources to prepare for the test. Not only does this expose you to a broader base of questions, but it helps avoid the "memorize the question and answer" issue that often arises from using a single sample source.

Registering for the Exam

When you feel confident in your ability to pass the exam, your next step is to register for the exam. To do so, navigate to docs.microsoft.com/en-us/learn/certifications/exams/az-900. There you will find information about the exam and links to register for the exam with a testing provider. The test might be administered in person at a testing site or remotely. In either case, you will need to provide photo identification when registering and provide that same identification when you take the exam. You will not be able to use any electronic devices or other resources during the exam. If taking the exam remotely, your device must have a camera through which a proctor can watch you throughout.

Taking the Exam

Unless you already have a strong background in Azure and taking the AZ-900 exam is a formality, I recommend you set aside a few days to prepare for the exam even after you complete your training and study. Spend several hours reviewing the material and the practice questions. Ensure that you are well rested the day of the exam.

When you are taking the exam, carefully read through each question in full, even if you think you know the intent of the question from samples that you have seen. Be deliberate about each question. As you review the possible answers, consider that one answer might provide a more complete answer than another, and choose the one that most completely suits the question. Think carefully about the scenario outlined by each question when choosing your answer.

Here is a summary of points to help you be successful:

- Arrive or go online early to give yourself time to review content and mentally prepare for the exam.

- As emphasized previously, read each question carefully and don't jump to a snap answer. Be deliberate about reading each question and choosing the correct answer.

- Answer all questions as you go along in case you run out of time. You will likely have time when you finish to go back through your answers and adjust as needed any answers you were unsure of on the first pass.

- Sometimes the additional information included in a question is relevant to the answer, but in others it only colors the scenario. Know that there are no trick questions. Read carefully to understand the intent of the question.

- If you are unsure of the correct answer, eliminate the answers that you know are incorrect to narrow the possibilities.

Who Should Read This Book?

IT administrators and other deeply technical roles are not the only ones who can benefit from Azure fundamentals training. If you are in technical sales, project management, or other less technical roles, understanding Azure and its services can help you in your role as well. That's why we have designed this book and its content to provide broad coverage of Azure fundamentals at an introductory level rather than a deep technical level. The book is appropriate for anyone who wants to understand Azure in a broad sense and prepare for the AZ-900 exam, even if you are not highly technical.

What's Included in the Book?

This book consists of seven chapters plus supplementary information: a glossary, this introduction, flashcards, and the assessment test after the introduction. The chapters are organized as follows:

- Chapter 1, "Cloud Concepts," explores the basic concepts of cloud computing to lay the foundation for the rest of the book. Chapter 1 covers categories of cloud computing, the financial benefits of cloud computing, and the various cloud models available with Microsoft Azure.

- Chapter 2, "Azure Core Services," explores the core services available with Azure, including key concepts such as subscriptions and billing, tenants, resources, and resource management. The chapter begins the exploration of key Azure services, including virtual machines, storage, and data services.

- Chapter 3, "Azure Core Networking Services," begins with an explanation of basic networking concepts to create a framework for the discussion of Azure-specific networking services. The chapter explores virtual networks, load balancers, VPN gateways, and content delivery networks.

- Chapter 4, "Security, Compliance, Privacy, and Trust," covers concepts, services, and solutions in Azure related to security, , compliance, privacy, and trust. Topics covered include Azure network security resources, authentication and authorization, and key Azure security services such as Security Center, Key Vault, and others. The chapter also covers governance methodologies, compliance resources, monitoring and reporting, privacy and compliance topics, and government implementations of Azure for the United States and China.

- Chapter 5, "Azure Solutions," covers services in Azure for Internet of Things (IoT), big data and analytics, artificial intelligence (AI), serverless computing, and DevOps.

- Chapter 6, "Azure Pricing, Service Levels, and Lifecycle," helps you understand subscriptions, ways to purchase Azure services, and how to estimate and manage costs in Azure. Pricing tools including the TCO Calculator and Pricing Calculator are explored, as are service level agreements (SLAs), ways to improve SLAs (and the potential effect of SLAs on cost), and other ways to manage cost in Azure.

- Chapter 7, "Creating and Managing Azure Resources," begins with an exploration of the tools you can use to create and manage Azure resources, including the Azure portal, PowerShell, the Azure CLI, the Azure Cloud Shell, and the Azure Mobile App. The chapter finishes with sections that step you through the process of creating several types of Azure resources.

Each chapter begins with a list of the objectives that are covered in that chapter. The book doesn't cover the objectives in order. Thus, you shouldn't be alarmed at some of the odd ordering of the objectives within the book. At the end of each chapter, you'll find a couple of elements you can use to prepare for the exam:

Exam Essentials   This section summarizes important information that was covered in the chapter. You should be able to perform each of the tasks or convey the information requested.

Review Questions   Each chapter concludes with review questions. You should answer these questions and check your answers against the ones provided after the questions. If you can't answer at least 80 percent of these questions correctly, go back and review the chapter, or at least those sections that seem to be giving you difficulty.

The review questions, assessment test, and other testing elements included in this book are *not* derived from the exam questions, so don't memorize the answers to these questions and assume that doing so will enable you to pass the exam. You should learn the underlying topic, as described in the text of the book. This will let you answer the questions provided with this book and pass the exam. Learning the underlying topic is also the approach that will serve you best in the workplace—the ultimate goal of a certification.

To get the most out of this book, you should read each chapter from start to finish and then check your memory and understanding with the chapter-end elements. Even if you're already familiar with a topic, you should skim the chapter; Azure is complex enough that there are often multiple ways to accomplish a task, so you may learn something even if you're already competent in an area.

Recommended Home Lab Setup

Microsoft Azure is a cloud-based offering, so you really don't need a home lab setup to learn about Azure. Instead, you need only a computer with a connection to the Internet and an Azure subscription for experimentation. As described in Chapter 7, you can create a free subscription in Azure and use a monthly credit included with that free subscription to work in Azure for up to a year without incurring any cost.

How to Contact Sybex

We want to ensure that you have the best resources and most up-to-date information as you take your Azure certification journey. On a periodic basis, visit www.wiley.com/go/Sybextestprep for updates, errata, and additional content as it becomes available.

Interactive Online Learning Environment and Test Bank

We've put together some great online tools to help you pass the AZ-900 exam. The interactive online learning environment that accompanies *Microsoft Certified Azure Fundamentals Study Guide: Exam AZ-900* provides a test bank and study tools to help you prepare for the exam. By using these tools, you can dramatically increase your chances of passing the exam on your first try.

The online section includes the following:

Sample Tests   Many practice questions are provided throughout this book and online, including the questions in the assessment test, which you'll find at the end of this introduction, and the review questions at the end of each chapter. In addition, we provide two bonus practice exams. Use these practice questions to test your knowledge of the study guide material. The online test bank runs on multiple devices.

Flashcards   The online text bank includes 134 flashcards specifically written to test your knowledge. Don't get discouraged if you don't ace your way through them at first. The purpose of the flashcards is to help ensure that you're ready for the exam. And no worries—armed with the review questions, practice exams, and flashcards, you'll be more than prepared when exam day comes! Questions are provided in digital flashcard format (a question followed by a single correct answer). You can use the flashcards to reinforce your learning and provide last-minute test prep before the exam.

Other Study Tools   A glossary of key terms from this book and their definitions are available as a fully searchable PDF.

Go to wiley.com/go/sybextestprep to register and get one year of free access after activation to the interactive online learning environment and test bank with study tools.

AZ-900 Exam Objectives

Microsoft Certified Azure Fundamentals Study Guide: Exam AZ-900 has been written to cover every exam objective at a level appropriate to its exam weighting. The following table provides a breakdown of this book's exam coverage, showing you the weight of each section and the chapter where each objective or subobjective is covered:

Subject Area	% of Exam
Describe cloud concepts	20–25%
Describe core Azure services	15–20%
Describe core solutions and management tools on Azure	10–15%
Describe general security and network security features	10–15%
Describe identity, governance, privacy, and compliance features	20–25%
Describe Azure cost management and service level agreements	10–15%
Total	100%

Domain 1: Describe Cloud Concepts

Subdomain 1a: Identify the benefits and considerations of using cloud services

Exam Objective	Chapter
1-1 Identify the benefits of cloud computing, such as High Availability, Scalability, Elasticity, Agility, and Disaster Recovery	1
1-2 Identify the differences between Capital Expenditure (CapEx) and Operational Expenditure (OpEx)	1
1-3 Describe the consumption-based model	1

Subdomain 1b: Describe the differences between categories of cloud services

Exam Objective	Chapter
1-4 Describe the shared responsibility model	1
1-5 Describe Infrastructure-as-a-Service (IaaS)	1
1-6 Describe Platform-as-a-Service (PaaS)	1
1-7 Describe serverless computing	1
1-8 Describe Software-as-a-Service (SaaS)	1
1-9 Identify a service type based on a use case	1

Subdomain 1c: Describe the differences between types of cloud computing

Exam Objective	Chapter
1-10 Define cloud computing	1
1-11 Describe Public cloud	1
1-12 Describe Private cloud	1
1-13 Describe Hybrid cloud	1
1-14 Compare and contrast the three types of cloud computing	1

Domain 2: Describe Core Azure Services

Subdomain 2a: Describe the core Azure architectural components

Exam Objective	Chapter
2-1 Describe the benefits and usage of Regions and Region Pairs	2
2-2 Describe the benefits and usage of Availability Zones	2
2-3 Describe the benefits and usage of Resource Groups	2

2-4 Describe the benefits and usage of Subscriptions   2

2-5 Describe the benefits and usage of Management Groups   2

2-6 Describe the benefits and usage of Azure Resource Manager   2

2-7 Explain Azure resources   2

Subdomain 2b: Describe core resources available in Azure

Exam Objective	Chapter
2-8 Describe the benefits and usage of Virtual Machines, Azure App Service, Azure Container Instances (ACI), Azure Kubernetes Service (AKS), and Windows Virtual Desktop	2
2-9 Describe the benefits and usage of Virtual Networks, VPN Gateway, Virtual Network peering, and ExpressRoute	3
2-10 Describe the benefits and usage of Container (Blob) Storage, Disk Storage, File Storage, and storage tiers	2
2-11 Describe the benefits and usage of Cosmos DB, Azure SQL Database, Azure Database for MySQL, Azure Database for PostgreSQL, and SQL Managed Instance	2
2-12 Describe the benefits and usage of Azure Marketplace	2

Domain 3: Describe Core Solutions and Management Tools on Azure

Subdomain 3a: Describe core solutions available in Azure

Exam Objective	Chapter
3-1 Describe the benefits and usage of Internet of Things (IoT) Hub, IoT Central, and Azure Sphere	5
3-2 Describe the benefits and usage of Azure Synapse Analytics, HDInsight, and Azure Databricks	5
3-3 Describe the benefits and usage of Azure Machine Learning, Cognitive Services, and Azure Bot Service	5

3-4 Describe the benefits and usage of serverless computing solutions that   5
include Azure Functions and Logic Apps

3-5 Describe the benefits and usage of Azure DevOps, GitHub, GitHub   5
Actions, and Azure DevTest Labs

Subdomain 3b: Describe Azure management tools

Exam Objective	Chapter
3-6 Describe the functionality and usage of the Azure Portal, Azure Power-Shell, Azure CLI, Cloud Shell, and Azure Mobile App	7
3-7 Describe the functionality and usage of Azure Advisor	7
3-8 Describe the functionality and usage of Azure Resource Manager (ARM) templates	7
3-9 Describe the functionality and usage of Azure Monitor	7
3-10 Describe the functionality and usage of Azure Service Health	7

Domain 4: Describe General Security and Network Security Features

Subdomain 4a: Describe Azure security features

Exam Objective	Chapter
4-1 Describe the basic features of Azure Security Center, including policy compliance, security alerts, secure score, and resource hygiene	4
4-2 Describe the functionality and usage of Key Vault	4
4-3 Describe the functionality and usage of Azure Sentinel	4
4-4 Describe the functionality and usage of Azure Dedicated Hosts	4

Subdomain 4b: Describe Azure network security

Exam Objective	Chapter
4-5 Describe the concept of defense in depth	4
4-6 Describe the functionality and usage of Network Security Groups (NSG)	4
4-7 Describe the functionality and usage of Azure Firewall	4
4-8 Describe the functionality and usage of Azure DDoS Protection	4

Domain 5: Describe Identity, Governance, Privacy, and Compliance Features

Subdomain 5a: Describe core Azure identity services

Exam Objective	Chapter
5-1 Explain the difference between authentication and authorization	4
5-2 Define Azure Active Directory	4
5-3 Describe the functionality and usage of Azure Active Directory	4
5-4 Describe the functionality and usage of Conditional Access, Multi-Factor Authentication (MFA), and Single Sign-On (SSO)	4

Subdomain 5b: Describe Azure governance features

Exam Objective	Chapter
5-5 Describe the functionality and usage of Role-Based Access Control (RBAC)	4
5-6 Describe the functionality and usage of resource locks	4
5-7 Describe the functionality and usage of tags	4
5-8 Describe the functionality and usage of Azure Policy	4
5-9 Describe the functionality and usage of Azure Blueprints	4
5-10 Describe the Cloud Adoption Framework for Azure	4

Subdomain 5c: Describe privacy and compliance resources

Exam Objective	Chapter
5-11 Describe the Microsoft core tenets of Security, Privacy, and Compliance	4
5-12 Describe the purpose of the Microsoft Privacy Statement, Product Terms site, and Data Protection Addendum (DPA)	4
5-13 Describe the purpose of the Trust Center	4
5-14 Describe the purpose of the Azure compliance documentation	4
5-15 Describe the purpose of Azure Sovereign Regions (Azure Government cloud services and Azure China cloud services)	4

Domain 6: Describe Azure Cost Management and Service Level Agreements

Subdomain 6a: Describe methods for planning and managing costs

Exam Objective	Chapter
6-1 Identify factors that can affect costs (resource types, services, locations, ingress and egress traffic)	6
6-2 Identify factors that can reduce costs (reserved instances, reserved capacity, hybrid use benefit, spot pricing)	6
6-3 Describe the functionality and usage of the Pricing Calculator and the Total Cost of Ownership (TCO) Calculator	6
6-4 Describe the functionality and usage of Azure Cost Management	6

Subdomain 6b: Describe Azure Service Level Agreements (SLAs) and service lifecycles

Exam Objective	Chapter
6-5 Describe the purpose of an Azure Service Level Agreement (SLA)	6

6-6 Identify actions that can impact an SLA (i.e. Availability Zones)   6

6-7 Describe the service lifecycle in Azure (Public Preview and General   6
Availability)

Exam domains and objectives are subject to change at any time without prior notice and at Microsoft's sole discretion. Please visit their website for the most current information.

Assessment Test

1. Microsoft Azure enables your organization to move IT expenditures to:
    A. Capital expenditures
    B. Operational expenditures
    C. A controlled expense model
    D. None of the above

2. Which of the following tools can you use to estimate the expense of moving a data center from on-premises to Azure?
    A. Azure Pricing Calculator
    B. Azure Cost Management + Billing
    C. Azure TCO Calculator
    D. Azure CLI

3. The term *agility* in Microsoft Azure refers to:
    A. The ease with which you can move workloads from on-premises to Azure and back again
    B. The ability to quickly adjust resources such as memory to adapt to changes in demand
    C. The ability to add more front-end web servers to a web application to adapt to increased demand
    D. The ability to quickly create redundancy in a solution

4. Which of the following describes the benefit *economy of scale* as it relates to Microsoft Azure?
    A. The capability to distribute resources across multiple regions to reduce cost
    B. The ability to place resources in less expensive Azure regions to reduce costs
    C. The capability to automatically scale down the number of virtual machines in an Azure solution to reduce costs when demand decreases
    D. The decrease in price per subscriber as more subscribers are added

5. Which of the following in an example of vertical scaling?

   A. Adding VMs to a web app as demand increases

   B. Reducing memory allocated to VMs when demand decreases

   C. Adding CPU cores to a VM when demand increases

   D. Both B and C

6. A service that provides the capability to deploy a SQL database without the need for you to set up a VM or install SQL Server is an example of:

   A. Infrastructure-as-a-service (IaaS)

   B. Software-as-a-service (SaaS)

   C. Platform-as-a-service (PaaS)

   D. Data-as-a-service (DaaS)

7. Accessing an application through a web page rather than installing the application on your local device is an example of:

   A. Infrastructure-as-a-service (IaaS)

   B. Software-as-a-service (SaaS)

   C. Platform-as-a-service (PaaS)

   D. Data-as-a-service (DaaS)

8. Deploying virtual machines (VMs) in a shared cloud environment is an example of:

   A. Infrastructure-as-a-service (IaaS)

   B. Software-as-a-service (SaaS)

   C. Platform-as-a-service (PaaS)

   D. Data-as-a-service (DaaS)

9. Which of the following accurately describes an Azure *geography*?

   A. It corresponds to a single country or to a market encompassing multiple countries.

   B. It always corresponds to a specific country.

   C. It represents a set of physical data centers.

   D. None of the above.

10. An Azure region:

   A. Describes a specific Azure data center

   B. Is usually paired with another region to ensure high availability

   C. Can span across multiple countries

   D. Encompasses the data centers in which all of your Azure resources reside

11. Azure China is a physically isolated instance of Azure available only to Chinese government entities.

   A. Yes

   B. No

12. You are deploying three VMs in a single region as web front ends to a web application. You need to ensure that power outages or other potential data center outages do not make your web application unavailable. Which of the following achieves this goal?

A. You place the VMs in an availability set.

B. You place the VMs in separate resource groups.

C. You place the VMs in different availability zones.

D. You deploy additional VMs to other regions.

13. What is the function of a resource group in Azure?

A. It provides automatic scaling of CPU cores, memory, and other resources for VMs.

B. It enables you to establish a higher SLA for VMs.

C. It protects resources from being deleted.

D. It serves as a logical container for Azure resources.

14. Is the underlined portion of the following statement true, or does it need to be replaced with one of the other fragments that appear below?

Azure Resource Manager <u>enables you to deploy multiple resources using JSON-based templates</u>.

A. is the primary tool you use to manage resources in Azure.

B. is the blade in Azure portal that provides access to resource management and monitoring tools, including management templates.

C. enables you to interactively allocate additional CPU cores and memory to VMs.

D. No change is needed.

15. Which of the following statements is not true regarding Azure subscriptions?

A. A subscription is aligned to a specific Azure region.

B. You can move resources from one subscription to another.

C. Subscriptions can help simplify Azure billing and cost management.

D. You can move a subscription to a new Azure AD tenant.

16. Azure App Service provides support for multiple development languages, containers, and Windows and Linux.

A. Yes

B. No

17. Which of the following can you use to orchestrate container management in Azure?

A. Azure Container Instance (ACI)

B. Azure Resource Manager

C. Azure Kubernetes

D. Azure CLI

18. Is the underlined portion of the following statement true, or does it need to be replaced with one of the other fragments that appear below? Containers that you deploy in a group Azure support only the Linux OS.

A. support only the Windows OS.

B. share the same OS as other containers in the group.

C. require configuration of the OS for each container.

D. No change is needed.

19. You need to set up a storage solution in Azure to enable you to store the state of an application from one execution of the application to the next. Which of the following storage solutions provide that capability?

A. Azure Disk

B. Azure Blob

C. Azure Files

D. Azure Archive

20. Which of the following data solutions would be the most cost-efficient solution for storing and retrieving sales data for your sales team using SQL statements?

A. Host a database using Azure SQL Database

B. Host a database using Azure Managed SQL Instance

C. Install SQL Server on a VM in Azure

D. Host a database using Cosmos DB

21. Which of the following does not provide load balancing between resources in Azure?

A. Azure Front Door

B. Azure Traffic Manager

C. Azure Load Balancer

D. Azure network security groups (NSGs)

22. You have deployed a web application in Azure and need HTTPS traffic to be routed to a specific endpoint based on the requested URL. Which of the following load-balancing solutions provides this capability?

A. Azure Traffic Manager

B. Azure Load Balancer

C. Azure Application Gateway

D. Azure network security groups

23. You need to ensure that network traffic between your on-premises data center and Azure is securely encrypted as it traverses the Internet, but you do not want your organization to manage the service. Which of the following should you choose?

A. Azure VPN Gateway

B. Azure Point-to-Point VPN

    C. Azure ExpressRoute

    D. Azure ExpressRoute Direct

24. Your organization has compliance restrictions that prevent your data from traversing the Internet between your on-premises data center and your resources in Azure. Which of the following provides a solution for this requirement?

    A. Azure Managed VPN

    B. Azure ExpressRoute Direct

    C. Azure VPN Gateway

    D. Azure ExpressRoute

25. Which of the following is an appropriate solution for placing video files and large documents close to where your globally dispersed users are located to reduce latency?

    A. A dedicated point-to-point VPN connection between the source files and each location.

    B. Azure DirectRoute

    C. Azure Content Delivery Network

    D. None of the above

26. Which of the following solutions would enable only you and one of your peers to access and manage an Azure VM using RDP on port 3389?

    A. Role-based access control (RBAC) and an Azure network security group (NSG)

    B. An appropriately designed Azure policy applied to the resource group containing the VM

    C. Azure Firewall

    D. Azure Front Door

27. You are deploying a VM-based solution, and due to security and compliance requirements, all traffic reaching that VM must come from a single endpoint located in a different subnet. Which of the following solutions meets this requirement?

    A. Create a network security group (NSG) with the appropriate routing and apply the NSG to all virtual networks.

    B. Create a user-defined route and apply it to all subnets in the virtual network.

    C. Use Azure Firewall to route traffic to the target VM based on the IP address in the resource request URL.

    D. Create a custom route in Azure Firewall to direct traffic to the endpoint based on source and destination address.

28. Replace the underlined section of the statement if needed to make the statement true:

Azure DDoS Protection Standard <u>alerts you to DNS attacks as they are happening</u>.

    A. begins protecting resources from DNS attacks as soon as you configure DDoS on the resource.

    B. begins protecting resources from DNS attacks as soon as you configure the service on a virtual network.

    C. provides protection and alerts against DDoS attacks but does not provide mitigation reporting.

    D. No change is needed.

29. Which of the following is an example of authorization?

    A. Providing a username and password when logging in to your device

    B. Receiving a text message on your mobile device after providing a username and password for a website

    C. Presenting a passport to enter another country

    D. Presenting a visa to enter another country

30. Which of the following capabilities requires Azure AD Premium?

    A. Enabling users to reset their own Azure AD passwords

    B. Enabling users to reset their own on-premises passwords

    C. Controlling access to resources in Azure through role-based access control (RBAC)

    D. All of the above

31. Which of the following Azure services offers security recommendations for improving security in your Azure environment?

    A. Azure Advanced Threat Protection (ATP)

    B. Azure Information Protection (AIP)

    C. Azure Security Center

    D. Azure Service Health

32. You are a developer and need to store security credentials for a web application in a secure store in Azure. Which of the following meets this need?

    A. Azure AD Premium

    B. Security Center

    C. Azure Credential Manager

    D. Azure Key Vault

33. Your CIO has directed you to implement a solution that enables your organization to protect emails and documents using policies, identities, and encryption. Which of the following satisfies this requirement?

    A. Azure Advanced Threat Protection (ATP)

    B. Azure Policies

    C. Azure Initiatives

    D. Azure Information Protection (AIP)

34. Because of a recent network intrusion, you need to present a solution to your CIO that will enable your organization to identify pass-the-hash and reconnaissance attacks. Which of the following is an appropriate solution?

A. Windows Defender

B. Advanced Threat Protection

C. Azure Information Protection

D. Security Center

35. Is the underlined portion of the following statement true, or does it need to be replaced with one of the other fragments that appear below?

A honeytoken attack tests multiple passwords against a username.

A. attempts authentication against an alphabetical list of usernames.

B. is an attempt to log in to a fake account that you have created.

C. is an example of a pass-the-token attack.

D. No change is needed.

36. Which of the following would you use to ensure that the VMs added to a resource group do not exceed certain limits for the number of CPU cores and memory?

A. Azure Initiatives

B. Azure Configuration Manager

C. Azure Policies

D. Resource Locks

37. Is the underlined portion of the following statement true, or does it need to be replaced with one of the other fragments that appear below?

Azure Policies enable you to specify what actions a user can take with a resource in Azure after they have authenticated in Azure.

A. apply policies to a single resource or to a resource group, with the latter causing all resources in the group to have the policy applied.

B. create policies in Security Center to control access to specific Azure resources.

C. deploy specific sets of RBAC permissions to new Azure users.

D. No change is needed.

38. Which of the following would you use to prevent resources in a resource group from being deleted?

A. Role-based access control (RBAC)

B. Policies

C. Resource locks

D. Azure Information Protection (AIP)

39. Which of the following should you use to implement a large, repeatable deployment of resources in Azure with associated role assignments and policies?

    A. Azure PowerShell

    B. Azure CLI

    C. Azure Initiatives

    D. Azure Blueprints

40. Which of the following accurately describes Azure Monitor?

    A. Azure Monitor supports only Windows operating systems and SUSE Linux.

    B. Azure Monitor begins monitoring a resource as soon as you create the resource.

    C. Azure Monitor is a component service of Azure Telemetry and Reporting.

    D. Azure Monitor requires you to create logs and metrics to begin monitoring resources.

41. Which of the following would you use to view status information about resources that your organization hosts in Azure?

    A. Azure PowerShell

    B. Azure Service Health

    C. Azure portal

    D. Azure Security Center

42. Which of the following should you use to view information about planned maintenance in Azure?

    A. Azure Advisor

    B. Azure Update Center

    C. Azure Service Health

    D. None of the above

43. Which of the following is not an example of a standards-based, nonregulatory organization or agency?

    A. GDPR

    B. ISO

    C. NIST

    D. All of the above

44. Which of the following statements are not true? (Choose all that apply.)

    A. Microsoft can share your personal information with vendors and third parties only with your authorization.

    B. You must provide personal information to use some Microsoft products.

    C. You cannot use a work email when setting up a Microsoft account that you will then use to access Microsoft services.

    D. You can use a personal email account when setting up a Microsoft account that you will then use to access Microsoft services.

45. Which of the following provides bidirectional communication between Internet of Things (IoT) devices and other Azure services?

    A. IoT Hub

    B. IoT Central

    C. IoT Connector

    D. None of the above

46. Which of the following would enable your organization to monitor and control thousands of sensors deployed in a manufacturing facility, including analyzing telemetry from the sensors?

    A. IoT Hub

    B. IoT Central

    C. IoT Connector

    D. Azure Sphere

47. Your organization needs to implement a solution that analyzes photos and videos. Which of the following should you consider as a solution?

    A. Azure Machine Learning

    B. Machine Learning Studio

    C. Cognitive Services

    D. Azure Analytics

48. Which of the following would you choose to add natural language question and answer capabilities to a web application?

    A. Azure Machine Learning

    B. Azure Cognitive Services

    C. Azure Bot Services

    D. Logic Apps

49. Which of the following enables developers to create serverless workflow solutions in Azure?

    A. Logic Apps

    B. Functions

    C. Bot Services

    D. PowerShell

50. Is the underlined portion of the following statement true, or does it need to be replaced with one of the other fragments that appear below?

Azure Functions is <u>a solution for creating serverless, stateless functions that can be called from other Azure services to perform data processing.</u>

    A. a solution for building workflow-based functions that integrate with other Azure services to perform data processing.

    B. a component of Azure DevOps that helps simplify development and deployment of serverless, stateful functions for data processing.

C. a library of functions you can implement in your web applications to monitor and manage Azure services.

D. No change is needed.

51. Which of the following is a popular code repository for open source software development?

A. Azure DevTest Labs

B. Azure DevOps

C. GitHub

D. Azure Artifacts

52. Your CIO has asked you to investigate Azure as an alternative to hosting resources in your on-premises data center. What is the first action you need to take before creating resources in Azure?

A. Create a storage account.

B. Create an account in Azure AD.

C. Create an Azure subscription.

D. Create an Azure AD tenant.

53. Is the underlined portion of the following statement true, or does it need to be replaced with one of the other fragments that appear below?

You can purchase Azure services <u>only through an enterprise agreement (EA)</u>.

A. as a component of your Unified Support agreement with Microsoft.

B. directly from Microsoft through the Azure portal.

C. only through a cloud solution provider (CSP).

D. No change is needed.

54. You have been tasked by the director of infrastructure at your organization to estimate the cost of moving a data center from on-premises to Azure. Which of the following should you use to estimate the cost?

A. Azure Advisor

B. Pricing Calculator

C. TCO Calculator

D. Azure Migration Planner

55. Which of the following should you use to estimate the cost of storage that you will include with three new VMs that you need to deploy to Azure?

A. Pricing Calculator

B. Storage Calculator

C. TCO Calculator

D. Azure Advisor

56. Which of the following statements is not true?

    A. Azure Advisor provides recommendations for cost management.

    B. Azure Advisor provides recommendations for operational excellence.

    C. Azure Advisor provides recommendations for security.

    D. Azure Advisor provides reporting for the health and status of Azure services.

57. Which of the following provides significant discounts for purchasing Azure services?

    A. Azure Reserved Instances (ARI)

    B. Azure Reservations

    C. Azure Managed Services

    D. Azure Enterprise

58. Is the underlined portion of the following statement true, or does it need to be replaced with one of the other fragments that appear below?

Your organization currently has two Azure subscriptions. Adding a third Azure subscription will increase your Azure consumption and costs.

    A. enable you to deploy Azure resources in other regions.

    B. require you to create a third Azure AD tenant.

    C. not cause any cost increase by itself.

    D. No change is needed.

59. Which of the following enables you to bring your existing licenses for SQL Server into Azure to save licensing costs?

    A. Azure Hybrid Benefit

    B. An enterprise agreement

    C. SQL Managed Instance

    D. Cosmos DB

60. You manage internal Azure billing for your organization, allocating costs to various departments based on their consumption of Azure services. Which of the following would you use to define budgets for subscriptions?

    A. Azure Cost Management + Billing

    B. Azure Cost Management

    C. Azure Monitor

    D. Azure Quota Management

61. You have a solution in Azure comprising two VMs, each with a 99.5% SLA. What is the composite SLA for the solution?

    A. 99.0%

    B. 99.5%

    C. 99.9%

    D. 99.99%

62. Which of the following statements are true regarding public preview features in Azure? (Choose all that apply.)

   A. They are available to all Azure customers.

   B. The are available only by invitation from Microsoft.

   C. They are subject to the same SLAs as generally available (GA) services.

   D. They are not subject to SLAs.

63. Is the underlined portion of the following statement true, or does it need to be replaced with one of the other fragments that appear below?

Microsoft provides at least <u>30 days'</u> notice before it retires an Azure service.

   A. 6 months

   B. 12 months

   C. 2 year

   D. 5 years

64. Which of the following would you choose to perform management tasks in Azure as an experienced Linux administrator?

   A. Azure PowerShell

   B. Azure CLI

   C. Azure Tools for Linux

   D. Azure Power Tools for Linux

65. What function does the Azure Cloud Shell provide?

   A. It enables you to run either PowerShell or the Azure CLI from a web browser.

   B. It is a library of management functions that you can integrate into your web apps to monitor Azure services.

   C. It enables you to run PowerShell commands within the Azure CLI.

   D. All of the above.

66. Which of the following is not a true statement?

   A. You can use the Azure Mobile App to run the Azure CLI.

   B. You can run Azure CLI directly in the Azure portal.

   C. You can run the Azure CLI from within the Azure Cloud Shell.

   D. You can install the Azure CLI on a Windows device.

67. Which of the following is a good option for deploying a single VM in Azure?

   A. Azure portal

   B. An Azure Resource Manager (ARM) template

   C. Azure Mobile App

   D. PowerShell

Answers to Assessment Test

1. B. Azure is a consumption-based cloud model in which you pay only for the services that you consume, enabling you to move from a CapEx model to an OpEx model. See Chapter 1 for more information.

2. C. The TCO Calculator helps you consider the costs of facilities, power, and related expenses associated with moving services hosted in a data center to Azure.

3. B. Agility refers to the ability to adjust resources to meet changes in demand. See Chapter 1 for more information.

4. D. As the number of subscribers increases, the cost to provide a service to those subscribers goes down because the cost is spread across more users, providing an economy of scale. See Chapter 1 for more information.

5. D. Vertical scaling refers to adding or removing resources such as CPU cores or memory as demand changes. See Chapter 2 for more information.

6. C. This is an example of PaaS. See Chapter 1 for more information.

7. B. This is an example of SaaS. See Chapter 1 for more information.

8. A. This is an example of IaaS. See Chapter 1 for more information.

9. A. An Azure geography can align to a single country or to a market that encompasses multiple countries, such as Europe. See Chapter 2 for more information.

10. B. Regions are usually paired with other regions in Azure to help ensure high availability. See Chapter 2 for more information.

11. B. Azure China is a physically isolated instance of Azure, but it is available to business as well as governmental organizations within China. See Chapter 4 for more information.

12. C. Distributing VMs across availability zones helps guard against data center outages. See Chapter 2 for more information.

13. D. Resources groups serve as a logical container for Azure resources. See Chapter 2 for more information.

14. D. The underlined fragment is correct. See Chapter 2 for more information.

15. A. Subscriptions are just logical containers and therefore are not limited to a single region. See Chapter 2 for more information.

16. A. The statement is true. See Chapter 2 for more information.

17. C. Azure Kubernetes provides orchestration services for containers that you create with ACI. See Chapter 2 for more information.

18. B. All containers in a group share the same OS. See Chapter 2 for more information.

19. C. Azure Files enables you to save application state from one execution to another. See Chapter 2 for more information.

20. A. The most cost-effective option is to use Azure SQL Database. See Chapter 2 for more information.

21. D. Azure NSGs do not provide load-balancing capability. See Chapter 4 for more information.

22. C. Azure Application Gateway provides URL-based routing. See Chapter 4 for more information.

23. C. Azure ExpressRoute is the appropriate solution to provide VPN across the Internet, managed by a third party. See Chapter 4 for more information.

24. B. Azure ExpressRoute Direct provides similar capabilities as Azure ExpressRoute but is not routed across the Internet. See Chapter 4 for more information.

25. C. Azure Content Delivery Network (CDN) enables you to place replicas of content geographically near the users who need to consume the content. See Chapter 4 for more information.

26. A. An Azure NSG enables you to restrict access to the VM based on port, and RBAC enables you to restrict access to specific individuals. See Chapter 4 for more information.

27. B. To implement custom routing, create a user-defined route and apply it to all relevant virtual networks. See Chapter 4 for more information.

28. D. No change is needed, since DDoS Standard provides alerting to ongoing distributed denial-of-service (DDoS) attacks. It also provides alerting and mitigation reporting. See Chapter 4 for more information.

29. D. In this example, the first three options are examples of authentication (identifying the holder), but do not authorize the user. The visa provides that authorization for entering the country. See Chapter 4 for more information.

30. B. Adding the capability to synchronize password changes to on-premises AD requires Azure AD Premium. See Chapter 4 for more information.

31. C. Security Center provides recommendations on improving security, as well as monitoring and alerts. See Chapter 4 for more information.

32. D. Azure Key Vault is the appropriate place to store secrets such as security credentials in Azure. See Chapter 4 for more information.

33. D. Azure Information Protection (AIP) provides the capability to protect emails and documents using policies, identities, and encryption. See Chapter 4 for more information.

34. B. Advanced Threat Protection (ATP) provides protection from many kinds of security threats, including pass-the-hash, pass-the-token, and others. See Chapter 4 for more information.

35. B. A honeytoken attack is an attempt to authenticate to a fake account that you have created as a "honeypot" to attract attackers. See Chapter 4 for more information.

36. C. You can use Azure Policies to enforce restrictions on VM resources.
See Chapter 4 for more information.

37. A. You can apply policies at the resource or resource group levels, and if at the resource group, the policies apply to all resources in the group. See Chapter 4 for more information.

38. C. Locking a resource with the CanNotDelete lock prevents resources in the resource group from being deleted. The lock must be removed before a resource in the group can be deleted. See Chapter 4 for more information.

39. D. Blueprints enable you to create large, repeatable deployments of resources in Azure with corresponding role and policy assignments. See Chapter 4 for more information.

40. B. You do not need to configure Azure Monitor for it to begin monitoring a resource. Instead, Azure Monitor begins monitoring as soon as you create a resource. See Chapter 4 for more information.

41. B. Azure Service Health enables you to view status information for resources that you host in Azure. See Chapter 4 for more information.

42. C. Azure Service Health enables you to view information about planned maintenance in Azure. See Chapter 4 for more information.

43. A. ISO and NIST are both standards-based, nonregulatory agencies. General Data Protection Regulation (GDPR) defines data protection and privacy requirements as a regulation in European Union law. See Chapter 4 for more information.

44. A, C. Microsoft can share your personal information with vendors and third parties without your consent, including in response to legal actions. You can use a work email when setting up a Microsoft account. See Chapter 4 for more information.

45. A. IoT Hub provides bidirectional communication between IoT devices in Azure. See Chapter 5 for more information.

46. B. IoT Central enables you to monitor and control IoT devices. See Chapter 5 for more information.

47. C. Cognitive Services provides human-like analysis services in Azure. See Chapter 5 for more information.

48. C. Azure Bot Services provides human-like interaction, including natural language question-and-answer capabilities. See Chapter 5 for more information.

49. A. Azure Logic Apps enables you to create serverless workflow solutions in Azure. See Chapter 5 for more information.

50. D. The statement is correct, so no change is needed. See Chapter 5 for more information.

51. C. Although Azure DevOps provides features and functions similar to GitHub, GitHub is intended for open source projects. See Chapter 5 for more information.

52. C. The first step before you create or use any resources in Azure is to create a subscription to host those resources. See Chapter 6 for more information.

53. B. Although you can purchase Azure through an EA, a CSP, and the Azure portal, only option B is correct as stated. See Chapter 6 for more information.

54. C. The TCO Calculator enables you to factor in facilities costs and other factors when estimating a move from on-premises to Azure. See Chapter 6 for more information.

55. A. The Pricing Calculator enables you to price individual Azure services based on factors such as CPU cores, memory, and storage capacity. See Chapter 6 for more information.

56. D. Azure Advisor does not provide reporting for health and status of Azure services. See Chapter 4 for more information.

57. B. Azure Reservations enables you to reserve Azure resources with a monetary commitment and receive potentially very significant discounts as a result. See Chapter 6 for more information.

58. C. Adding an Azure subscription does not by itself result in additional costs, because a subscription is just a logical container for Azure resources, which could be existing resources that you move to the new subscription. See Chapter 6 for more information.

59. A. Azure Hybrid Benefit enables you to potentially use your Windows Server and SQL Server licenses in Azure to save costs. See Chapter 6 for more information.

60. B. Azure Cost Management enables you to define budgets for your Azure subscriptions and track expenditures. See Chapter 6 for more information.

61. A. Composite SLAs are the product of the individual SLAs in the solution, and in this case, would be 0.995 × 0.995. See Chapter 6 for more information.

62. A, D. Services in public preview are available to all Azure subscribers and are not subject to service level agreements (SLAs). See Chapter 6 for more information.

63. B. Microsoft provides 12 months' notice before retiring an Azure service. See Chapter 6 for more information.

64. B. Azure CLI is an implementation of the Bash shell, making it an excellent management tool for experienced Linux administrators. See Chapter 7 for more information.

65. A. The Azure Cloud Shell enables you to run either PowerShell or the Azure CLI from the Azure portal. See Chapter 7 for more information.

66. B. You cannot run the Azure CLI directly in the Azure portal, but instead must open the Azure Cloud Shell from the portal and then choose Azure CLI. See Chapter 7 for more information.

67. A. Although you could use any of these options to deploy a VM, the Azure portal is the easiest option for deploying a single resource. See Chapter 7 for more information.

Chapter

1

Cloud Concepts

MICROSOFT EXAM OBJECTIVES COVERED IN THIS CHAPTER:

DESCRIBE CLOUD SERVICES

✓ **Identify the benefits and considerations of using cloud services**

- Identify the benefits of cloud computing, such as High Availability, Scalability, Elasticity, Agility, and Disaster Recovery

- Identify the differences between Capital Expenditure (CapEx) and Operational Expenditure (OpEx)

- Describe the consumption-based model

DESCRIBE CLOUD SERVICES

✓ **Describe the differences between categories of cloud services**

- Describe the shared responsibility model

- Describe Infrastructure-as-a-Service (IaaS)

- Describe Platform-as-a-Service (PaaS)

- Describe Software-as-a-Service (SaaS)

- Identify a service type based on a use case

DESCRIBE CLOUD OBJECTIVES

✓ **Describe the differences between types of cloud computing**

- Describe cloud computing

- Describe Public cloud

- Describe Private cloud

- Describe Hybrid cloud

- Compare and contrast the three types of cloud computing

The first objective in the Microsoft Azure AZ-900 Certification Exam covers basic cloud concepts. These concepts lay a foundation for understanding why companies choose cloud computing and what types of services are available in Azure. These concepts include the various cloud computing models in Azure, the economic benefits of using Azure, and the three primary service categories in Azure—software-as-a-service (SaaS), infrastructure-as-a-service (IaaS), and platform-as-a-service (PaaS).

First, we'll explore cloud computing.

Understanding Cloud Computing

Microsoft currently offers three cloud computing solutions: Microsoft Azure, Microsoft 365, and Microsoft Dynamics 365. Azure, which is covered on the AZ-900 Certification Exam, provides a broad spectrum of cloud services. These services encompass both server-based and end user–based computing services, along with database services and analytics, artificial intelligence, networking, infrastructure, and much more.

The second Microsoft cloud offering, Microsoft 365, is geared primarily toward providing end-user SaaS solutions like Windows, Office, Share-Point, and OneDrive. Microsoft Dynamics 365 encompasses enterprise resource planning and customer relationship management applications. Microsoft 365 and Microsoft Dynamics 365 are not covered on the AZ-900 exam.

Both Microsoft cloud offerings enable organizations to eliminate computing infrastructure that they might normally host themselves. Larger organizations typically host their own servers, networking equipment, and other IT resources in a *data center,* which is a facility specifically designed and constructed to house servers and other IT hardware and related infrastructure. Some organizations maintain their own data centers, whereas others contract with a third-party data center provider to host their IT equipment and resources.

Smaller organizations generally either use a third-party data center or place their servers and other IT infrastructure in one or more *server rooms,* which are essentially very small data centers housed inside the company's facility.

A cloud offering such as Azure enables organizations to move some—if not all—of their servers, networking equipment, and other IT resources into a data center managed by another company. In the case of Azure, Microsoft owns and maintains numerous data centers around the world to host these resources for all sizes of organizations. Managing these resources then becomes a shared responsibility between the organization and Microsoft. The extent of that shared management depends on the scope of what Microsoft is hosting and the services the organization is using in Azure.

Figure 1.1 shows an example of an organization that is hosting some of its IT infrastructure and services in Azure. As Figure 1.1 illustrates, some of the organization's IT resources remain on site in their own data center, whereas other resources are hosted in Azure, and services interact between the two environments.

FIGURE 1.1   A hybrid cloud scenario

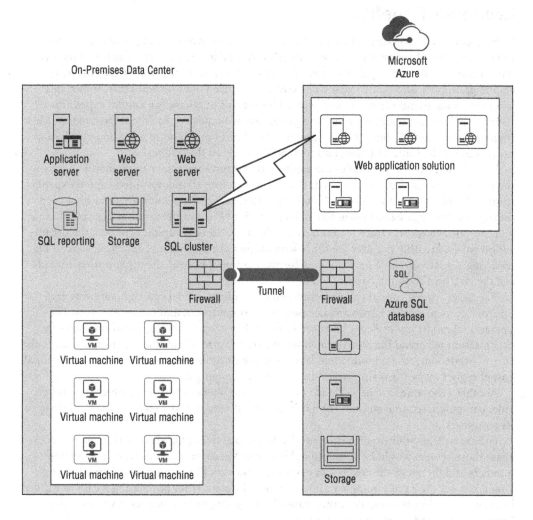

Whatever the case or the extent of services hosted in the cloud, offloading these resources to a cloud provider like Microsoft offers several benefits, which are discussed in the next section.

Benefits of Cloud Computing

Leveraging a cloud computing model offers several benefits, both in financial cost and human resources. This section explores these primary benefits.

Economic Benefits

IT hardware, infrastructure, and related resources can be extremely expensive. In an on-premises model where an organization hosts its own IT infrastructure, whether in its own data center or a third-party data center, the organization bears the cost of the hardware, shipping, support, and related costs. The cost is amortized over several years, sometimes longer than the useful life of the hardware. This type of purchase is a *capital expenditure (CapEx)*, which is money spent by an organization to acquire or maintain fixed assets. Most organizations carefully budget their capital expenditures and require a yearlong budgeting process to set the CapEx budget, and then hold strictly to the budget.

With Azure, Microsoft handles the capital expenditures necessary to maintain and grow the service. An organization using Azure services therefore eliminates those capital expenditures and replaces them with *operational expenditures (OpEx)*, which are monthly expenditures that the organization uses to run its operation. For example, rather than purchasing a license for Microsoft Office for each user (which would be a capital expense), the organization pays a monthly per-user fee for Microsoft 365 (an operational expense). Instead of incurring a relatively large up-front cost for the perpetual license, the organization spreads out the cost on a monthly basis.

The move from a capital to an operational expenditure model can eliminate very large up-front costs to deploy hardware, licenses, support contracts, and other resources. The operational model not only avoids those large up-front expenditures, but also enables the organization to spread the cost throughout the year. It also allows the organization to tie the cost to headcount, so if an individual leaves the organization, the corresponding operational cost also goes away (or is simply reallocated to an incoming resource).

Another economic benefit to cloud computing is *economy of scale*, in which a cloud provider can purchase large amounts of hardware at a discount and pass that discount along to its customers.

For example, if your organization needed to replace five aging servers, the cost to purchase those servers would be substantial. However, Microsoft purchases servers in large numbers and therefore the cost is less per server and very likely much less than what you would pay for the same equipment. It's not much different from purchasing a case of canned beans at a warehouse store. Per can, a case of 24 is going to be much less expensive than buying a single can. That's economy of scale.

Storage offers another good example of economy of scale. As cloud providers like Microsoft purchase large amounts of storage at a significant discount, that discount is passed to their customers. The result is that storage you purchase from Microsoft is generally much less expensive than storage and related infrastructure that you purchase yourself. As with that can of beans, the cost is shared across many customers, further decreasing the cost to each customer.

Scalability and Elasticity

Two additional benefits of cloud computing are *scalability* and *elasticity*. Scalability is the ability to add computing resources to adjust to increased demand. For example, assume your organization deploys a web farm to handle e-commerce business. For seven or eight months out of the year, your needs are relatively stable. During a peak holiday season, however, you might need several additional servers to handle the increased traffic from sales. You can *scale out* your servers, adding additional ones to meet the increased demand, then *scale in* (eliminate the additional servers) when the peak season is over. This is called horizontal scaling. Instead of incurring the up-front capital expenditure cost of the equipment, you have an increased operational cost only while you are using those servers. Figure 1.2 illustrates an example of horizontal scaling.

FIGURE 1.2 Horizontal scaling adds additional resources when they are needed and removes them when they are no longer needed.

Three-node web application solution

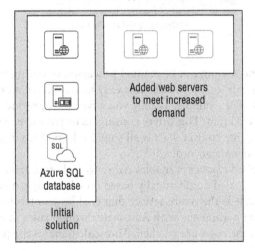

Added web servers to meet increased demand

Azure SQL database

Initial solution

There are two types of scalability. The previous example described scaling out and its reverse, scaling in. *Scaling up*, also called *vertical scaling*, refers to adjusting capacity in existing resources to accommodate demand changes. For example, increasing the amount of memory available to a virtual server is an example of scaling up. Adding more processor cores to an existing server is another example of scaling up. As with horizontal scaling, you can go the other way with vertical scaling. When you remove the extra memory when you no longer need it, you're *scaling down*. Figure 1.3 illustrates an example of vertical scaling.

FIGURE 1.3   Vertical scaling adjusts the capacity of existing resources to accommodate demand changes.

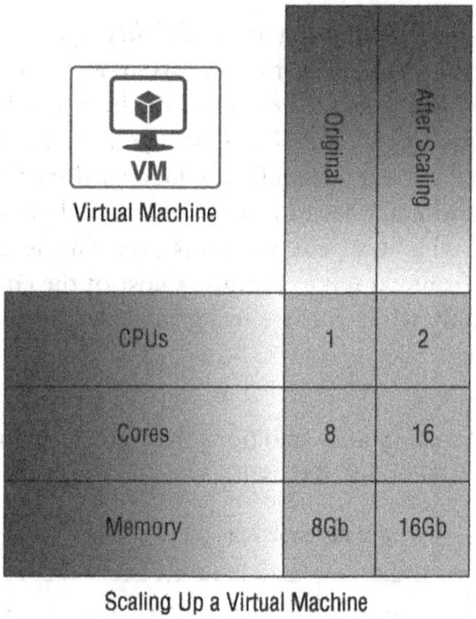

	Original	After Scaling
VM Virtual Machine		
CPUs	1	2
Cores	8	16
Memory	8Gb	16Gb

Scaling Up a Virtual Machine

Vertical and horizontal scaling can be manual processes, requiring you to take specific action to scale resources. Although it's relatively easy to scale resources in Azure, automatic scaling is often desirable. For example, assume you advertise a product during a television show that airs at 11:00 p.m. This drives consumers to your site, where demand starts to increase around midnight. Your IT staff is all sound asleep. Who is going to notice the demand and take steps to scale accordingly?

Automatic scaling, called *elasticity*, enables Azure to scale resources for you without interaction. Resources can be scaled automatically based on CPU usage, memory usage, storage usage, and so on. Autoscale is the Azure service that enables you to configure automatic scaling. You configure the parameters with Autoscale through rules that you create. When the thresholds defined in the rules are reached, Autoscale handles the process of scaling as defined in the rule.

See https://docs.microsoft.com/en-us/azure/azure-monitor/ platform/autoscale-get-started for more information on configuring and using Autoscale.

Azure makes it very easy to scale resources to meet demand requirements, and Autoscale—once configured—can make it almost effortless
to scale resources. The capability to rapidly adjust resources to meet
demand is one aspect of *cloud agility*. Another aspect of cloud agility is
the capability to quickly adapt to changing business requirements. The
latter is not a concept covered in the Azure Fundamentals certification
but is nevertheless an important concept to consider when evaluating
cloud computing options.

High Availability

High availability (HA) describes a system that is available for use without significant outages and that is generally backed by a *service level agreement (SLA)*. For example, if a service has an SLA of 99.9 percent, the service is guaranteed to be available 99.9 percent of the
time. Translated to the real world, that means the service can be unavailable no more than
43.2 minutes in a 30-day period to meet the 99.9 percent SLA for that month. A financially
backed SLA provides a credit for the time in which the service was unavailable.

Service level agreements are discussed in detail in Chapter 6, "Azure Pricing, Service Levels, and Lifecycle."

There are many reasons why a service might become unavailable. Servers might go down,
a network issue might prevent traffic to or from the servers, a server application might fail,
or a peripheral service might fail. For example, if your line-of-business application relies on
a database to host its data and the database goes offline, your application will likely not be
available.

It's important to note that "available" does not necessarily translate to
performance. If an Azure service is available but at reduced performance,
it is nonetheless considered available in the context of the SLA.

Fault Tolerance

The term *fault tolerance* describes a characteristic of a system that enables it to continue
functioning when one or more components of the system fails. For example, a typical
SharePoint farm consists of at least one database server, a web server, and an application
server. These servers together provide the SharePoint services that users consume. If the
web server goes down, the service becomes unavailable. To make the SharePoint farm more
fault tolerant, you can add a second web server and balance traffic between them. So, if
one web server goes down, the other continues to serve web requests. Users might notice a

degradation in responsiveness, but the service remains functional. The SharePoint farm is now fault tolerant to a degree. Figure 1.2 (shown earlier) illustrates this example.

In this SharePoint example, the farm is not fully fault tolerant because points of failure remain in the single application server and database server. When building a fault tolerance strategy for a service, you should consider other points of potential failure, such as a single network path.

Disaster Recovery

Fault tolerance generally applies at the component level of a service. For example, adding a second web server, ensuring that a virtual machine can quickly fail over to another instance, or creating a clustered database instance are examples of fault tolerance. Fault tolerance generally comes into play when a single resource fails.

Disaster recovery refers to the process of recovering from a situation where multiple systems or services fail. For example, assume that your company's primary data center is hit by a tornado, destroying all the IT infrastructure and services hosted at that location. This is certainly a disaster. Recovering from that disaster, however, might be as difficult as setting up all new servers and restoring their configuration and data from backups, or it could be as (relatively) simple as pointing all of your users to a backup data center where all of your infrastructure has been actively duplicated, updated, and ready to become your primary data center.

There is no right answer for a disaster recovery strategy, and it is very much situational and tied to your business continuity needs and defined by the IT services you provide. A very small company, for example, might only need a complete set of backups of its only server and data so that it can quickly restore to a new server. A large organization naturally requires a much more complex disaster recovery plan that can include multiple data centers, active mirroring of services between data centers, and much more. Many organizations are turning to Azure to not only provide a higher level of fault tolerance than they could otherwise implement on-premises, but to implement a disaster recovery environment in Azure for their on-premises systems. Other organizations are turning to Microsoft 365 and Azure to host all of their IT services, with no on-premises IT infrastructure at all, to attain a high level of flexibility, elasticity, fault tolerance, and disaster recovery.

Chapter 2, "Azure Core Services," describes key concepts and services in Azure that provide both fault tolerance and disaster recovery capabilities.

Human Resources

How cloud computing affects human resources is not a major topic on the AZ-900 exam, but the topic does bear some discussion in the context of the benefits of cloud computing.

Organizations move to a cloud model for many reasons: to leverage services that would be very difficult or expensive to deploy on their own, to gain cost savings through economies of scale and shared responsibility, to gain higher elasticity and scalability, or to implement a more effective disaster recovery plan, to name a few.

The indirect consequence of outsourcing IT infrastructure and services to a cloud provider like Microsoft always has some effect on the IT staff who are managing the infrastructure and services that move to the cloud. The following list describes three common scenarios:

- **Staff reduction:** Outsourcing to a cloud provider can potentially reduce the number of IT staff you need to manage those services because Microsoft manages some, if not most, of the infrastructure and services. However, there is a shared responsibility between the organization and Microsoft, and some staff is always required to manage at least some aspects of your cloud footprint.

- **Staff repurposing:** A better approach can be repurposing your staff to more strategic purposes and tasks. Instead of "keeping the lights on," your staff can focus on optimizing the services hosted in the cloud, rolling out new services, and in general playing a more strategic technology role for the business.

- **Staff increase:** It's also possible in some scenarios that an organization will need more IT staff as they transition to the cloud. New services can mean additional staff to direct and manage those services. For example, if you are new to AI and leveraging the AI-related services in Azure, you'll need staff to implement and manage those services.

Financial Models

The section "Economic Benefits" earlier in this chapter briefly described different financial models associated with deploying and managing IT services to meet business needs. The topic bears some additional discussion to further explore the economic benefits offered by cloud computing.

You learned earlier in this chapter that organizations generally budget in two specific areas, capital expenditures and operational expenditures. Organizations typically budget once a year for capital expenditures, which are funds they spend to acquire hard assets like servers and other infrastructure hardware, laptops for employees, company vehicles, buildings and building improvements, and so on. Operational expenses are those funds the organization spends on a monthly basis to operate the business. Outside the context of cloud computing, operational expenses can include electricity and other utilities, fuel for the company vehicles, and mundane things like snacks for the break room.

Organizations that host their own IT infrastructure and related services almost always incur capital expenditures to deploy those services. The cost of servers, routers, switches, firewalls, software licenses, support contracts, and similar items are usually capital expenditures, and in most cases, very expensive expenditures. Moving to a cloud solution that is paid for via a monthly subscription service based on consumption represents a shift to an operational expense. This shift from capital to operational can mean a huge savings for an organization, as well as greater flexibility and agility.

For example, assume an organization wants to create a proof of concept that requires a dozen servers, storage, server application licenses, a new firewall device, a new load balancer, and other resources. Deploying that as an on-premises solution would require the up-front purchase of those resources. Let's assume that the price for all of that is $500,000.

Deploying that same proof of concept in Azure could be a small fraction of the cost of the on-premises solution. Why? Instead of purchasing servers, you create virtual machines in Azure, which you only pay for while they are turned on. If you purchase the hardware yourself, you incur the cost whether or not those servers are ever operational.

The other infrastructure, including firewalls, load balancers, and other resources, are also paid for on a consumption basis. So, you stand up the proof of concept, evaluate and determine your go-forward strategy, and then turn off all those services when the project evaluation is completed. You've perhaps paid a few thousand dollars for a month of consumption, rather than the $500,000 investment required by the on-premises solution.

The previous example illustrates both the agility and cost savings associated with moving to a cloud platform. It also highlights the benefits of moving from a capital expenditure model to an operational expenditure model. You avoid large, up-front capital expenses and instead transition to monthly operational costs based on your consumption of Azure services.

Cloud Computing Models and Responsibilities

Azure provides three cloud computing models, and each of these results in different levels of shared responsibility between Microsoft and Azure subscribers. The following sections explore these models and how each varies in shared responsibility.

Software-as-a-Service

Azure services fall generally into three categories. The first of these categories is *software-as-a-service (SaaS)*.

SaaS is a licensing model in which an organization licenses software on a subscription basis from a provider that centrally manages and distributes the software. A perfect example of SaaS is Microsoft 365, where Microsoft provides Office applications (Word, Excel, and others) on a subscription basis (see Figure 1.4). Rather than purchase a perpetual license for Microsoft Office for each user, an organization pays a monthly subscription fee per user to enable that user to access and use the software.

FIGURE 1.4   Microsoft 365 is an example of an SaaS offering.

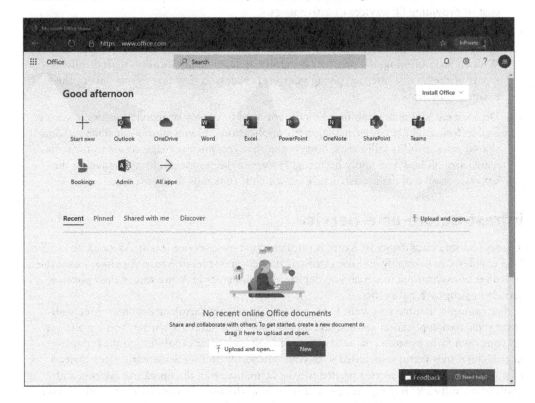

With a perpetual license, the organization is responsible for deploying the software to the user's device and managing updates. There are exceptions, but generally the organization must purchase a new license to upgrade to the next version of the software.

With an SaaS subscription, the user often uses the software through a web interface. With a Microsoft 365 subscription, for example, the user can use Word, Excel, and the other Office applications through a web browser. A Microsoft 365 subscription gives the user the capability to install the applications on a device and use it locally as well.

A typical Azure SaaS offering is Azure SQL Database. Rather than deploy a physical server or virtual machine, install Microsoft SQL Server on that server, and create a database, you simply create a SQL database in Azure. You don't need to worry about managing the server or the SQL Server application—you only manage the database itself.

SaaS offers a number of benefits:

- **Operational expense:** Instead of incurring a capital expenditure to obtain a perpetual license, you move licensing cost into an operational expenditure model. This not only reduces potentially high, lump-sum payments but also enables you to more easily tie the cost of providing IT services to active users.

- **Updates:** With most perpetual licensing models, you must purchase upgrade licenses or even another full license when you want to move to the next version of an application. With an SaaS offering, the provider generally updates the application periodically as a part of the service offering, giving your users access to new features as part of their existing subscription.

- **Deployment and manageability:** You do not need to deploy or manage software with an SaaS offering. The provider manages the application and you simply consume it. Some shared responsibility still exists, however, in that you must manage access to the software through how you apply licensing. However, the responsibility of managing the software itself and the infrastructure on which it runs falls to the provider.

Infrastructure-as-a-Service

The second service category in Azure is infrastructure-as-a-service (IaaS). As its name implies, IaaS enables you to deploy and use infrastructure components in Azure. A primary example of IaaS is *virtualization*, in which you deploy virtual servers in Azure rather than physical servers in your own data center.

For example, assume you want to stand up a SharePoint farm consisting of three web front ends, two application servers, and a two-node SQL database cluster. You have to set up your own farm because you need customization and other capabilities not available in the SharePoint features included with your Microsoft 365 implementation. So, instead of purchasing the seven servers needed for the farm, licensing the operating systems and application software, buying storage, and setting up the farm in your own data center, you stand up seven virtual machines in Azure (see Figure 1.5). These virtual machines are provisioned and run on virtualization hardware that Microsoft manages. Microsoft also manages the networking infrastructure, physical storage, and other resources needed by the Share-Point solution.

The first advantage of this solution is that you don't incur a capital expenditure for the hardware or for the operating system licenses. You also only incur operational costs when the servers are running. So, if you spend a week getting the virtual servers and the farm configured, then shut them down for a couple of weeks while you work on other aspects of the project, you don't incur any costs for the time those servers are turned off.

FIGURE 1.5   A simplified illustration of a virtualized SharePoint farm in Azure

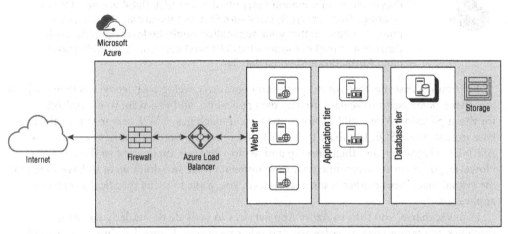

Scalability is another important aspect of IaaS. Using the same SharePoint example, you can easily add resources to the web front ends (vertical scaling) or add additional web front ends (horizontal scaling) to accommodate increased traffic to the farm.

Flexibility is another important benefit of IaaS over using dedicated hardware. Assume your team spends a few days standing up the virtual machines and getting the SharePoint farm operational, and then the business makes the decision to take the project in a different direction or to cancel the project altogether. You shut down the servers and related services, ending the infrastructure costs associated with the project. You aren't stuck with hardware and other infrastructure that you now need to repurpose for something else.

IaaS generally has a higher shared responsibility than SaaS. Although Microsoft manages the hardware that supports your virtualized infrastructure, you still need to manage the virtual servers, operating systems, and applications installed on the virtual machines. You will learn more about the different responsibilities later in this chapter in the section "Shared Responsibility."

Platform-as-a-Service

Conceptually, platform-as-a-service (PaaS) is a combination of IaaS and SaaS in that it incorporates both infrastructure and software. Microsoft provides and manages the virtualized infrastructure (virtual machines, networking, and so forth) and provides additional software and resources to facilitate application development. So, think of PaaS as providing the capability to quickly develop and deploy web-based applications without the need to manage the underlying servers, operating systems, and other resources that are part of the developed application.

Previously in this chapter I identified Azure SQL Database as an SaaS offering. That is correct, but Azure SQL Database can also be a component of PaaS in that your application might be leveraging Azure SQL Database as part of the solution. The next section, "Shared Responsibility," provides additional details.

For example, assume that your organization needs to develop and deploy a web application that uses a database to store data used by the application, and you want to use ASP.NET for the application. You could deploy some virtual machines, a SQL server to host the database (or use Azure SQL Database to host it), and other required software to provide for ASP.NET integration, and then develop and deploy the web application to those servers. However, you want to streamline your development effort and don't want to have to manage the virtual machines or other resources. Instead, you want to focus specifically on the web application.

In this scenario, you turn to Azure App Services to provide the underlying virtual machines, operating systems, software, and other resources. Figure 1.6 shows an example of a web app service being created in Azure. As the figure illustrates, this web app is called JBTestApp99 and uses ASP.NET 4.7 on Windows.

FIGURE 1.6 Creating a web app named JBTestApp99 to use ASP.NET 4.7 and run on Windows

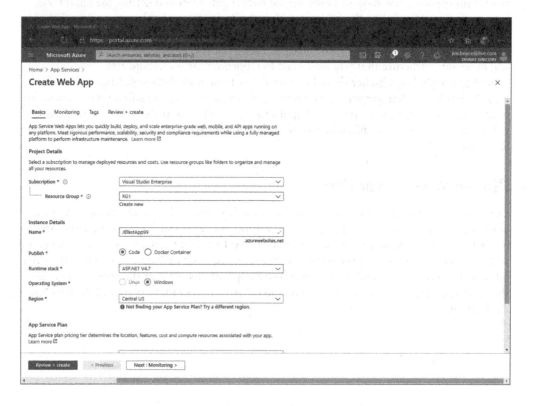

Even though this solution is running on Windows and uses ASP.NET, you don't need to deploy or manage the Windows environment, ASP.NET, or other resources. Instead, you focus solely on the application development.

There are many other aspects to creating web applications using Azure, including the capability to create multiple app service plans, configure automatic monitoring and application insights for the app, and more. For the purposes of the AZ-900 exam, however, just understand that PaaS provides a development platform that you can use to create and deploy many different types of web applications without worrying about deploying or managing the servers and other infrastructure that support that application.

Shared Responsibility

In an on-premises IT scenario, your organization is generally responsible for all aspects of a service, including physical space, hardware, power, cooling, operating systems, applications, networking, and more. With cloud computing, you have a shared responsibility with the cloud provider. In the case of Azure, Microsoft manages certain aspects of the services that you host in Azure, and you are responsible for other aspects.

Figure 1.7 shows the relationship of different cloud computing elements and how they fit into the categories described previously in this chapter. As the figure illustrates, different categories overlap, with IaaS being a subcomponent of both PaaS and SaaS.

FIGURE 1.7   IaaS, PaaS, and SaaS are all categories of cloud computing and share a nested relationship.

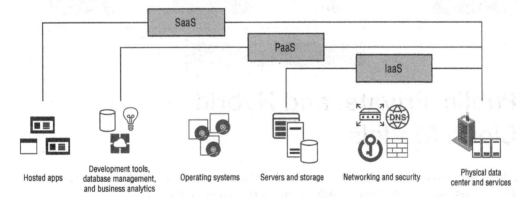

| Hosted apps | Development tools, database management, and business analytics | Operating systems | Servers and storage | Networking and security | Physical data center and services |

Each category of cloud computing in Azure involves different levels of responsibility from your organization and Microsoft. Figure 1.8 illustrates the various levels of responsibility with each of these categories, with IaaS having the highest level of responsibility for the customer and SaaS having the least responsibility.

FIGURE 1.8 The three categories of Azure cloud computing have different levels of shared responsibility between your organization and Microsoft compared to on-premises/self-hosted.

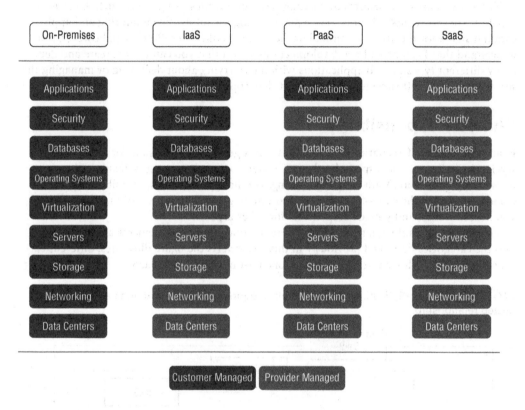

Public, Private, and Hybrid Cloud Models

A key topic covered on the AZ-900 exam is the difference between cloud computing models. This section explores the three models: public, private, and hybrid.

Public Cloud

A public cloud is one in which the services offered in the cloud are available for public use over the Internet. This doesn't mean that the services you deploy in Azure are available to the public. In a public cloud, many boundary layers segregate your services from those hosted in Azure by other organizations. The services and data that you host in Azure are secure and inaccessible by people outside of your organization (unless you specifically provide guest access to certain services, such as your company website).

Using a public cloud to host some of your IT services doesn't mean that all of your services are moved to the cloud. You might put some of your services in Azure but still maintain other services on-premises in your own data center.

Private Cloud

A private cloud is one in which the cloud serves a single organization, whether hosted in your own data center or by someone else. A private cloud offers many of the same benefits of scalability, elasticity, and other aspects of a public cloud. Because a private cloud is dedicated to one organization, it offers some additional capabilities to meet regulatory requirements because you can impose controls and processes in the private cloud that would not necessarily be available in a public cloud. Security is also another aspect where a private cloud offers some advantages. Many organizations have regulatory requirements to prevent certain types of data from being exposed to the Internet, and hosting that data in a private cloud can help that organization meet that requirement.

Although a private cloud offers many benefits, it also has several potential drawbacks. For example, hosting services in a private cloud is often no less expensive than simply hosting those same services on-premises in your own data center because the hardware and most of the infrastructure is dedicated to your organization, even if it is hosted by a third party. You either pay for the hardware yourself or the hosting provider passes the cost on to your organization in some fashion. Any cost savings you realize from a third-party private cloud generally come from the fact that the hosting company manages the data center for multiple customers, which provides some economy of scale.

Hybrid Cloud

A hybrid cloud is one in which an organization integrates on-premises services with cloud-hosted services, whether in a public or a private cloud. Using Microsoft 365 as an example, you might continue to host your own Exchange servers in your data center to provide certain internal functions but also have mailboxes hosted in Exchange Online. The on-premises Exchange servers and Exchange Online service work together to provide a consolidated messaging solution.

An example of an Azure hybrid scenario is one in which you host data on-premises in a SQL Server cluster but have applications hosted in Azure that use that data. The two services work together to provide the end solution to your users.

The key to differentiating between a hybrid cloud scenario and a mix of on-premises and cloud services is whether there is service interaction between your on-premises service and the related service(s) in the cloud. For example, assume you use Microsoft 365 to provide messaging and Office applications to your users and use on-premises servers and applications to provide line-of-business applications such as accounting and billing. If the two environments exist separately with no interaction between services in each environment, then you don't have a hybrid cloud scenario. If you do have interaction between services, then you do have a hybrid cloud scenario.

Summary

The Cloud Concepts objective of the AZ-900 exam is intended to help you understand what cloud computing is, its benefits, and different cloud models without diving into specific Azure services, pricing models, or other details (except where needed peripherally to understand a basic concept).

This chapter covered the following concepts:

- **Benefits of cloud computing:** Cloud computing offers a number of economic benefits, including economies of scale and the opportunity to move from a capital expenditure model to an operational expenditure model. Scalability and elasticity enable you to scale your Azure services to meet changes in demand, adding resources when needed to meet increased demand and scaling back as demand decreases, with associated changes in cost. Cloud computing also provides improved capabilities for both high availability and fault tolerance, enabling your services to respond to issues and outages.

- **Cloud computing models and responsibilities:** The three cloud models—software-as-a-service, infrastructure-as-a-service, and platform-as-a-service—each provide different capabilities with different levels of shared responsibility aligned to each. Trade-offs exist within each model between flexibility and control. For example, IaaS gives you the most control over the services hosted in Azure, whereas SaaS is generally the easiest to manage.

- **Public, private, and hybrid cloud models:** These three cloud models each offer certain benefits and can be used individually or together to achieve business goals through IT services. All of the models offer significant potential savings in both cost and effort over on-premises hosting models. A public cloud generally offers the lowest cost, a private cloud a higher cost but greater flexibility to meet certain regulatory requirements, and a hybrid cloud the capability for integrating systems on-premises and in the cloud.

Exam Essentials

Describe terms such as high availability, scalability, elasticity, agility, fault tolerance, and disaster recovery.   High availability is a characteristic of Azure that refers to the availability of specific services, measured as a percentage (available/total time). For example, a service with a service level agreement (SLA) of 99.9 percent is guaranteed to be unavailable no more than 43.2 minutes in a 30-day period. Reduced performance is not counted as unavailable.

Scalability is a characteristic of Azure that enables services to adjust to changes in demand. Vertical scaling refers to adding resources to an existing system, such as adding more memory or CPU cores to a virtual machine. Horizontal scaling refers to adding additional systems, such as adding additional virtual machines. Scaling down and scaling in are the reverse of scaling up and scaling out. Scalability is a function of elasticity.

Agility refers to the capability to quickly deploy services with reduced effort and cost.

Fault tolerance is a characteristic of a system that enables it to tolerate the failure of one or more of its components.

Disaster recovery is the process of recovering systems and data following a major failure or disaster.

Describe the principles of economies of scale. Technical economies of scale are achieved when a cloud provider can purchase a large amount of hardware and other infrastructure at a discount, resulting in a cost savings to its consumers, and/or when those resources are used by multiple organizations, effectively reducing the cost per user or per organization.

Describe the difference between capital expenditure (CapEx) and operational expenditure (OpEx). A capital expenditure (CapEx) is the acquisition of hard assets, such as the purchase of servers and other IT hardware. Operational expenditures (OpEx) are expenses incurred in operating a business, such as monthly consumption fees for using Azure services.

Describe the consumption-based model. In a consumption-based model, an organization pays for the resources the organization and its users consume, generally resulting in a cost savings because costs are incurred only when the resources are in use.

Describe infrastructure-as-a-service (IaaS). IaaS refers to compute, networking, and related services that your organization consumes from a pool of resources hosted by a cloud provider. The provider manages the physical hardware and supporting infrastructure, and your organization manages the operating system, applications, networking configuration, and related services.

Describe platform-as-a-service (PaaS). PaaS describes a system that enables organizations to quickly develop and deploy applications without the need to obtain or manage the underlying hardware or other infrastructure required by the application.

Describe software-as-a-service (SaaS). SaaS describes a model in which an organization consumes software hosted by a cloud provider. The cloud provider manages the application and updates, and the consumer manages access to the applications by its users. Microsoft 365 is an example of SaaS.

Compare and contrast the three different service types. IaaS is generally tied to virtualization and the capability to quickly stand up and manage virtual servers in the cloud with consumer control over the operating system and applications running on the VMs. PaaS abstracts the hardware and underlying support applications (*middleware*) and instead focuses on the interaction between the consumer and the service, simplifying the capability to consume development-related services. SaaS fully abstracts all hardware and application support, enabling the organization's users to use an application without needing to manage any aspect of the application or its underlying infrastructure. Office applications in Microsoft 365 are an example of applications served through an SaaS model.

Describe a public cloud. A public cloud is one in which services are provided to multiple organizations through a publicly accessible network such as the Internet. In general, physical compute and networking hardware, along with other supporting infrastructure, is shared among the organizations consuming services from the public cloud. Various physical and virtual boundaries securely separate one organization's services and data from those of others. Reduced cost is the primary advantage to a public cloud model.

Describe a private cloud.   A private cloud is one in which services are provided to a single organization, whether managed internally by the organization or by a third party. Greater control over systems, applications, and data is the primary advantage of a private cloud.

Describe a hybrid cloud.   A hybrid cloud model is one in which non-cloud services hosted on-premises directly interact with services hosted in either a public or a private cloud.

Review Questions

1. Is the underlined portion of the following statement true, or does it need to be replaced with one of the other fragments that appear below?

   As a cloud service, Microsoft Azure enables your organization to budget IT infrastructure costs <u>as a capital expenditure</u>.

   A. as an operational expenditure.

   B. on an annual basis.

   C. using the Azure Pricing Estimator.

   D. No change is needed.

2. The cost per subscriber decreases as the number of Azure subscribers increases. Which benefit of cloud computing does this statement describe?

   A. Agility

   B. Scalability

   C. Economy of scale

   D. Elasticity

3. You are an IT manager for a small company that hosts a web application for e-commerce. The web application uses two web servers and a small database cluster. As demand increases through a peak season, you want to add additional web servers to handle the increased demand, then remove those additional servers as demand decreases. You propose moving the application to Azure. Which of the following statements is true?

   A. The web servers can be moved to Azure but the database cluster must remain on-premises, which represents a hybrid cloud model.

   B. Horizontal scaling enables you to add and remove web servers to meet demand changes.

   C. Vertical scaling enables you to add and remove web servers to meet demand changes.

   D. Azure will automatically add the web servers for you as demand approaches a threshold set by the Azure App Service.

4. You are an IT director for Contoso and are preparing a proposal to your CIO to move all IT infrastructure to Azure. Which of the following is an advantage to moving your infrastructure to a public cloud provider?

   A. You will have complete control over all infrastructure, network, applications, and all other resources in the cloud.

   B. You can scale your infrastructure horizontally or vertically without capital expenditure costs.

   C. You will reduce your operational expenditures.

   D. The cloud provider will manage all infrastructure for you, enabling Contoso to reduce IT staff.

5. Contoso is building a web application that uses a SQL database to store data. Which of the following represents a hybrid cloud scenario? (Choose all that apply.)

    A. A virtual machine in Azure that hosts the web application and a second virtual machine in Azure running SQL Server

    B. A two-node SQL cluster in a third-party data center that hosts the data and two virtual machines in Azure running the web application

    C. A web application hosted in Azure that stores its data in an Azure SQL database

    D. A web application hosted in Azure that sends data to and from a database hosted in Contoso's on-premises data center

6. Is the underlined portion of the following statement true, or does it need to be replaced with one of the other fragments that appear below?

    Moving servers from an on-premises data center to virtual machines in Azure <u>enables you to reduce IT staffing because Microsoft manages the infrastructure for you.</u>

    A. enables you to pay for only the Azure resources you consume on a monthly basis.

    B. represents a platform-as-a-service (PaaS) solution.

    C. enables you to use additional firewall services only available in Azure to protect against security risks.

    D. No change is needed.

7. You are the application development director for Contoso. Your team needs to develop and bring a new web application online quickly with minimal expense. You consider using Azure Web Apps, Azure Functions, and Azure Database for MySQL. Which Azure service category does this represent?

    A. Infrastructure-as-a-service (IaaS)

    B. Platform-as-a-service (PaaS)

    C. Software-as-a-service (SaaS)

    D. Development-as-a-service (DaaS)

8. Your company currently installs Microsoft Office on each user's computer using perpetual licenses that you have purchased from a licensing vendor. You propose to the CIO to transition your users to Microsoft 365 to use Office applications hosted by Microsoft, which enables your organization to work with documents in a web browser and also receive Office application updates automatically. This represents which service category?

    A. Infrastructure-as-a-service (IaaS)

    B. Platform-as-a-service (PaaS)

    C. Software-as-a-service (SaaS)

    D. None of the above

9. You are a server administrator for Wingtip Toys, a small company that makes and distributes wooden toys. You manage a custom line-of-business (LOB) application for order management and shipping. The solution is hosted on aging servers in a server room in your manufacturing facility. You want to eventually move the application's functions to Microsoft Dynamics 365 and eliminate the custom application. You propose to your manager that you first migrate the servers into virtual machines hosted in Azure to avoid purchasing new, up-to-date hardware. The current application will run on these new VMs. This proposal represents which of the following?

A. Software-as-a-service (SaaS)

B. Infrastructure-as-a-service (IaaS)

C. Platform-as-a-service (PaaS)

D. A hybrid cloud scenario

10. You are the CIO for a company and are concerned about the security of your data in the cloud. You need to implement a cloud solution in which you gain the flexibility and agility of a cloud solution but maintain full control of your data and infrastructure. You propose to your CEO that you contract with a third-party cloud vendor to host your IT services, and the infrastructure on which your services will be hosted will not be used by any other organization. This represents which type of cloud model?

A. Public cloud

B. Private cloud

C. Hybrid cloud

D. Both A and B

11. You deploy a custom data analytics application to Azure that includes a single web front end through which the users access the application. At peak times during the day, the web server experiences very high memory usage and temporarily enters an unresponsive state due to a bug in your application. As a stopgap measure while your developers research the issue, you add a second web server and balance the load between the two web servers. Although the service sometimes slows down, the servers are able to independently recover from the memory issue and the service remains available. Scaling out the web servers resulted in improvements in which two areas?

A. Disaster recovery

B. Agility

C. Fault tolerance

D. High availability

12. You deploy a web app using Azure App Services and configure autoscaling for it so that it can request additional compute resources when the app experiences high increases in demand. What is this an example of?

A. Elasticity

B. PaaS

C. Fault tolerance

D. High availability

Azure Core Services

MICROSOFT EXAM OBJECTIVES COVERED IN THIS CHAPTER:

DESCRIBE CORE AZURE SERVICES

✓ **Describe the core Azure architectural components**

- Describe the benefits and usage of Regions and Region Pairs
- Describe the benefits and usage of Availability Zones
- Describe the benefits and usage of Resource Groups
- Describe the benefits and usage of Subscriptions
- Describe the benefits and usage of Management Groups
- Describe the benefits and usage of Azure Resource Manager
- Explain Azure resources

DESCRIBE CORE AZURE SERVICES

✓ **Describe core resources available in Azure**

- Describe the benefits and usage of Virtual Machines, Azure App Services, Azure Container Instances (ACI), Azure Kubernetes Service (AKS), and Windows Virtual Desktop
- Describe the benefits and usage of Container (Blob) Storage, Disk Storage, File Storage, and storage tiers
- Describe the benefits and usage of Cosmos DB, Azure SQL Database, Azure Database for MySQL, Azure Database for PostgreSQL, and SQL Managed Instance
- Describe the benefits and usage of Azure Marketplace

DESCRIBE CORE SOLUTIONS AND MANAGEMENT TOOLS ON AZURE

✓ **Describe Azure management tools**

- Describe the functionality and usage of Azure Resource Manager (ARM) templates

Microsoft Azure consists of a multitude of services. Even though the number of different Azure services can be bewildering, there are nevertheless core services and concepts that underpin many of the Azure offerings. Understanding the role that these core services play is instrumental in understanding Azure holistically. The exam objectives explored in this chapter are designed to help you build that understanding.

First, let's explore concepts that will help you understand where and how Azure services are deployed geographically, how high availability works, and ways to manage those services.

The AZ-900 exam covers several network services that are core services supporting almost every Azure service in some way. These networking services and concepts are covered in Chapter 3, "Azure Core Networking Services." Azure solutions and management tools are covered in Chapter 5, "Azure Solutions."

Core Azure Architectural Components

Azure is a distributed cloud offering with data centers located in many geographical regions across the world. That global distribution primarily provides a means of serving customers close to where their users are; enables customers to meet legal, compliance, or tax requirements; and enhances opportunities for high availability. The following sections explain these core concepts by examining the roles that regions, availability zones, resource groups, and Azure Resource Manager play in enabling and supporting that distributed cloud model.

Geographies and Regions

As explained previously in this chapter, Azure has multiple data centers distributed around the globe. Those data centers house the servers and other infrastructure on which Azure is built. The data centers are distributed into various *geographies*. The Azure geographies generally align to specific countries such as the United States, Canada, Australia, and so on. However, Azure geographies can also be aligned to specific markets, such as Europe and Asia.

Compliance and data residency are key aspects of an Azure geography, and China is a good example. Azure China is a physically isolated instance of Azure located wholly in China. Azure China is operated by Shanghai Blue Cloud Technology Co., Ltd. (21Vianet). Azure China enables Chinese companies and entities to host their data and applications within China and meet strict Chinese regulatory requirements. Azure China is not limited to Chinese government entities.

Within each geography are Azure *regions*. A region is a grouping of data centers that interact to provide redundancy and availability for the services hosted within that region. For example, West US, Central US, and North Central US are three of many regions in the United States. Each region is paired with another in the same geography to allow for replication of resources across multiple data centers to reduce the effects of natural disasters, outages, or other potential events that would affect a given data center's ability to serve up the services hosted in that data center. For example, West US and East US are paired regions, North Europe and West Europe are paired, and UK West and UK South are paired. Figure 2.1 shows the relationship between geographies, region pairs, regions, and data centers.

FIGURE 2.1 The relationships between geographies, regions, region pairs, and data centers

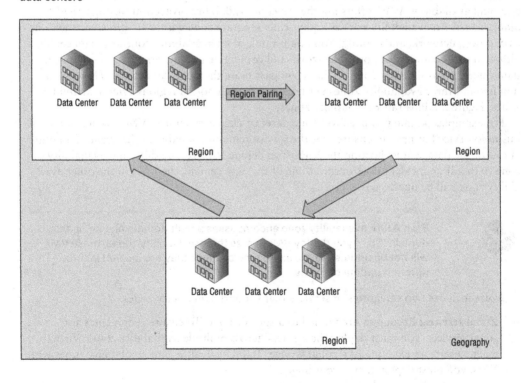

Microsoft establishes and controls the pairing relationships between regions, which means that you cannot choose a region pair. However, you choose the region in which to deploy a service, which indirectly determines which other region is in the pair.

You are not limited to choosing a single region to deploy your Azure services, nor are you limited to a specific region pair. In fact, you don't have to use a regional pair at all and can instead host all your services in a single region. However, using region pairs offers many benefits for redundancy, resiliency, and business continuity.

Visit https://azure.microsoft.com/en-us/global-infrastructure/ geographies to learn more about Azure geographies and regions, and to view information about region location and pairing, which will help you choose the right region(s) to host your services in Azure.

Availability Zones

As Figure 2.1 illustrates, there is a nested nature to Azure that provides both fault tolerance and availability. Azure offers another level of availability protection through *availability zones*. An availability zone is a physically separate zone within a region, each with its own power, network, and cooling. You might think of an availability zone as a data center, although the separation of power, network, and cooling defines the zone, not the physical data center. An availability zone might encompass more than one data center. There are a minimum of three availability zones per region, although not all regions offer availability zones. Figure 2.2 illustrates availability zones.

For example, assume you need to deploy a set of virtual machines (VMs) to host a line-of-business service but need to ensure that the service remains available in the event of a failure at one of the data centers hosting the VMs. You deploy VMs to an additional availability zone so that if an incident does occur at one of the data centers, the VMs in the other availability zone will be unaffected.

Each Azure availability zone encompasses a fault domain and an update domain. So, if you deploy VMs across three availability zones, those VMs will not be updated at the same time because they are located in three different update domains.

Azure includes two categories of services that support availability zones:

- **Zonal services:** Resources are pinned to a specific zone. To ensure redundancy for zonal services, you must deploy the services across multiple availability zones. Virtual machines are an example of a zonal service. To take advantage of availability zones with VMs, you must deploy them accordingly.

- **Zone-redundant services:** Azure replicates the service automatically across zones. Storage is a good example. When you deploy a new storage account, choosing ZRS (Zone Redundant Storage) will result in the storage automatically being replicated across availability zones. SQL databases are another example of a zone-redundant service.

You must use availability zones if you want to achieve certain SLAs. For example, deploying VMs to two or more availability zones results in an SLA of 99.99 percent.

FIGURE 2.2   Availability zones offer an additional layer of service availability.

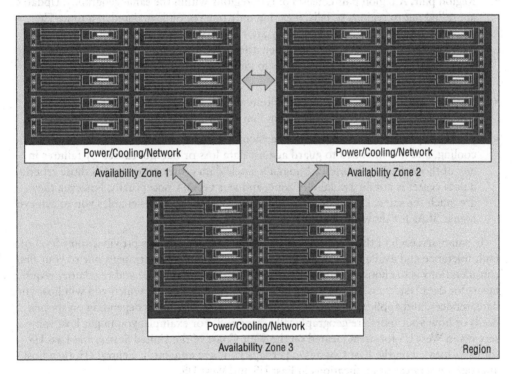

 There is no additional cost for VMs deployed in an availability zone, although you will incur charges for VM-to-VM data transfers between zones.

Bringing It All Together

As the previous sections describe, Azure offers multiple levels of availability and fault protection. The following list summarizes each:

- **Geography:** A geography defines a discrete market that preserves data residency and compliance boundaries. Geographies typically contain two or more regions. Although often defined by country, Azure geographies are not constrained to a specific country.

- **Region:** A region is a collection of data centers that interact to provide data redundancy and service availability.

- **Region pair:** A region pair consists of two regions within the same geography. Updates are rolled out to regions serially, meaning only one region is updated at a time. The second region in a pair is updated only after the first is successfully updated. An issue with an update or an outage would then affect only one region in the pair. Some Azure services take advantage of region pairs to guard against data loss, replicating data between regions.

- **Data center:** Individual data centers within a region host the servers and other infrastructure needed to host services within that region.

- **Availability zones:** An availability zone encompasses separate power, networking, and cooling, and it is intended to guard against data loss or outages caused by failures in any of those three categories. Although a single data center generally fits those criteria, a data center is not an availability zone, and vice versa. Conceptually, however, they are much the same. Deploying services across availability zones enables you to achieve higher SLAs for those services.

In summary, each of the topics discussed in the previous sections provides some level of fault tolerance and availability. When you're developing an Azure strategy, one of your first considerations is to choose a geography that meets your compliance and regulatory requirements for data residency. The next consideration is the region(s) in which you will host your data, services, and applications. You might choose multiple regions depending on specific needs or how your users are geographically dispersed. For example, you might host some services in West US for users located on the West Coast of the United States, and East US for users located on the East Coast. Or, perhaps you host content in Central US, then host appropriate services or applications in East US and West US.

Once you've identified the regions you'll be using and how those regions are paired, you can begin making decisions regarding not only where you will host storage and other services, but what additional types of fault tolerance and availability are appropriate. That might take the form of replicating storage, data, or other services between regions, or it might mean using other services to provide fault tolerance, redundancy, and high availability. Selecting the appropriate geography and region(s) underpins all of those considerations.

For more details on regions and availability zones, see `https://docs.microsoft`
`.com/en-us/azure/availability-zones/az-overview`.

Resources and Resource Groups

Azure *resources* are manageable items in Azure such as virtual machines, databases, virtual networks, and storage accounts. Figure 2.3 shows an example of creating a resource in Azure.

FIGURE 2.3   Creating a resource in Azure

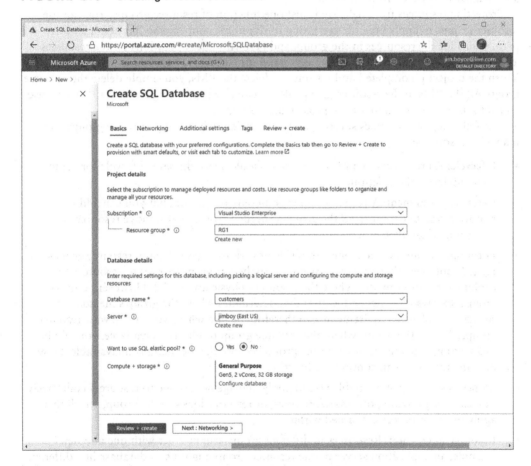

If you deploy only a few resources to Azure, managing them will likely not be a significant challenge. However, your Azure solution may grow to encompass a very large number of resources of different types, all potentially scattered across multiple regions. As the number of resources grows, your ability to manage them individually quickly becomes difficult. *Resource groups* provide a means for organizing and managing resources.

Think of a resource group as a logical container for one or more resources. You can apply various properties to the resource group, and those properties apply to all the resources in that resource group. For example, assume you have a group of resources that you want to prevent from being deleted but want resource admins to be able to modify. You can create a resource group, assign the resources to that group, and apply a CanNotDelete lock on the resource group. Any resources that you later apply to the resource group will also be automatically protected from deletion.

Protecting resources from deletion is just one function of resource groups. You can use resource groups to apply policies to a group of resources, control who has administrative permissions for the resources in the group, and perform other operations on the resources as a single entity. For example, assume you stand up 10 VMs for a proof-of-concept project. When the project is completed and it's time to delete the VMs, you simply delete the resource group. All the VMs in the resource group, along with any supporting resources that you also added to the resource group for the project, are deleted.

The following list describes several points to consider when using resource groups and managing resources:

- **Lifecycle:** All resources in a resource group should share the same lifecycle for deployment, updates, and deletion.

- **Resource assignment:** A resource can exist in only one group, but you can add or remove a resource to or from the group as needed. You can also move resources from one group to another.

- **Location:** Resources in a group can reside in various regions (again, resource groups are *logical* containers that provide a means to apply various properties to resources they contain—it doesn't matter where the resources physically reside). However, resource groups do have an assigned location that determines where the group's metadata is stored. Compliance requirements can therefore dictate where you create your resource groups. Also, if the region where the resource group resides is unavailable, you will be unable to update the resources in the group because the metadata is unavailable. However, the resources can continue to function.

- **Scope:** Resource groups enable you to apply management scope to resources collectively. You can assign Azure policies, Azure roles, or resource locks to the group, which then apply to the resources contained within it.

- **Resource interaction:** Resources in different groups can interact with one another. For example, an application server in one resource group might use a database in a different resource group.

- **Deletion:** When you delete a resource group, all resources in the group are deleted.

- **Creation:** You can use the Azure portal, PowerShell, Azure CLI, or an Azure Resource Manager template to create a resource group.

- **Tags:** You can apply tags to a resource group. For example, you might use tags to differentiate production from development or user acceptance testing (UAT) resources. The tag applies only to the resource group and not to the resources inside the group. Think of the tag as a label you add to the box, not to the contents of the box. However, the resources in the resource group can have their own tags.

Azure Resource Manager

Azure Resource Manager (ARM) is the service that enables you to manage resources, serving as the deployment and management service for Azure. ARM is not a tool or interface. Rather, as a service it functions as the broker between management tools like the Azure portal and resource providers. For example, when you create a VM in the Azure portal, the portal sends the properties to the ARM application programming interface (API). ARM then communicates with the resource provider to create the VM.

ARM supports the use of templates for creating, managing, and monitoring resources. ARM templates are JavaScript Object Notation (JSON) files that define one or more resources and their properties to deploy a tenant, management group, subscription, or resource group. So, you can automate the deployment of an entire Azure environment by using templates. ARM templates significantly simplify the creation of resources because you only need to declare in the template what you want to create and what its properties will be, and ARM then passes that information to the Azure providers, which then actually create the resources.

Azure Subscriptions and Billing Scope

As explored in Chapter 1, "Cloud Concepts," Azure is a consumption-based service where you pay only for those Azure services that you use. This section explores the different ways to pay for Azure services and how to manage costs, billing, and related topics.

Azure Subscriptions

Just as a resource group serves as a logical container for resources, an Azure subscription serves as a logical container for your Azure resources but at a higher level. Think of a subscription as a big box that contains all your resource group boxes. Also, a resource group can only exist in one subscription. Using the box analogy, imagine you have two subscription boxes side by side. A resource group box could only exist inside one of them; it cannot be in two places at once.

In a simple Azure environment, you will likely have a single Azure subscription that contains all your Azure resources. As the complexity of your environment grows, however, you might want to use multiple Azure subscriptions to simplify resource management, billing, and cost containment.

Azure subscriptions serve multiple purposes. First, a subscription is a legal agreement associated with a specific Azure offer, each with its own rate plan, terms and conditions, and benefits. For example, a free trial offer is an example of an Azure offering that would be tied to a specific Azure subscription. If you choose an Azure free trial offer, that choice creates an Azure subscription tied to that trial offer.

Azure subscriptions also represent a payment agreement. If you choose a pay-as-you-go offer tied to a credit card, for example, the resulting subscription includes the credit card number and related billing information required to bill your Azure consumption each month to that credit card.

Subscriptions also serve as scale boundaries for Azure, imposing limits for scaling Azure resources. For example, there is a limit to the number of VMs you can create in each subscription.

Lastly, Azure subscriptions can serve as administrative boundaries, enabling you to control security, resource administration, and policies. For example, you might have administrative permissions in a subscription managed by your business group but not in a subscription managed by a different business group. Or, perhaps you manage all the VMs for your organization as part of the server team but members of the data team manage the SQL Server resources. Your server resources would be in one subscription, and the data resources would be in another. Subscriptions therefore provide a good means for segregating resources and administrative responsibilities between different business units, technical silos, and so forth.

Subscriptions are not the only mechanism to segregate administrative responsibilities in Azure. For example, you can use resource groups with different role-based access (RBAC) permissions on those resource groups to control administrative permissions on the resources they contain.

Many factors drive your decisions on how many subscriptions to have, how to manage the resources in them, whether to move resources among subscriptions, and so on. Some of these factors are explained in more detail in other chapters of this book where appropriate.

Azure Billing Accounts

A *billing account* is a mechanism that you use to pay for Azure services. You manage invoices and payments with your billing account, as well as track costs. Azure currently supports the following types of Azure billing accounts:

- **Microsoft Online Services Program:** This type of billing account is added when you sign up for Azure services through the Azure website, such as an Azure Free Account, an account with pay-as-you-go billing, or through a Visual Studio subscription.

- **Enterprise agreement:** An enterprise agreement (EA) enables you to purchase software and services from Microsoft under a (typically) multiyear agreement. For example, your organization might purchase on-premises licenses, Office 365 licenses, Azure services, and Unified Support services through your organization's EA for a given three-year period. An annual true-up reconciles the licenses that you have used and adjusts the next year's cost accordingly.

- **Microsoft Customer Agreement (MCA):** An MCA consolidates monthly Azure, Azure Marketplace, and Microsoft AppSource invoices. In some regions, an MCA is created automatically when you subscribe to pay-as-you-go or Azure free subscriptions.

You can have more than one Azure billing account. For example, you might have an MCA with a corresponding billing account, and then your company signs an EA, which would potentially give you another billing account. This can become significant (and confusing) because the different types of billing accounts have different scope, as explained in the next section.

A fourth type of billing account for Microsoft Partner Agreements specific to cloud solution providers exists but is not covered in this book.

Billing Scope

An Azure billing *scope* is a node within a billing account that enables you to manage invoices, payments, accounts, and other Azure billing-related data. As such, billing scope helps you manage Azure costs and billing in a relatively granular way.

Azure billing scopes are not directly evaluated on the AZ-900 exam, but understanding billing scope will help you better understand subscriptions, which are covered on the exam.

Each of the three types of billing accounts offers different scope options. Table 2.1 describes the scopes for the Microsoft Online Services Program; Table 2.2 describes the scopes for enterprise agreements; and Table 2.3 describes the scopes for Microsoft Customer Agreements.

TABLE 2.1   Billing scopes for Microsoft Online Services Program

Scope	Definition
Billing account	This node represents a single administrator account for one or more Azure subscriptions.
Subscription	A subscription is a grouping of Azure resources, and the Subscription scope enables invoices to be generated for each subscription, each with its unique associated payment methods.

TABLE 2.2   Billing scopes for enterprise agreements

Scope	Definition
Billing account	This node represents a single administrator account for one or more Azure subscriptions.
Department	This scope is an optional grouping of enrollment accounts.
Enrollment account	This scope represents a single account owner under which subscriptions are created.

TABLE 2.3   Billing scopes for Microsoft Customer Agreements

Scope	Definition
Billing account	This node represents a customer agreement for various Microsoft services and products. The billing account is then structured using the billing profile and invoice sections, which are described later.
Billing profile	This scope represents an invoice and its corresponding payment methods. Invoices are generated at the billing profile scope, but the invoice can include multiple invoice sections.
Invoice section	This scope represents a group of costs within an invoice, with subscriptions and other costs associated with specific invoice sections.

It's perhaps easiest to visualize billing scopes with an illustration. Figure 2.4 illustrates the scope relationships within a billing account for a Microsoft Customer Agreement.

FIGURE 2.4   Billing scopes for a Microsoft Customer Agreement account

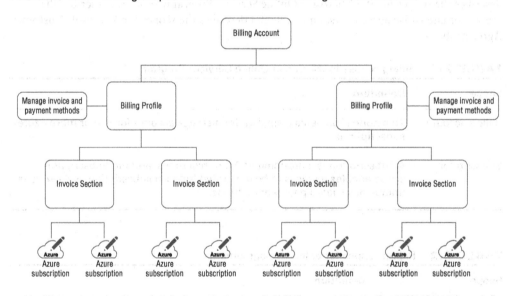

The most important thing to understand about billing scopes at this point is that they make it possible for you to more effectively manage billing and cost management within your Azure environment.

Azure Tenants

Azure tenancy bears some discussion when considering Azure billing and subscriptions. An Azure *tenant* is a specific instance of Azure Active Directory (AAD) that contains accounts and groups. In simpler terms, a tenant is a group of users. The tenant provides authentication services for your cloud resources, whether solely or in concert with onsite AD services.

Your Azure implementation is not limited to a single tenant. A *multitenancy* implementation is one in which more than one tenant share Azure resources. Figure 2.5 illustrates an example of a multitenant app deployed in Azure.

FIGURE 2.5   A shared application is an example of multitenancy.

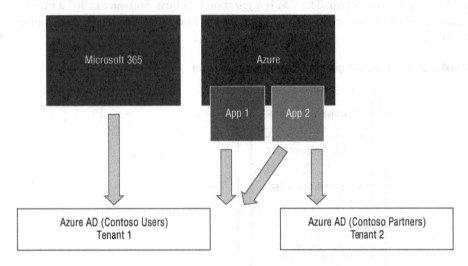

As you might have guessed, you can use a single tenant for multiple Microsoft cloud offerings. For example, you might deploy Microsoft 365, Dynamics 365, and Azure resources all associated with a single AAD tenant. Or, you might have multiple tenants in different scenarios. It all depends on your organization's needs.

Core Azure Services

Now that you have some understanding of how Azure is structured in terms of resource management, you are ready to begin learning about the core services available within Azure. The following sections explore these core services.

Virtual Machines

In the early days of computing, systems were always physical, meaning that a computer was a discrete collection of hardware that ran an operating system and often used various input and output devices. Imagine a data center where every computer is a separate, physical device. You can also imagine that the requirements for power, cooling, networking, and management would be significant.

Virtualization changed that model. Although physical computers are still a major component of many organizations' IT infrastructure, organizations are increasingly moving toward the use of *virtual machines* (VMs). A virtual machine is an emulation of a computer system that provides the functionality of a physical computer. The VM still runs on a physical device generally referred to as a *host*. The VM is a *guest* on that host. Software called a *hypervisor* manages the VMs running on the host. Figure 2.6 illustrates a virtual host with multiple guests.

FIGURE 2.6   Multiple guest VMs on a physical host

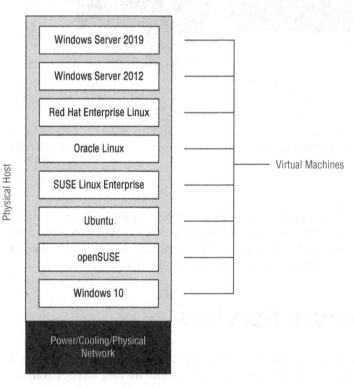

Virtual machines offer many advantages over physical machines. First, they reduce power and physical space requirements because multiple VMs can run on a single host. Granted, the physical host must have sufficient physical CPUs, memory, and other hardware to host the VMs, but they nevertheless host virtual systems more efficiently. For example, the data center rack space needed to host 10 physical servers might host 100 or more virtual servers. There is no specific ratio of physical-to-virtual machines because the requirements of each VM might vary. However, you can see that virtualization offers significant potential for reducing data center footprint.

VMs also offer considerable flexibility over physical machines. Because VMs are software based, you can create them very quickly by specifying their parameters and handing the actual creation task over to the hypervisor. A physical server that might take a day or more to deploy and get operational could take just minutes to deploy virtually.

Scalability is another advantage to using VMs. You can easily add resources like CPUs, cores, and memory to a VM by modifying its configuration settings. When you need to add another server for horizontal scaling, you can do so in a matter of minutes, either by initiating the process yourself or by allowing a preconfigured virtual machine scale set (described in the next section) to scale out automatically.

VMs are not limited to running whatever operating system is deployed on the host. A physical host might be running Windows Server, for example, but you might have several VMs on that server running Windows 10, Windows Server, and a selection of various Linux distributions.

Finally, VMs can be moved easily from one host to another because they are software based. You only need to move the metadata that defines the VM, not a physical server. For example, assume you need to move a VM from one region to another to accommodate a reorganization. The best method to achieve the move is to configure site recovery with the target region, move the VM using site recovery, and then fail over from the original VM to the new one.

The Azure Site Recovery service enables organizations to easily replicate virtual machines and physical servers from a primary site to a secondary site in support of business continuity. Not only can you replicate VMs between regions, but you can also replicate physical servers or VMs from your own data center to Azure.

Virtual Machine Scale Sets

A virtual machine scale set simplifies creating and managing a group of load-balanced VMs. A scale set can automatically scale out or scale in to adjust to changes in demand. Load balancing adjusts automatically to ensure that the access to the VMs in the set is balanced across VMs appropriately as VMs are added or removed from the set. Scale sets therefore enable high availability for your VMs and the services that rely on them. Scale sets also make it very simple to manage many VMs.

A scale set supports up to 1,000 standard VM instances, or up to 600 instances if you create and upload your own custom images.

The VMs in a scale set are all created from the same OS image, which ensures consistency across all VMs in the scale set. So, if a VM in the scale set hangs or is removed through a scale-in event, the remaining VMs can continue to service requests. If you need to include applications and other required components in the VMs, you create an instance with the appropriate services and configuration, save the image, and then use that image to create the scale set. All VMs in the set will then have the same components, applications, and configuration.

Azure scale sets can use either Azure Load Balancer or Azure Application Gateway to balance traffic to the VMs in the set. Which one you choose depends on the requirements of the app hosted on the VM.

Although scale sets offer high availability in themselves, you can also use availability zones to further improve availability by distributing the VMs across multiple data centers. If a data center experiences an outage, the VMs in other data centers can continue to function and service application requests.

Availability Sets

Availability sets are another feature of Azure that help you avoid potential outages caused by hardware issues, updates, or other events. Two elements that enable availability sets are *update domains* and *fault domains*. A fault domain is a logical grouping of hardware that shares a power source and network switch, similar to a physical rack in a data center. An update domain is a logical group of hardware that undergoes maintenance activities or reboot events at the same time.

An availability set distributes VMs across multiple fault domains and update domains (see Figure 2.7). Distributing the VMs in this way helps guard against outages caused by a power or networking event in a fault domain and also enables the VMs to be updated or otherwise maintained within their respective update domains without causing the set as a whole to be unavailable.

The use of availability zones affects your SLA. As of this writing, the following scenarios are available:

- 99.99 percent: All virtual machines with two or more instances deployed across two or more availability zones in the same Azure region will have connectivity to at least one instance 99.99 percent of the time in a specified SLA period.

- 99.95 percent: All virtual machines with two or more instances deployed in the same availability set will have connectivity to at least one instance 99.95 percent of the time in a specified SLA period.

- 99.9 percent: Any single instance virtual machine using Premium SSD or Ultra Disk for all operating system and data disks will have connectivity to that instance 99.9 percent of the time in a specified SLA period.

- 99.5 percent: Any single instance virtual machine using Standard SSD Managed Disks for all operating system and data disks will have connectivity to that instance 99.5 percent of the time in a specified SLA period.

- 95 percent: Any single instance virtual machine using Standard HDD Managed Disks for operating system and data disks will have connectivity to that instance 99.5 percent of the time in a specified SLA period.

FIGURE 2.7   Availability sets distribute VMs across multiple fault domains and update domains.

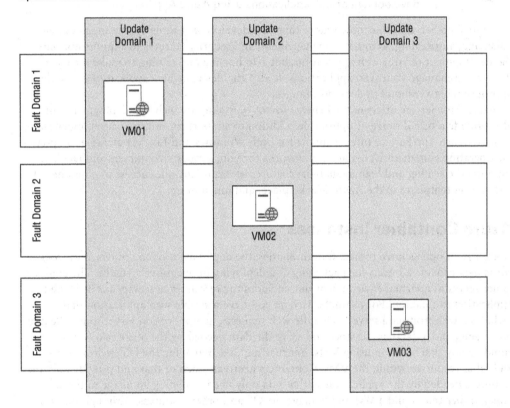

Based on this list, achieving 99.95 percent or higher SLA for your VMs requires the use of availability sets or availability zones. However, you can achieve 99.9 percent SLA on a single VM instance by using premium storage, which uses solid-state drive (SSD) storage on the same physical device hosting the VM.

Azure App Service

The Azure App Service is a PaaS offering that enables you to quickly develop and deploy web applications. Azure App Service supports many development languages, including .NET, Java, Ruby, and Python, among others. Web apps developed and deployed using Azure App Service run and scale on Windows and Linux environments.

 The Azure App Service also enables you to quickly build and deploy mobile back ends and REST APIs, but this chapter focuses specifically on development of web applications using Azure App Service.

Azure App Service offers much more than just development tools. It encompasses load balancing, autoscaling, automated management, and security features to support not only the development of your web application, but also hosting and scaling to make it easy to deploy and manage your web applications. It also enables your web applications to scale appropriately to respond to demand changes.

Azure App Service offers many benefits to not only simplify web app deployment but also provide a broad range of options. In addition to support for multiple development languages, Azure App Service offers support for both Windows and Linux, patches and updates the operating system and language frameworks for you, supports containers and Docker, supports the scaling and high availability features of Azure, includes access to a number of application templates in the Azure Marketplace, and much more.

Azure Container Instances

Docker is an open source project for automating the deployment of containers, and Docker *containers* provide a means for packaging and deploying applications virtually. The container serves as a virtual environment that includes the resources necessary for its hosted application to function. For example, assume you have a simple web application that includes a web front-end server to handle web requests, an application server to handle app processing, and a database to store and serve the data needed by the other two servers. You could deploy that solution using VMs, but that requires managing the OS environments and other resources within the VMs. Containers abstract much of that and provide only the resources needed by the application so that you only need to deploy an image to the container, rather than build a VM and manage the OS and other resources. Although the container relies on the underlying OS on which it runs, you don't have to configure or manage the VM. Instead, you focus solely on the application.

Azure Container Instances (ACI) is the Azure service that gives you the ability to create and deploy containerized applications. ACI supports both Windows and Linux containers. Containers offer a potentially significant cost savings because you are only paying for consumption of CPU and memory resources used by the container, rather than paying for a VM instance. In addition, containers can easily scale out to accommodate demand changes for the containerized app.

Although ACI supports only single container instances for Windows as of this writing, ACI supports container groups for Linux. A container group is a collection of containers that run on the same host machine and share the same operating system, lifecycle, local network, resources, and storage. The group shares a single IP address and DNS name. Figure 2.8 illustrates a container group.

FIGURE 2.8   An example of a container group

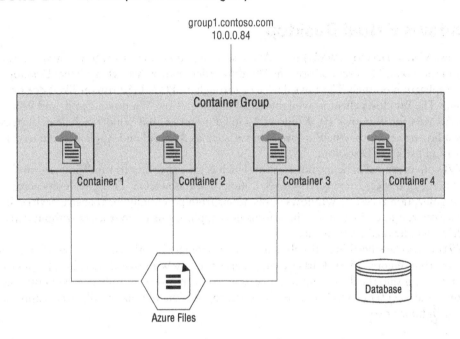

group1.contoso.com
10.0.0.84

Container Group

Container 1   Container 2   Container 3   Container 4

Azure Files

Database

 ACI supports Azure Files (discussed later in this chapter) to store data used by a container, enabling the container to persist data for stateful applications.

Azure Kubernetes Service

Managing a few container instances is relatively easy, but as the number of containers increases, deployment and management become much more complex. That is where Azure Kubernetes Service (AKS) comes into play.

AKS is a container *orchestration service* that monitors container health, provides container scalability, and enables resource sharing among containers in a Kubernetes cluster. Each of the containers in the Kubernetes cluster is called a *node*. AKS simplifies deployment because once you've defined a container image, you can use AKS to easily deploy as many instances of that image as needed within a cluster, as well as deploy multiple clusters.

> Within the context of the AZ-900 exam, anywhere you see a reference to container orchestration and large-scale management of containers, it is referencing Kubernetes.

Windows Virtual Desktop

Windows Virtual Desktop (WVD) is an Azure service that enables users to run a Windows client in the cloud. The user accesses the Windows client either through a Virtual Desktop client application on their Windows device or through an HTML 5 browser like Edge or Chrome. The Windows client is available for Windows 64-bit, Windows 32-bit, and Windows ARM64 for Windows 10, Windows 10 IoT Enterprise, and Windows 7 client devices. Using a browser enables non-Windows devices, such as Android and Apple devices, to connect to and use a WVD session.

WVD offers several benefits, not least of which is the capability to run Windows on a broad range of devices running Windows, Linux, iOS, and macOS. This gives users across your organization access to Windows applications from potentially inexpensive devices. It also enables you to easily roll out line-of-business applications to your users without deploying them to individual users' devices.

WVD is also beneficial in a distributed work environment, with users often working from home or from remote offices. Rather than provision a new Windows device, install applications on it, and ship the device out to a new user, you can instead simply provision the user in Azure, and the user can then connect to a desktop session and potentially access applications in an hour or so.

Core Azure Storage

The previous sections discussed several core Azure services. None of those services could function without storage, and Azure offers several core storage offerings. This section describes these storage offerings.

Blob Storage

Azure Blob storage is optimized to store very large amounts of unstructured data such as text and binary data. For example, if you need to store many documents of various types, Blob storage is a great solution. Blob storage can be accessed in several ways, including through HTTP or HTTPS, the Azure Storage REST API, Azure PowerShell, Azure CLI, or an Azure Storage client library.

When you think of Blob storage, think of situations where you need to store either many files or large files. Examples include documents, as already discussed; video and audio files; large amounts of data to be analyzed; and backup and recovery data.

Blob Storage Tiers

How you use storage and the type of storage you choose will determine how expensive that storage will be. You should take into account how you will access data to determine which storage solution is right for each situation. For example, you might access some data frequently and other data only seldom, if ever. In this scenario you should choose the least expensive option that meets your overall needs. At the opposite end of the spectrum, you might have data that is accessed frequently and therefore requires a different, more expensive storage option.

Azure Storage provides three *access tiers* for Blob storage to enable you to not only fine-tune the type of storage you need but also minimize costs. These tiers are as follows:

- **Hot access:** This tier is optimized for storing frequently accessed data.
- **Cool access:** This tier is optimized for data that you access infrequently and for a relatively limited period of time, and that typically would move to a lower tier of storage when access is no longer likely.
- **Archive access:** This tier is intended for data that you rarely access, if at all. An example is long-term storage for backups.

Hot and cool access tiers store data online, and the archive access tier stores data offline. The hot access tier has a lower access cost than the cool access tier but also has a slightly higher SLA and higher storage cost. Choosing the cool access tier means lower storage cost but higher access cost. This is generally a sound trade-off because you should access data stored in the cool access tier less frequently. The archive access tier provides the lowest storage cost of the three but has the highest cost to rehydrate the data from offline to storage. As you begin to develop a storage hierarchy and overall plan, keep these trade-offs in mind.

Disk Storage

Azure disks are virtualized storage presented as a disk and attached to a virtual machine, much like a physical disk in a server. Azure disks are designed for 99.999 percent availability through replicas, with a disk encompassing three replicas of the data. Even if two replicas fail, the third enables the disk to persist and the data to remain available.

Azure offers three main disk roles: data disk, OS disk, and temporary disk. OS and data disks are persistent, meaning they don't go away if you reboot a VM or redeploy it. Temporary disks are not managed and do not *necessarily* persist during maintenance events and reboots, although data stored on a temporary disk will persist during a normal, successful reboot of the VM that hosts it. Temporary disks therefore should be used only for swap files, temporary files, and other data that could be lost.

TIP   Azure supports direct upload of local virtual hard disks (VHDs) to Azure managed disks, making it relatively easy to move on-premises VMs to Azure and to move or back up large data disks to Azure.

Azure managed disks support two types of encryption: server-side encryption and disk encryption. Server-side encryption provides encryption-at-rest to safeguard your data and meet compliance and policy requirements. Server-side encryption is enabled by default for all managed disks, snapshots, and images. Disk encryption on Windows volumes uses Bit-Locker, and Linux volumes use DM-Crypt. Disk encryption enables you to encrypt OS and data disks.

File Storage

Azure Files is another storage type supported by Azure. Think of Azure Files as files that are available securely from anywhere in the world but not associated with a specific VM or volume letter. Files stored using this service can be accessed by using the Server Message Block (SMB) protocol or Network File System (NFS) protocol. Azure file shares can be concurrently accessed by on-premises as well as Azure services.

Azure Files support many file sharing scenarios, including replacing your existing on-premises file servers or NFS file shares, moving data from on-premises to Azure, and sharing application settings or other files that your applications need to access. You can also use Azure Files to store persistent data that enables you to build stateful containers, where the container instances access the shared file system at startup.

NOTE   The types of storage discussed in this section are only some of the storage types available in Azure, but these are the core storage services used by multiple Azure services.

Storage Accounts

Before you can begin using storage in Azure, you must create a *storage account*. A storage account contains Azure Storage objects and provides a unique namespace through which you can access those storage objects via HTTP and HTTPS. As you might expect, Azure offers several types of storage accounts, each intended for specific purposes and each with different costs. The following list provides a brief overview of each type of storage account:

- **General-purpose v1:** This is a legacy account type intended for blobs, files, queues, and tables.

- **General-purpose v2:** This storage account type is also intended for blobs, files, queues, and tables, as well as Data Lake Gen2.

- **BlockBlobStorage:** This storage account type is intended for block blobs and append blobs in high-performance scenarios such as high storage transaction rates, or where storage consists of small objects and/or low latency.

- **FileStorage:** This storage account type is intended for files-only storage scenarios where premium performance is required.
- **BlobStorage:** This is a legacy blob-only storage account type.

Creation and use of storage accounts is more complex than what is described here, but for the purposes of the AZ-900 exam, understand that there are various types of storage accounts suited to specific uses and you must create a storage account before you can create and use Azure storage.

Core Data Services

Azure is not just about VMs, storage, and applications. In reality, data is always the most important aspect of any IT system. There are exceptions but the role of infrastructure, storage, and applications is almost always to host and present data. As you might expect, Azure offers many types of data services.

Structured and Unstructured Data

Understanding Azure data services requires a brief discussion of *structured* and *unstructured* data. Structured data is defined by a schema that determines the characteristics and types of data stored in a data set. A table in a relational database like SQL Server is an example of structured data. The table includes columns that define which discrete data items are stored in the table, including the name of the column, its data type (like text, number, date, and so on), allowed length of the data, and other properties. Each row in the table defines a specific record or collection of columns that describe a discrete data item.

Unstructured data, as its name implies, does not have a defined structure and is not organized in a predefined way. Unstructured data often encompasses text—potentially large amounts of it—but can also contain other types of data, such as numbers and dates. Past studies have determined that the majority of data owned and managed by most organizations is unstructured data. To illustrate, consider the data that resides in all the emails, documents, spreadsheets, instant messages, and other data items you touch daily. In general, these data items represent unstructured data.

Semi-structured data is a hybrid of structured and unstructured data. Semi-structured data is not constrained to a data model like a relational data set containing tables of data, but the data does contain tags or markers that describe and enforce a hierarchy of records and fields within the data.

Azure SQL Database

To host your own database in SQL Server on-premises, you generally must deploy a server (physical or virtual), install Microsoft SQL Server on it, and use that server application to create and manage a SQL database. Standing up and managing that server and application can be time consuming and expensive.

Azure SQL Database abstracts all the infrastructure needed to host a SQL database. It is a PaaS offering in which Microsoft hosts the SQL platform and manages maintenance like upgrades and patching, monitoring, and all other activities needed to ensure a 99.99 percent uptime for your SQL databases. The only task you focus on is creating the SQL database and managing the tables, views, and other elements within the database. So, if your organization hosts SQL Server today, moving your databases to Azure SQL Database will eliminate a significant amount of management overhead and cost.

Microsoft rolls out new features to Azure SQL Database before rolling those same features out to SQL Server. Azure SQL Database therefore gives you the best means of testing and deploying new SQL features. Best of all, you don't have to deploy servers or applications to do so.

SQL Managed Instance

SQL Managed Instance offers many of the same benefits as the Azure SQL Database service. Like Azure SQL Database, SQL Managed Instance is a PaaS offering that provides a scalable cloud data service without the need to deploy or manage hardware or SQL. Instead, you focus specifically on managing your databases.

Although these two offerings are similar, SQL Managed Instance offers additional features for auditing, authentication, backups, change data capture (CDC), common language runtime (CLR), linked servers, OPENQUERY, and several other features. A key differentiator for SQL Managed Instance is its integration with the Azure Data Migration Service, enabling organizations to easily move existing on-premises SQL instances into Azure Managed Instance.

Cosmos DB

Azure Cosmos DB is a multimodel database service that enables you to scale data out to multiple Azure regions across the world. Scaling out your data in this way makes it readily available to your users worldwide, with response times in milliseconds. Cosmos DB also provides excellent elasticity in both throughput and storage, adjusting to changes in data storage requirements and high usage during peak hours.

Cosmos DB supports SQL for querying data stored in Cosmos, but also supports other APIs, including Cassandra, MongoDB, Gremlin, and Azure Table Storage, all of which are NoSQL solutions. A NoSQL database provides the mechanism needed to store and retrieve data in nonrelational databases.

A key advantage to using Azure Cosmos DB is its support for the Gremlin API. The Gremlin API enables you to use Azure Cosmos DB to store and query massive graphs at any scale, including those with potentially billions of vertices and edges. For context, a graph database uses a graph data type to store sets of vertices and ordered or unordered pairing of the vertices to model complex relationships. Azure Cosmos DB provides for a highly scalable solution to build and query graph-based data solutions.

Azure Database for MySQL

MySQL is an open source relational database management system that supports Structured Query Language (SQL). You can think of MySQL as an open source alternative to Microsoft's proprietary implementation of SQL.

Azure Database for MySQL gives you the capability to deploy, manage, and use MySQL databases without deploying MySQL on a server or VM. Instead, as with Azure SQL Database—which enables you to focus specifically on a SQL database rather than its infrastructure—Azure Database for MySQL lets you focus on your MySQL databases without worrying about the underlying infrastructure. Azure Database for MySQL is therefore appropriate in situations where you need to deploy and manage MySQL databases without having to manage the server, application, or other resources.

If you are familiar with web development, you might be familiar with LAMP, which stands for Linux, Apache, MySQL, and PHP. This is a common technology stack that organizations use to create web applications and websites. If you are considering moving from on-premises servers to Azure for your web applications and websites and use the LAMP stack for development, you should consider Azure Database for MySQL as an option. In the context of the AZ-900 exam, if you see a reference to LAMP, think MySQL.

Azure Database for PostgreSQL

PostgreSQL is an open source relational database management system with its origins in POSTGRES, which was a successor to the Ingress database developed at the University of California, Berkeley. Azure Database for PostgreSQL is an Azure-based implementation of PostgreSQL that supports the PostgreSQL database engine with the scalability, elasticity, high availability, and other cloud features you would expect from an Azure service. PostgreSQL is appropriate in situations where you want to deploy and manage PostgreSQL databases without worrying about underlying infrastructure.

Azure Database Migration Service

Azure Database Migration Service supports a variety of database migration scenarios for both one-time (*offline*) and continuous synchronization (*online*) migrations. In an offline migration, the source is offline while the migration takes place, making the application(s) supported by that data unavailable. In an online migration, the data is synchronized from the live source to the target and then the application is cut over to the new instance of the database.

Microsoft Marketplace

Microsoft's cloud offers incredibly rich environments with a very diverse user base. Like many Microsoft offerings, third-party providers supplement Microsoft's cloud offerings. These offerings are available through the Microsoft Marketplace, which encompasses two online stores: Microsoft AppSource and Azure Marketplace.

Microsoft AppStore offers business solutions for Azure, Dynamics 365, Microsoft 365, web apps, and Power Platform. The apps are available through the Microsoft Appstore site at `https://appsource.microsoft.com`, and through in-product experiences in M365, D365, and Power Platform.

Azure Marketplace is an online store that enables you to find and purchase a variety of Azure solutions and managed services. Think of it like Google Play in the Android world or the App Store for Apple devices. You search for apps, content, and so on in those stores on your mobile device, the content that you purchase is downloaded to your device, and you pay for it on your next phone bill.

Azure Marketplace lets you access Azure services that are built on or designed to work with Azure, as well as Azure managed services and consulting services (services delivered by third parties to help you deploy and manage Azure solutions). The resources that you obtain through Azure Marketplace are billed through your Azure account.

Summary

The services described in this chapter form the core services offered in Azure. Understanding the role these core services play will help you begin to understand how to achieve some of your initial goals in Azure and also to begin to understand some of the relationships between the various services in Azure.

This chapter covered the following concepts:

- **Core Azure Architectural Components:** Azure is a global cloud offering deployed to various geographies across the globe. Within those geographies (markets) are multiple regions, with regions paired with other regions for availability, fault tolerance, and redundancy. Availability zones ensure those same characteristics within regions.

- **Azure Subscriptions and Billing Scope:** Azure billing is tied to an Azure account, with three types of billing accounts available, including enterprise agreement, Microsoft Online Services Program, and Microsoft Customer Agreement. Your Azure subscriptions are associated with an Azure billing account. Subscriptions act as containers for Azure resource groups and, along with billing accounts, enable you to control how your Azure services are billed and paid for.

- **Core Azure Services:** Azure includes several core compute services, including virtual machines (VMs), which can leverage virtual machine scale sets and availability sets for scalability and high availability. Azure App Service makes it easy to build and deploy web applications without worrying about the underlying infrastructure needed for development or deployment. Container instances are another example of a core Azure service. Containers enable you to easily roll out and manage VM instances tailored for specific uses. Azure Kubernetes is a container orchestration service that you use to monitor and manage large numbers of container instances.

- **Core Azure Storage:** Supporting most Azure services in some way are the various storage services available in Azure. Blob storage is used for storing large amounts of data for access in various ways, disk storage is used primarily for virtual disks for VMs, and file storage lets you store files independently of a logical disk.

- **Core Data Services:** Azure includes many types of data management services for structured, semi-structured, and unstructured data. These data services encompass relational database solutions such as SQL Server for storing tabular data and NoSQL solutions such as Cosmos DB for storing and managing unstructured and semi-structured data.

Exam Essentials

Describe the core Azure architectural components.   Geographies align to markets but can generally be considered as aligning to countries or regions. For example, Europe is a geography that encompasses multiple countries. The United States is another geography that represents a single country. Within each geography are regions. Within the regions, availability zones enable services to be distributed across multiple physical data centers to ensure high availability, resiliency, and fault tolerance. An availability zone has its own power, cooling, and network resources, so that if an incident occurs in one availability zone, that incident does not affect resources in other availability zones.

Resource groups are logical containers that you use to group together Azure resources and enable you to control access to the resources and their management, and otherwise manage the resources in the group as a whole. The service that enables management of resources is Azure Resource Manager (ARM). ARM lets you create resources in a declarative way using templates, which it then passes to the target Azure service provider to create the service.

Billing is another key concept in Azure. Azure billing accounts are the mechanism by which you are billed for Azure services. Subscriptions serve as a container for Azure resources, and a resource can exist only in one subscription, although you can move resources between subscriptions. Subscriptions serve as a billing boundary, enabling you to charge different groups within your organization for various Azure resources.

Describe some of the core products available in Azure.   Although certainly not the only Azure service, virtual machines (VMs) are in some ways one of the most easily understood and certainly one of the most common Azure products. A VM is a virtual instance of a computer running as a guest operating system on a physical host device. A given host can run both Windows and Linux guests.

Virtual machine scale sets enable you to easily scale VMs out or in as needed to accommodate demand changes. The scale set includes load balancing to distribute load among the VMs in the set. Because all of the VMs in a scale set are based on the same image, scale sets also make it easy to roll out many VMs at once.

An availability set distributes VMs across multiple fault domains and update domains. Distributing the VMs in this way helps guard against outages caused by power or networking events in a fault domain, and it also enables the VMs to be updated or otherwise maintained within their respective update domains without causing the set as a whole to be unavailable.

Azure App Service is a PaaS offering that simplifies developing and deploying web applications. The Azure App Service takes care of the underlying infrastructure so that you can focus on developing the app, and the service also provides for deployment, load balancing, and other resources necessary to deploy and manage your app.

The Azure Container Instance service supports the creation and management of containers, which is a virtualized environment that includes the resources necessary for its hosted application to function.

Review Questions

1. Is the underlined portion of the following statement true, or does it need to be replaced with one of the other fragments that appear below?

    An Azure geography <u>always corresponds to a specific country.</u>

    A. corresponds to a single country or a market encompassing multiple countries.

    B. determines where your resources can reside.

    C. represents physical data centers.

    D. No change is needed.

2. An Azure region _____. (Choose all that apply.)

    A. corresponds to a specific data center.

    B. is paired with another region to help ensure high availability.

    C. can span multiple countries.

    D. specifies the location of Azure resources.

3. Is the underlined portion of the following statement true, or does it need to be replaced with one of the other fragments that appear below?

    Azure China <u>is only available to Chinese government entities.</u>

    A. has less restrictive regulations than other Azure geographies.

    B. is a physically isolated instance of Azure.

    C. includes Azure services that are only available in China.

    D. No change is needed.

4. An Azure region _____.

    A. specifies the location of Azure resources.

    B. is always paired with another region.

    C. contains one or more data centers.

    D. All of the above.

5. You need to deploy three virtual machines that will host an application. You want the VMs to reside in the same region, but you want to guard against power or other potential outages. You also need to ensure minimum latency between the instances. Which option describes a scenario that meets your requirements and is the most cost effective?

    A. You deploy an additional set of three VMs to a different region and use continual replication between the two regions, then fail over to the other region in the event of an outage.

    B. You place the VMs in separate resource groups in the same region.

    C. You use separate availability zones for the VMs.

    D. You use separate availability sets for the VMs.

6. Which of the following correctly describes an availability set? (Choose all that apply.)

   A. Protects against power, cooling, or other physical outages but requires distribution of additional instances to other availability zones to enable rolling updates.

   B. Two or more VM instances deployed to the same availability set results in a 99.99 percent SLA.

   C. Distributes VM instances across multiple fault and update domains to guard against outages caused by a data center outage and to enable VMs to be updated without making all instances in the set unavailable.

   D. A and B.

7. Is the underlined portion of the following statement true, or does it need to be replaced with one of the other fragments that appear below?

   A resource group in Azure serves as a logical container for Azure resources.

   A. provides high availability for resources within the resource group.

   B. protects resources in the group from being deleted.

   C. contains resources only from the region in which the resource group resides.

   D. No change is needed.

8. Is the underlined portion of the following statement true, or does it need to be replaced with one of the other fragments that appear below?

   Applying a tag to a resource group propagates the tag to all resources contained in the group.

   A. prevents resources in the resource group from being deleted if the tag is a CanNotDelete tag.

   B. determines the actions that administrators can take on resources in the group.

   C. applies the tag only at the container level.

   D. No change is needed.

9. You are planning a deployment of resources in Azure of various types to support a new project, and you want to use templates to simplify deployment and ensure that the new resources are configured the same as your existing Azure resources. Which one of the following would you use?

   A. Resource groups

   B. Azure Resource Manager

   C. Azure Resource Templates

   D. None of the above

10. Your CIO suggests the possibility of moving some of your organization's resources to Azure to cut costs and improve availability and DR options. She asks you to explain how Azure subscriptions work. Choose all answers that are correct.

   A. An organization can have multiple Azure subscriptions associated with either the same or different Azure AD tenants.

   B. A subscription can contain resources only from a single region.

    C.   You can use Azure multiple subscriptions to distribute costs to multiple groups within your organization.

    D.   A subscription can be moved to a new Azure AD tenant.

11. As a consequence of organizational changes that require restructuring some of your IT infrastructure, you need to move virtual machines from one region to another. Which of the following methods presents the easiest solution?

    A.   You back up the VM, restore it to the new region, and delete the original VM.

    B.   You move the VM to a resource group located in the new region.

    C.   You use Azure Resource Manager to move the resource to the new region.

    D.   You configure site recovery between the regions, migrate the VM to the new region using site recovery, and fail over to the new VM.

12. Which of the following is *not* a feature of Azure App Service?

    A.   Support for multiple development languages, including Java and Python

    B.   Support for Windows and Linux

    C.   Firewall protection for apps you develop with Azure App Service

    D.   Support for containers

13. You decide to use Azure Container Instances (ACI) to deploy containers as part of a project to deploy a new solution. You need to describe the benefits of using containers to your project team. Which of the following does not describe containers in Azure?

    A.   Containers can run on either Windows or Linux.

    B.   Containers represent a single application and the application's dependencies.

    C.   All containers in a container group share the same operating system.

    D.   Containers require setup and configuration of a virtual machine hosting them.

14. You need to deploy a stateful application using Azure Container Instances. Which of the following provides storage, enabling the application to store and retrieve persistent state?

    A.   Azure Disk

    B.   Azure Files

    C.   Azure Blob

    D.   Azure Archive

15. Your organization is planning to deploy a containerized solution in Azure and needs a container orchestration service that enables you to coordinate application upgrades and easily scale out containers. Which solution meets these goals?

    A.   Deploy the solution using Azure Container Instances (ACI).

    B.   Deploy containers using scale sets.

    C.   Deploy the containers using the Docker Management Portal (DMP).

    D.   Deploy the solution using Azure Kubernetes Service (AKS).

16. You want to deploy a solution that uses SQL to store and retrieve data on sales managers, sales quotas, and seller attainment. You want to minimize cost and configuration effort. Which solution achieves these goals?

    A. Use Cosmos DB to host the data.

    B. Use Azure SQL Database to host the data.

    C. Use a VM with SQL Server installed to host the data.

    D. None of the above.

17. Which of the following Azure services is designed for storing nonstructured data and includes support for NoSQL?

    A. Azure SQL Database

    B. Azure HDInsight

    C. Azure Database for MySQL

    D. Azure Cosmos DB

18. Your organization needs to provide a consistent user experience for running Windows applications across your enterprise, including for macOS, iOS, and Android devices. Which of the following Azure resources provide that consistent experience?

    A. Azure Client Emulator

    B. Windows 10 Enterprise

    C. Windows Virtual Desktop

    D. Microsoft 365

19. You have been tasked by your CIO with moving a large amount data from on-premises to Azure. The data needs to be maintained for compliance reasons but will not be accessed unless required by an audit or litigation. Which type of storage is the most cost effective?

    A. Cool access storage

    B. File storage

    C. Disk storage

    D. Archive access storage

20. You have set up a new Azure subscription and need to deploy storage to support a virtual machine. What is the first thing you must do to add storage?

    A. Enable the subscription to support storage.

    B. Create a storage account.

    C. Choose the appropriate blob storage tier.

    D. Nothing, because the VM includes blob hot access tier storage by default.

21. You are considering migrating several SQL instances from on-premises to Azure. Which of the following PaaS solutions provides the best support for SQL and the easiest migration path?

A. Azure Database for MySQL

B. Azure SQL Database

C. Azure SQL Database Premium

D. SQL Managed Instance

22. You are a project manager for a project to move several key web applications from on-premises to Azure. The development team has stated that support for LAMP is critical to simplifying the development effort. Which of the following is the most likely choice to support LAMP development?

A. Azure Database for MySQL

B. Azure SQL Database

C. Azure Cosmos DB

D. Azure Database for PostgreSQL

Chapter

3

Azure Core Networking Services

MICROSOFT EXAM OBJECTIVES COVERED IN THIS CHAPTER:

DESCRIBE CORE AZURE SERVICES

✓ Describe core resources available in Azure

- Describe the benefits and usage of Virtual Networks, VPN Gateway, Virtual Network peering, and ExpressRoute

The previous chapter explored several core Azure architectural components and core Azure services, with a focus on compute, data, and storage services. This chapter continues coverage of Azure core services focused on networking. A good grasp of these core networking services will not only help you understand how some of the other core services connect with one another, but will also prepare you to dive into security aspects of Azure, which are covered in Chapter 4, "Security, Compliance, Privacy, and Trust."

Networking Concepts

The Azure Fundamentals exam is not just for deeply technical roles—sales professionals, power users, solution specialists, and other less technical roles can benefit from a fundamental understanding of Azure. If you are in a role that is not deeply technical, you might not understand networking concepts sufficient to the requirements of the AZ-900 exam. This section lays the groundwork for the remainder of the sections in this chapter by covering some basic networking concepts. If you are a technical professional, you can skip this introductory section.

Client-Server and Serverless Computing

Until relatively recently, a *client-server* model prevailed in IT, with discrete servers hosting applications and services that were consumed by client systems (like desktop, notebook, and mobile devices). The servers were either physical or virtual. That model is still the most common, but as described in Chapter 1, "Cloud Concepts," PaaS and SaaS cloud offerings are evolving the way services are delivered to clients. In addition to discrete servers hosting applications and services, *serverless computing* means that the server is abstracted (or essentially hidden from the service consumers) and the service becomes the primary focus. Azure SQL Database is a great example. When you need a SQL database, you simply provision one and Azure handles all the server-related resources on the back end without any intervention from you.

Regardless of the model your solutions use, the servers, serverless applications, and clients need a way to communicate with one another. Networks provide that means of communication. For example, your email application needs to know where to find the mail server so that it can send and receive your email. Your web browser needs to turn a web address like www.microsoft.com into something that enables it to send requests to and receive responses back from the web server. Network addressing and the Domain Name System (DNS) are the primary mechanisms that make that communication possible.

Network Addressing

Each device on a network, whether physical or virtual, needs a unique identification that enables other devices and services to communicate with it. Each device is assigned a *network address* that serves as its address, much like a street address identifies the place where you live. For the AZ-900 exam, you don't have to understand network addressing in detail, so for now, think of a network address space as describing the building addresses in a specific neighborhood. Within that network address space, *subnets* further segregate parts of the address space into virtual networks. Using the neighborhood analogy, think of the subnet as describing a specific street in the neighborhood.

The two network address protocols used today to route traffic across local networks and the Internet are IPv4 and IPv6. The IP in the names stands for Internet Protocol. IPv4 uses a four-octet address to uniquely identify devices, such as 192.168.0.107. IPv6 uses eight groups of hexadecimal digits separated by colons, such as 0:0:0:0:0:FFFF:C0A8:006B.

Your personal computer (and other network devices including your mobile phone) receives a network address when it boots. The mechanism of how that works is not relevant to this discussion, but understand that the address identifies your device uniquely on its network. The address is defined by the network address space and a *subnet mask* that defines the virtual network on which your device resides.

If you are connected to a home Wi-Fi network, for example, your device is assigned an address from your Wi-Fi access point and the network uses that address to route traffic (information) to and from your device. Other devices on the network can also use that address to communicate with your device. For example, when you print a document to a network-connected printer, that data is routed from your network address to the printer's network address. Figure 3.1 illustrates an example of a home network.

Computers and other devices have no problem using numbers for addresses, but people do. That is where the Domain Name System comes into play.

Domain Name System

The Domain Name System (DNS) maps numeric IP addresses to *hostnames* that are more easily recognized and understood by people. For example, DNS maps the hostname www.microsoft.com to an IP address of 23.35.205.40. So, when you want to visit the Microsoft website, you type **www.microsoft.com** into your web browser instead of the numeric address. A *DNS resolver* on your computer communicates with a DNS server whose job it is to look up addresses associated with hostnames and return the hostname to your web browser. It is a bit like asking a directory service, "What's the street address for Joseph Q. Brown in Fargo, North Dakota?"

FIGURE 3.1   A simple home network

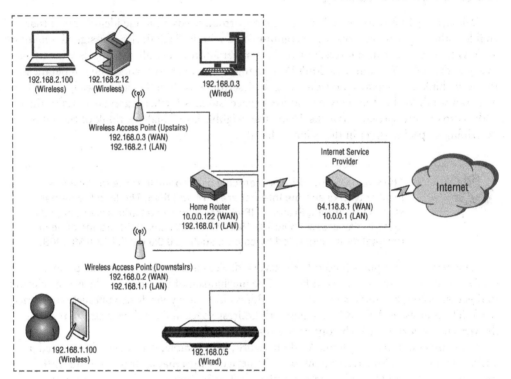

DNS is complex, but a deep understanding of how it works is not necessary to understand the topics in the AZ-900 certification exam. The key point is that client applications communicate with DNS servers to obtain the IP addresses associated with hosts like web servers, database servers, printers, and other network resources. The client applications then communicate with those hosts using their IP addresses. Likewise, servers and server applications communicate with one another using IP addresses that they obtain by looking up the address from a DNS server.

One key DNS topic to understand for the exam is denial-of-service (DoS) attacks, in which an attacker floods a system with traffic to overwhelm it and prevent it from functioning. Chapter 4 discusses DoS attacks that target DNS.

Routing

Earlier in the section "Network Addressing," you learned that networks are segmented into subnets (subnetworks), much like buildings are organized by their street. Your home network is a simple example of a network subnet. Figure 3.1, shown previously, illustrates a typical home network that includes a 192.168.0.x subnet for wired devices, a 192.168.1.x subnet for one Wi-Fi network, a 192.168.2.x segment for another Wi-Fi network, and a 10.0.0.x network for the Internet service provider (ISP).

The wireless access points (WAPs) in Figure 3.1 function as *routers*, routing data between the two subnets that they host and the local network. The home router handles traffic between those WAPs and the ISP's network. The ISP's router handles traffic to the Internet. For example, when you open a web page on your wireless tablet, the WAP manipulates the address information before sending it on so that the next router up the chain knows where to send the response. The next router does the same thing until the data reaches the web server. Then, the process is reversed until the data gets back to your WAP, which sends the response to your tablet.

Address translation and the other aspects of routing are complex and well outside the scope of this book. The key point to understand is that routers move data between subnets, manipulating the data so that the traffic can reach its intended destination and responses can come back to the requesting system.

There are two types of subnet—private and public. A private subnet is one that does not have a presence on the Internet. Your home Wi-Fi network is an example of a private subnet. Because it is private, that same subnet can be used by your neighbor. Your subnet is hidden from the Internet by your router. Public subnets have a presence on the Internet and corresponding host entries in the DNS system. Think of it this way: strangers know how to get to your home address because it is public but do not know where the television is in your home. The router is like a director at your front door who directs traffic intended for your television.

The main point to understand for the AZ-900 exam is that servers and services in Azure need IP addresses to route data. As with your home network, your subnets in Azure are private subnets, but at the point where your Azure networks meet the Internet, you have public network addresses. The public addresses are owned and managed by Microsoft, and the private addresses are assigned and managed by you.

Virtual Networks

A core concept for Azure and for any networking discussion is *virtual networks*, and the Azure Virtual Network (VNet) service is a fundamental component of your private Azure networks. VNet enables virtual machines and other Azure services to communicate among themselves, with the Internet, and in the case of a hybrid environment, with your on-premises networks. As you might expect from an Azure service, VNet adds availability and scalability to your network resources in Azure.

As you do with other Azure resources, you must create VNet resources in Azure. When you create a VNet, you specify the private IP address space that the VNet will use. Within that address space, subnets that you define enable you to segregate network segments for various resources. A virtual network is scoped to a single region and a single subscription. However, you can create multiple virtual networks within a region and subscription.

You can use virtual network peering to connect virtual networks, including across regions. This enables your resources to communicate across virtual networks (globally, if necessary), with the traffic traversing Microsoft's private backbone network. Resources in the peered virtual networks can communicate at the same latency and with the same bandwidth as they would if they were on the same virtual network.

Load Balancers

Load balancing refers to distributing network traffic across multiple resources to improve responsiveness, reliability, and availability. For example, if you deploy a web application with three web servers, you will use a load balancer to distribute the traffic among the three web servers. Client systems see a single hostname and IP address for the balanced services, and the load balancer distributes the traffic across the hosts in the balanced group. Not only does this distribute the load for performance reasons, but if one of the web servers fails, the load balancer can exclude the failed server from the group and begin sending all the traffic to the remaining two. Or, if you scale out with additional servers, the load balancer will begin sending traffic to the new servers.

Azure offers four load balancing services:

- **Azure Front Door:** Azure Front Door is designed for global or multiregion routing and site acceleration of Internet-facing web traffic. It uses the Microsoft global edge network to enable fast, secure, and scalable web applications.

- **Azure Traffic Manager:** This service is an application layer DNS-based traffic load balancer that balances traffic at the domain level. It can balance traffic across global Azure regions. Traffic Manager offers several options for routing traffic and detecting endpoint health.

- **Azure Application Gateway:** This is an application layer load-balancing service that provides an application delivery controller (ADC) as a service. You can configure Application Gateway as Internet-facing, internal-only, or a combination of the two. Azure Application Gateway is applicable for HTTP(S) traffic and can route traffic based on several criteria, including incoming URL, URI path, and host headers.

- **Azure Load Balancer:** The Azure Load Balancer service is a transport layer service designed for high performance and low latency and is zone-redundant to provide high availability across availability zones. It is applicable for non-HTTP(S) traffic.

> What do layers mean in the context of load balancing? The OSI model is a conceptual model created by the International Organization for Standardization (ISO) to enable communication between various systems. The OSI model encompasses seven layers: (1) physical, (2) data link, (3) network, (4) transport, (5) session, (6) presentation, and (7) application. The layers referenced in the discussion of the types of load balancers refers to the OSI layers. Azure Traffic Manager and Azure Application Gateway both function at layer 7, whereas Azure Load Balancer service functions at layer 4. A load-balancing service can support different functionality based on the level at which it functions. The OSI model and the details surrounding the layer-specific benefits are outside the scope of the AZ-900 exam.

Figure 3.2 shows an example of two Azure load-balancing services working together to balance traffic.

FIGURE 3.2   The load-balancing services in Azure can work individually or in concert, as in this example.

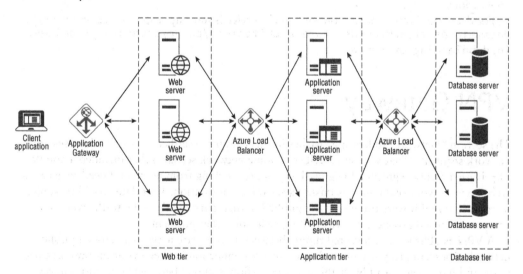

Which load-balancing service you choose depends on the scenario, and you might use one in some situations and more than one in others. Azure Load Balancer is generally the appropriate solution for non-HTTP(S) traffic based on the IP address of the target service. For example, you would use Azure Load Balancer when balancing traffic among multiple database VMs.

Azure Application Gateway is designed to support regional load balancing for HTTP(S) traffic and offers support for path-based routing. For example, assume you want to route traffic to a set of web servers. When the URL includes /videos in the path, you want to direct the traffic to a specific pool of servers that are optimized to handle video requests. Azure Application Gateway gives you that capability.

Like Azure Application Gateway, Front Door supports URL path-based routing. However, Azure Front Door is intended for globally distributed web applications where speed, user location, fast failover, caching, and high availability are critical. If you are configuring regional routing, think Azure Application Gateway. For global routing, think Front Door.

Azure Traffic Manager is appropriate for DNS-based global routing. Traffic Manager supports a variety of methods for routing traffic and for detecting endpoint health, enabling Traffic Manager to support a wide range of applications and usage scenarios where region or global load balancing is needed.

For the purposes of the AZ-900 exam, consider Azure Load Balancer as the service you would choose to balance traffic evenly across multiple virtual machines based on IP address. Application Gateway performs URL-based routing across multiple instances. Traffic Manager routes traffic to the data center that is geographically closest to the user. Front Door also provides that capability, but it offers additional features for global deployment of web applications.

For details and recommendations on which service is most appropriate, see https://docs.microsoft.com/en-us/azure/architecture/guide/technology-choices/load-balancing-overview.

VPN Gateway

The section "Network Addressing" earlier in this chapter described network addresses and network segments. That section described a home network scenario that included a couple of private network segments. Imagine that you are working from home and need to access a web server at work that contains business-sensitive information. That data would be subject to compromise if it were traversing the public Internet, particularly if the traffic were not encrypted. Virtual private networks (VPNs) help solve that problem.

A VPN establishes an encrypted tunnel between two private networks across a public network. For example, you can establish a secure connection between your on-premises network and Azure using a VPN, enabling traffic to flow securely between your on-premises data center and your resources in Azure. Similarly, you can use a VPN connection between your home network and office network to access the web server that hosts that business-sensitive data, protecting the data from prying eyes as it travels between the server and your computer. Figure 3.3 illustrates VPN connections.

FIGURE 3.3   A VPN connection establishes a secure tunnel between networks.

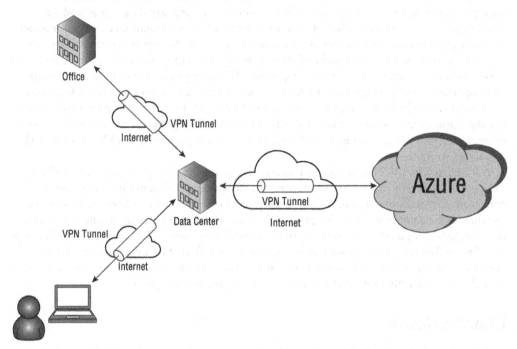

Even if your organization hosts all its IT resources in Azure, you will certainly need a VPN connection between your users and Azure to ensure that traffic between client applications and the services that host them in Azure is encrypted and secure. One option for creating a VPN connection to Azure is to use the Azure VPN Gateway service, discussed next.

Azure VPN Gateway

Azure VPN Gateway enables you to create VPN connections between Azure virtual networks and between Azure and your on-premises network. VPN Gateway supports multiple VPN configurations:

- **Site-to-site:** Establishes a VPN tunnel between two sites, such as between your on-premises data center and Azure.
- **Multi-site:** A variation of site-to-site, a multi-site VPN establishes VPN tunnels between Azure and multiple on-premises sites.
- **Point-to-site:** Establishes a VPN tunnel from a single device (point) to a site.
- **VNet-to-VNet:** Establishes a VPN tunnel between two Azure VNets.

A site-to-site VPN connects two sites, such as an on-premises facility and Azure. For example, you might use a site-to-site VPN to connect your primary data center and Azure, enabling secure, encrypted traffic between the on-premises servers and services that interact with resources in Azure. Or you might use a site-to-site VPN to connect your primary office location to Azure to secure user-related data traffic between the office and Azure. A multi-site VPN provides an expanded site-to-site capability. For example, you might use a multi-site VPN to create a secure connection to Azure from separate data center and office locations.

A point-to-site VPN is similar to a site-to-site VPN in that it creates an encrypted tunnel, but the connection is between a single device and a site. If only one server or service at one of your locations needs to connect to Azure, you can use a point-to-site VPN to connect that one server to Azure.

A VNet-to-VNet VPN connects two Azure VNets with an encrypted tunnel. The VNets can be from different regions and subscriptions. Connecting VNets in this way enables you to connect resources and networks in different Azure locations without traversing the Internet. One common use for a VNet-to-VNet VPN is to enable georedundancy of services. Assume, for example, that you want to build a highly available SQL Server solution that uses SQL Server Always On to replicate databases between different regions in an availability group. A VNet-to-VNet VPN tunnel between the two regions where the virtual servers reside provides the connectivity needed for replication between those regions.

ExpressRoute

Azure ExpressRoute enables you to extend your on-premises networks into Azure over a private connection managed by a third-party connectivity provider. The route does not traverse the Internet, enabling higher reliability, faster speeds, less (and more consistent) latency, and higher security. Figure 3.4 illustrates an ExpressRoute connection.

ExpressRoute Direct, as an alternative to ExpressRoute, enables you to connect directly to the Microsoft global network without traversing the Internet. Consider ExpressRoute Direct if you require physical isolation as a regulated industry or government entity, or if you need to move massive amounts of data into Azure. See https://docs.microsoft.com/en-us/azure/expressroute/expressroute-introduction for more information on both ExpressRoute and ExpressRoute Direct.

FIGURE 3.4   ExpressRoute establishes a secure route from your on-premises
network to Azure.

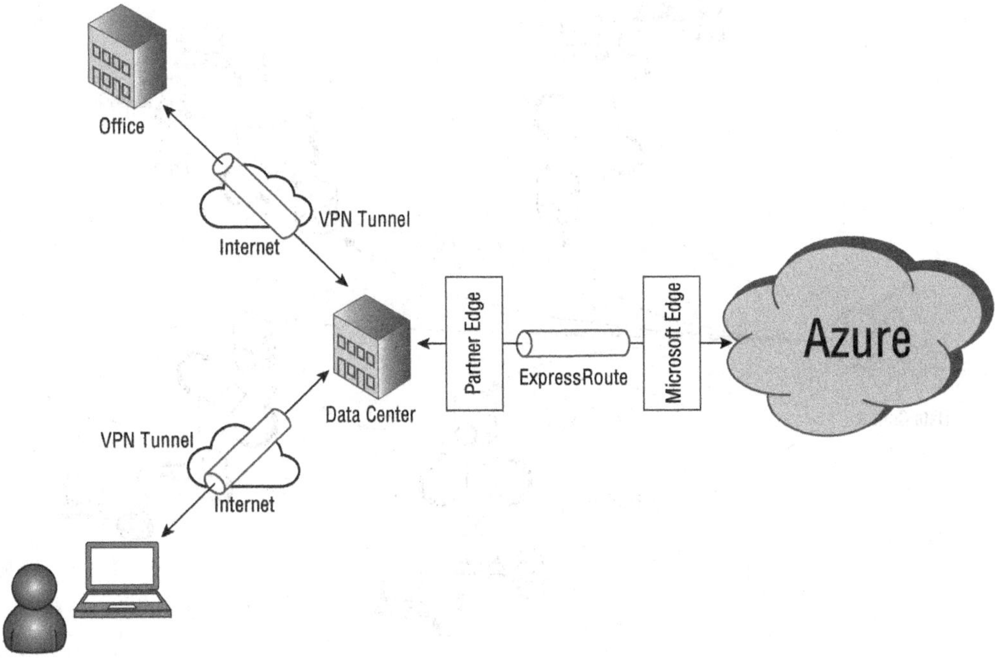

Content Delivery Networks

Azure Content Delivery Network (CDN) places web content across a distributed network of
servers to make that content readily available to users based on their location. For example,
if your organization is based in the United States but you have large video files that you
need to make available to users in Switzerland, you could place those files on a CDN that
has a point of presence (PoP) in Zurich or Geneva. When the users access those files, the files
come from the cached copies in the CDN, rather from your servers in the United States. This
reduces latency and improves performance. Figure 3.5 illustrates CDNs.

Each file has a time-to-live (TTL) property that determines when the file should be
refreshed from the source to the cache. If the TTL has expired and a user requests the file,
Azure CDN refreshes the data from the source to the cache and resets the TTL. This helps
ensure that the file is up to date, but also helps reduce network traffic for files that do not
change often, if at all. In the latter case, you could set a long TTL for the file to reduce how
often it is copied to the cache.

FIGURE 3.5   A CDN places content close to users geographically.

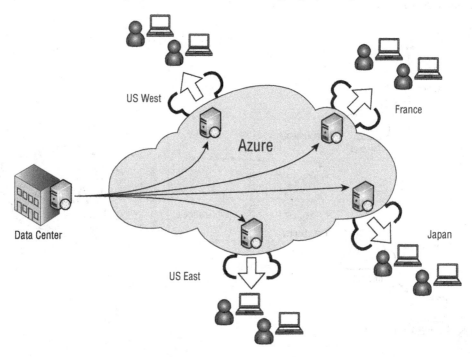

Azure CDN supports CDN caching rules, compression, geofiltering, scalability, and several other features. For more details, visit `https://docs.microsoft.com/en-us/azure/cdn/cdn-overview`.

Summary

The services described in this chapter are the core networking services offered in Azure. Becoming familiar with these services will help you begin to understand how various Azure resources communicate with one another, how your organization can connect to the Azure network, and how to secure traffic between VNets in Azure and between your on-premises network and Azure.

This chapter covered the following concepts:

- **Networking addressing:** Devices on a network are assigned a network address, which uniquely identifies the device on the network and enables network traffic to be routed to and from the device. Subnets create virtual networks to segregate devices within an address space. When you create a resource in Azure, you specify the address segment in which it will reside and either assign it a static address or allow it to take a dynamic address.

- **Routing:** Routers move network traffic between network segments. They make it possible not only for public network segments to communicate, but also for private network segments to communicate with public network segments.

- **Domain Name Service (DNS):** DNS provides host-to-address resolution, enabling applications and services to determine the IP address associated with a hostname.

- **Virtual private network (VPN):** A VPN creates an encrypted tunnel between two private networks across a public network, enabling secure network traffic between the two networks. You can establish a VPN connection between Azure network segments, your on-premises network and Azure, or between specific hosts.

- **Load balancer:** A load balancer distributes traffic to a group of servers or services, enabling the load to be shared among them. Load balancing also enables fault tolerance by detecting failed resources and directing traffic away from them.

- **ExpressRoute:** Azure ExpressRoute enables you to establish a secure VPN connection between your on-premises network and Azure through a third-party provider, bypassing the Internet. ExpressRoute Direct enables you to connect your on-premises network directly to the Microsoft global network.

- **Content Delivery Network (CDN):** A CDN places content near users, enabling them to consume that content without pulling the data from a geographically distant server. CDNs reduce network traffic and latency.

Exam Essentials

Describe core resources available in Azure.   You create VNets in Azure to segregate and organize hosts and services. Each VNet is scoped to a single subscription and region, but you can create multiple VNets. Virtual Network Peering enables you to connect VNets across regions.

The load-balancing services in Azure balance network traffic across multiple servers. Azure Load Balancer is used when you need to balance traffic based on IP address. Azure Application Gateway is used for regional load balancing of web applications, and Azure Front Door is intended for globally distributed web applications. Azure Traffic Manager is intended for regional or global DNS-based load balancing, but because it is DNS based it's not able to fail over as quickly as Front Door.

Virtual private networks (VPNs) enable you to connect two private networks using a tunnel through a public network such as the Internet. Use Azure VPN Gateway to establish VPN tunnels between Azure VNets and between Azure and your on-premises networks. VPN Gateway supports site-to-site, multi-site, point-to-site, and VNet-to-VNet connections. Azure ExpressRoute provides VPN connectivity between your on-premises network and Azure with higher possible speeds using third-party network providers. ExpressRoute Direct offers even higher speeds and connects directly to the Microsoft network rather than tunneling through the Internet.

Lastly, content delivery networks (CDNs) enable you to place content near where users are located, improving performance, minimizing network traffic, and reducing latency.

Review Questions

1. You are deploying a web application in Azure and need to distribute traffic based on a single public IP address to the virtual machines that are hosting the database. Which of the following best satisfies that requirement?

   A. Azure Application Gateway

   B. Azure Traffic Manager

   C. Azure Load Balancer

   D. Azure Front Door

2. Is the underlined portion of the following statement true, or does it need to be replaced with one of the other fragments that appear below?

   Your organization hosts its public website in Azure. You want to use URL path-based routing to accommodate processing for videos and images by sending traffic to server pools optimized for each content type. Your organization operates globally, and you also want to ensure the best possible performance regardless of where your consumers are in the world. You should use <u>Application Gateway</u> as a load-balancing solution to meet these requirements.

   A. Traffic Manager

   B. Front Door

   C. Azure Load Balancer

   D. No change is needed.

3. You are developing a solution in Azure that requires sending HTTPS traffic within a region to a specific endpoint based on the requested URL. Which of the following is the appropriate load-balancing service?

   A. Azure Application Gateway

   B. Azure Traffic Manager

   C. Azure Load Balancer

   D. Azure Front Door

4. Your organization is building a hybrid Azure environment where several on-premises services need to interact with resources in Azure, and vice versa, over a secure connection. You require high-speed connectivity through an encrypted tunnel across the Internet. The connection will be provided and managed by a third party. Which Azure service does this scenario describe?

   A. Azure Client VPN

   B. Azure VPN Gateway

   C. Azure ExpressRoute Direct

   D. Azure ExpressRoute

5. Your organization maintains two on-premises data centers named Alpha and Bravo, and you are considering moving some or all the resources hosted in those data centers to Azure. As part of an Azure proof of concept, you need to establish a connection to Azure from a server named vmtest01 in data center Alpha. Which VPN solution meets the requirement for minimum setup and cost?

    A. An ExpressRoute connection between Alpha and Azure

    B. A multi-site VPN connection between Alpha, Bravo, and Azure

    C. A site-to-site VPN from vmtest01 to Azure

    D. A point-to-site VPN from vmtest01 to Azure

6. You are an IT infrastructure manager for a large bank. You propose moving some of your IT infrastructure and services to Azure. You need to provide a secure, high-bandwidth connection from your primary data center to Azure, but the connection cannot traverse the Internet. Which of the following meets these requirements?

    A. Azure VPN Gateway

    B. Azure ExpressRoute Direct

    C. Azure ExpressRoute

    D. None of the above

7. Your global organization hosts an intranet that serves training content in the form of videos and large drawing files used by service personnel. These resources need to be available to users in the United States, Canada, the UK, and France with minimal network latency. Which of the following options meets these requirements with minimal cost?

    A. Use Azure Content Delivery Network to host the files geographically close to your users.

    B. Use VNet-to-VNet connections between regions to enable the documents and videos to flow rapidly between regions.

    C. Use ExpressRoute to provide higher bandwidth for user connections.

    D. None of the above.

Chapter

4

Security, Compliance, Privacy, and Trust

MICROSOFT EXAM OBJECTIVES COVERED IN THIS CHAPTER:

DESCRIBE GENERAL SECURITY AND NETWORK SECURITY FEATURES

✓ **Describe Azure security features**

- Describe basic features of Azure Security Center, including policy compliance, security alerts, secure score, and resource hygiene
- Describe the functionality and usage of Key Vault
- Describe the functionality and usage of Azure Sentinel
- Describe the functionality and usage of Azure Dedicated Hosts

DESCRIBE GENERAL SECURITY AND NETWORK SECURITY FEATURES

✓ **Describe Azure network security**

- Describe the concept of defense in depth
- Describe the functionality and usage of Network Security Groups (NSG)
- Describe the functionality and usage of Azure Firewall
- Describe the functionality and usage of Azure DDoS Protection

DESCRIBE IDENTITY, GOVERNANCE, PRIVACY, AND COMPLIANCE FEATURES

✓ **Describe core Azure identity services**

- Explain the difference between authentication and authorization
- Define Azure Active Directory
- Describe the functionality and usage of Azure Active Directory
- Describe the functionality and usage of Conditional Access, Multi-Factor Authentication (MFA), and Single Sign-On (SSO)

DESCRIBE IDENTITY, GOVERNANCE, PRIVACY, AND COMPLIANCE FEATURES

✓ **Describe Azure governance features**

- Describe the functionality and usage of Role-Based Access Control (RBAC)

- Describe the functionality and usage of resource locks

- Describe the functionality and usage of tags

- Describe the functionality and usage of Azure Policy

- Describe the functionality and usage of Azure Blueprints

- Describe the Cloud Adoption Framework for Azure

DESCRIBE IDENTITY, GOVERNANCE, PRIVACY, AND COMPLIANCE FEATURES

✓ **Describe privacy and compliance resources**

- Describe the Microsoft core tenets of Security, Privacy, and Compliance

- Describe the purpose of the Microsoft Privacy Statement, Product Terms site, and Data Protection Addendum (DPA)

- Describe the purpose of the Trust Center

- Describe the purpose of the Azure compliance documentation

- Describe the purpose of Azure Sovereign Regions (Azure Government cloud services and Azure China cloud services)

DESCRIBE CORE SOLUTIONS AND MANAGEMENT TOOLS ON AZURE

✓ **Describe Azure management tools**

- Describe the functionality and usage of Azure Advisor

- Describe the functionality and usage of Azure Monitor

- Describe the functionality and usage of Azure Service Health

Chapter 3, "Azure Core Networking Services," introduced several key networking concepts and Azure networking resources. This chapter expands on those concepts to describe Azure services and resources that enable you to apply various security methods to protect network traffic between Azure and your services and users. Topics covered in this chapter include Azure Firewall, network security groups, application security groups, user-defined routes, and Azure DDoS Protection.

This chapter also describes the key security-related topics of authentication and authorization, differentiating the two, and covers Azure AD and multifactor authentication. Continuing the security focus, the chapter explores Azure services, including Azure Security Center, Azure Key Vault, and Azure Information Protection.

This chapter also introduces several governance topics covered in the exam, including initiatives and policies, controlling access with role-based access control (RBAC), locking resources, and using Azure Advisor and Azure Blueprints. Reporting and monitoring options are also included.

The chapter rounds out with a discussion of compliance and data protection standards to help you begin to understand how to implement compliant solutions in Azure, as well as topics relevant to governmental and geopolitical requirements.

Network Security

Chapter 3 laid the foundations for understanding networking concepts and described resources and services in Azure that provide for networking Azure resources, securing network traffic with VPN options, connecting your data centers to Azure, using load balancing, and moving content close to your users with content delivery networks (CDNs). This chapter turns the focus from networking to resources and service in Azure that help secure your networks and network traffic.

Before exploring specific Azure services for networking security, let's discuss an underlying concept: *defense in depth*.

Defense in Depth

Bad actors have many ways to compromise an organization's security, from physical access to your building and facilities to attacks on your IT services and user devices. These attacks can come in many forms. Protecting against these bad actors is therefore obviously more difficult than simply deploying a firewall or ensuring your users have an antivirus application installed on their devices. This is where the concept of defense in depth comes into play.

Defense in depth defines a strategy for multiple layers of defense to protect your facilities, data, services, and users from compromise. These defense layers begin with physical security and extend to multiple points of potential compromise. The following list summarizes the key defense layers:

- **Physical security:** Controlling physical access to your facilities, including offices, data centers, and ancillary facilities such as warehouses and manufacturing plants, is critical to prevent unauthorized access to data in multiple forms and to servers, user devices, and other potential points of physical compromise.

- **Identity and access:** This layer protects services and data by ensuring that only authenticated users can access resources and that authorization ensures users can access only those resources allowed to them. Protection options include but are not limited to access control, single sign-on, multifactor authentication, and auditing.

- **Perimeter:** The perimeter of your network is the first point at which bad actors can potentially gain access to servers and other resources or execute attacks against your network. Firewalls help prevent intrusion, and services such as Azure DDoS Protectioncan guard against large-scale attacks.

- **Network:** Even within an internal network that is protected at the perimeter by a firewall, it's important to protect against potential threats. This includes ensuring that traffic can flow only between allowed endpoints, denying access by default and allowing access by exception only, highly restricting incoming access, limiting outbound traffic as necessary, and ensuring a highly secure connection between your on-premises networks and Azure.

- **Compute:** At this layer it is important to limit and secure access to servers, implement endpoint protection on all virtual servers, and ensure that all systems are patched against all potential threats.

- **Application:** At this layer protection begins with developing applications with security as the first and primary consideration. Third-party applications should be kept patched against vulnerabilities. You can use Azure Key Vault to protect secrets used by your applications.

- **Data:** This layer applies protection to your data in multiple locations, including databases and storage.

The specifics of fully implementing protection at each of these layers goes beyond the scope of this book and of the AZ-900 exam. However, the Azure services that are key to developing and implementing a defense-in-depth strategy are covered through the remainder of this chapter.

Azure Firewall

A *firewall* is a device or service that inspects network traffic flowing through it and applies actions to that traffic based on rules that you specify. Firewalls protect networks from intrusion and different types of network attacks. For example, if the only endpoints that you need to serve to your users are HTTP (port 80) and HTTPS (port 443), you would create a rule in your firewall to block all traffic inbound for ports other than 80 and 443. Firewalls can provide other capabilities as well. For example, some firewalls analyze network traffic for viruses, worms, and other network-borne threats.

Azure Firewall is a managed firewall service. It is a *stateful* firewall in that it inspects sessions of network traffic and can act based on the context and state of the packets. By contrast, a stateless firewall inspects individual data packets and is more limited in the information it gleans and therefore the actions it can take.

Azure Firewall can filter traffic based on several criteria, including port number, protocol type, network address, and fully qualified domain name (FQDN), among others. You create rules to specify how Azure Firewall will treat incoming and outgoing network traffic. If the traffic matches a rule that denies that type of traffic, the traffic is blocked. If the traffic matches a rule that allows that type of traffic, the traffic is allowed to flow through the firewall. If no rule applies, the traffic is blocked (denied). The firewall can also modify the traffic—for example, changing the source or destination addresses to route traffic. This latter mechanism is known as network address translation (NAT) and enables traffic to be routed between different network segments. Figure 4.1 illustrates an example of Azure Firewall in use.

FIGURE 4.1   Use Azure Firewall to scan and filter network traffic.

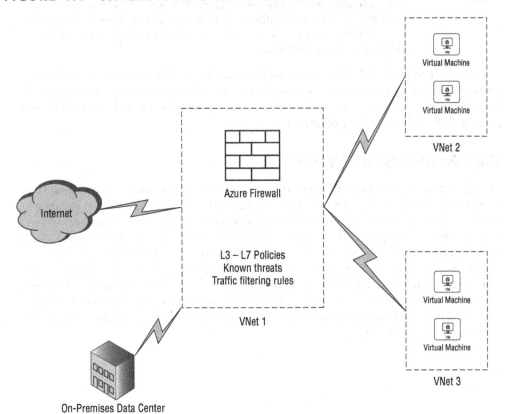

A fully qualified domain name uniquely identifies a host on a network, incorporating the hostname itself and the full domain name in which it resides. An example of a FQDN is www.microsoft.com, where www is the host and microsoft.com is the domain. If a host resides in a subdomain, the FQDN would include the subdomain, such as owa.mail. microsoft.com.

Azure Firewall supports three types of rule collections:

- **NAT rules:** As explained previously, NAT rules enable traffic to be forwarded between network segments, such as from the Internet to Azure resources.

- **Network rules:** These rules allow or deny traffic based on protocol type, inbound or outbound address, and inbound or outbound port.

- **Application rules:** These rules allow specific applications to communicate across the firewall and control traffic by FQDN. For example, you could block traffic to a specific website using an application rule.

Azure Firewall supports FQDN tags to simplify traffic routing. An FQDN tag represents a group of FQDNs that are associated with well-known Microsoft services. For example, you might use an FQDN tag in a rule to allow Windows Update traffic through Azure Firewall. Microsoft manages the FQDN tags, and you only need to include a tag in a firewall rule to allow the appropriate traffic.

In the context of the AZ-900 exam, consider Azure Firewall whenever you need to filter traffic based on source IP address and port, destination address and port, and/or protocol. Azure Firewall is not specific to certain types of applications. For example, it is not limited to filtering traffic only for web applications.

Web Application Firewall

Chapter 3 described the load-balancing offerings of Azure Application Gateway and Azure Front Door, as well as Azure Content Delivery Network (CDN). Azure Web Application Firewall (WAF) is a firewall service that you can deploy with each of these services to provide firewall services specifically for your web applications. WAF provides features tailored to each of these services. Figure 4.2 illustrates WAF being used with Application Gateway.

WAF protects your web applications against common vulnerabilities and exploits, such as SQL injection and cross-site scripting. As with Azure Firewall, policies and rules determine how WAF functions in each deployment. WAF offers Azure-managed rules, which are pre-configured rules that you can deploy easily to guard against common threats. You can also create custom rules as needed.

FIGURE 4.2   Web Application Firewall works in conjunction with the Application Gateway, Front Door, and CDN services.

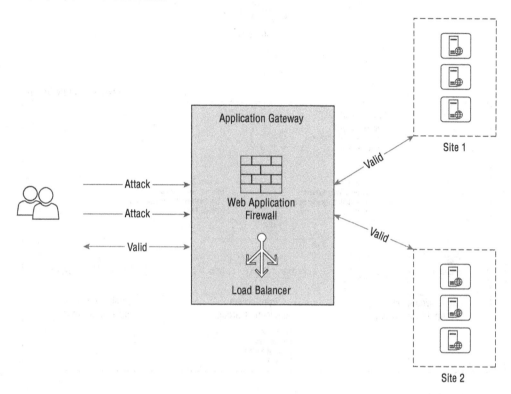

The key points to understand about WAF in the context of the AZ-900 exam are that it works in concert with Application Gateway, Front Door, and CDN, and it is specific to web application scenarios. If you are looking to protect other services and resources, turn to Azure Firewall and/or the additional network security services described in the following sections.

Network Security Groups

Network security groups (NSGs) are an additional firewall service offered in Azure. NSGs enable you to filter network traffic between Azure resources in an Azure virtual network. An NSG can be scoped to a subnet or to a network interface on a VM, and a single NSG can apply to multiple VMs or subnets. As with other Azure firewall services, you can create rules to determine which actions an NSG will take. NSGs also have default rules applied to them to allow communication between resources in a virtual network. NSGs can filter traffic based on protocol, source IP address, source port, destination IP address, and destination port. Figure 4.3 illustrates an implementation of an NSG. The NSG applies to all VMs within the subnet.

FIGURE 4.3   A network security group is a simple firewall offering in Azure.

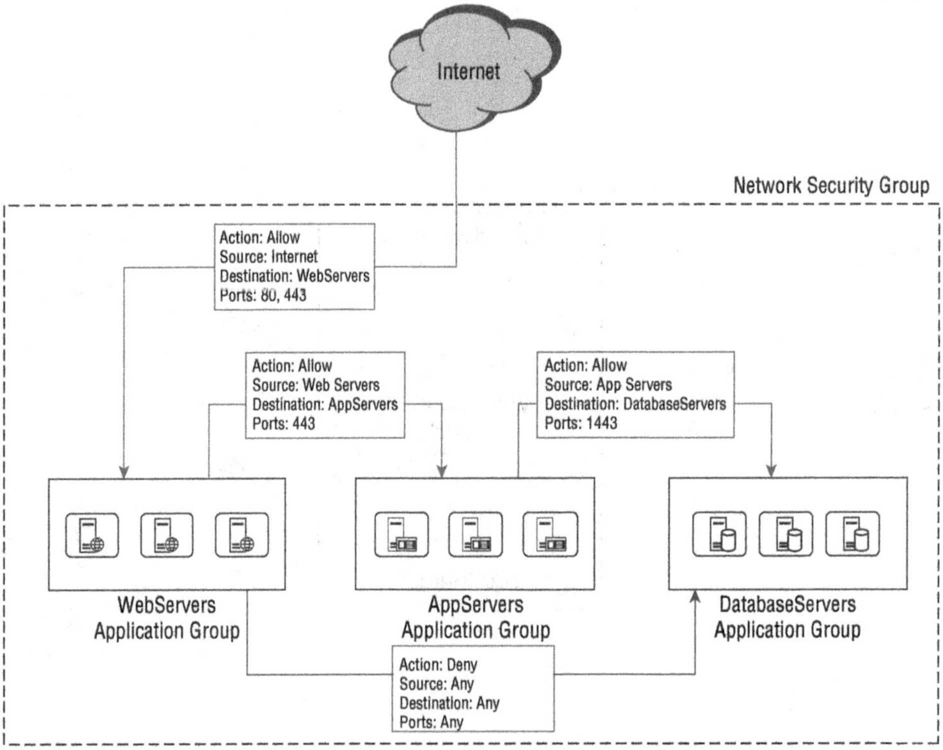

Your Azure implementation will likely incorporate various levels of protection using many, if not all, of the firewall- and security-related services available in Azure to provide defense in depth. For example, if you do not host any web applications in Azure, the Azure Firewall might be the only solution you choose. But you might use Azure Firewall as a frontline defense with NSGs and application security groups (discussed in the next section), providing further protection for specific applications and networks. Or you might use Application Gateway in concert with NSGs to protect networks where web applications are hosted without employing Azure Firewall. The key point is that you must consider protection at multiple levels within your Azure environment and implement the service or combination of services that offers the appropriate protection.

In the context of the AZ-900 exam, keep in mind that NSGs provide protection at the subnet or individual VM level and are often deployed using application security groups, which are discussed next.

Application Security Groups

An application security group (ASG) enables you to group servers based on the applications running on them and then manage security for them as a group. The ASG is an object reference within a network security group, enabling you to easily apply the rules in the NSG to the virtual machines contained in the ASG. So, rather than apply a network security group to specific VMs where application servers reside, you create the ASG and add VMs to it, and then create the NSG and reference the ASG in it. The NSG rules then apply to the VMs in the ASG.

ASGs simplify how you apply NSGs to virtual machines. For example, you create an ASG and reference one VM in it. Then you create an NSG and reference the ASG in it. Now, that one VM in the ASG has those rules applied to it. All you need to do to apply the same NSG to a dozen other servers is to add them to the same ASG. Those servers now have the NSG applied to them.

User-Defined Routes

Chapter 3 described routing in general and how network traffic is routed between network subnets. When you define a subnet in Azure, Azure creates default routes to determine how resources in the subnet will communicate with resources in other subnets. Those routes are stored in a routing table that is used to determine the next hop for the traffic. Default routes work fine for many scenarios, but not for all. That is where user-defined routes (UDRs) come into play.

What is a network *hop*? Remember the discussion from Chapter 3 about your home network? When traffic from your wireless device hits the wireless access point (WAP), a routing table stored and managed by the WAP tells it where to send the traffic. Assume the traffic is destined for the Internet. The WAP determines that the destination address is a service on the public Internet and, based on its routing table, sends the traffic to the home router, which it knows is the next hop (the next way-point on the traffic's journey) to the Internet. From there, the home router uses its own routing table to determine where to send the traffic. In this case, it sends the traffic to the ISP's router (the next hop). The process repeats until the network traffic reaches its destination.

A UDR enables you to define a custom route to override the default route. For example, assume you have a secure service hosted on a VM within a specific subnet and you want all traffic destined for that VM to go through a specific firewall instead of taking the default route. The target firewall is configured with rules to manage that traffic and scan it for certain vulnerabilities that would affect that specific VM. The solution is to create a UDR that directs traffic destined for the IP address of the VM through the firewall.

For the purposes of the AZ-900 exam, simply keep in mind that UDRs enable you to create a custom routing table and direct traffic through nondefault routes.

Azure DDoS Protection

As explored in Chapter 3, distributed denial-of-service (DDoS) attacks overwhelm a service by flooding the service with requests. When the number of requests increases significantly, the service's performance begins to suffer as resources are consumed. If enough requests are received by the service, it can fail altogether, making the service unavailable and denying access to the service (hence the name).

Azure DDoS Protection provides a means of defense against DDoS attacks. Azure DDoS guards against the following types of attacks:

- **Volumetric attacks:** These attacks flood an endpoint with a very large volume of traffic to overwhelm the service and/or consume all of the network bandwidth available within the network or between the endpoint and the rest of the Internet.

- **Protocol attacks:** These attacks target specific server resources through weaknesses in the protocol stack. An example is the Ping of Death attack, which floods the endpoint with ping requests, consuming service resources or overwhelming intermediate services such as the upstream firewall.

- **Resource layer attacks:** These attacks target the application layer of the protocol stack to affect web application traffic between hosts.

Azure provides DDoS Protection Basic and DDoS Protection Standard. The Basic offering provides active traffic monitoring and automatic attack mitigation. The Standard offering adds several other features, including an availability guarantee, mitigation policies, metrics and alerts, reporting, and more. So, if you only need detection and mitigation, Basic provides that function. When alerting, reporting, and customization are needed, DDoS Protection Standard is the appropriate offering.

Authentication and Authorization

The AZ-900 exam measures your knowledge about Azure Active Directory, authentication, and authorization. This section explores these topics, beginning with Azure Active Directory.

Azure Active Directory

Azure Active Directory (Azure AD) is Microsoft's cloud-based identity and access management service. Azure AD enables users to log into cloud services such as Microsoft 365 and access resources in Azure, including custom applications that you create and host in Azure. You can also use Azure AD to provide access for your users to resources hosted on-premises.

If you subscribe to Microsoft 365, Office 365, Azure, or Dynamics 365, you already have Azure AD because these subscriptions automatically get an Azure AD tenant with access to all of the free Azure AD services offered by Microsoft. You can also take advantage of paid Azure AD plans when you need additional capabilities. The following list explores these options:

- **Azure Active Directory Free:** This option provides management of users and groups, synchronization with on-premises Active Directory, basic reporting, self-service password change for accounts in Azure AD, and single sign-on (SSO) for Azure, Microsoft 365, Dynamics 365, and other applications hosted in the cloud.

- **Azure Active Directory Premium P1:** This option includes all features in Free along with the capability to access on-premises resources as well as cloud resources, support for dynamic groups, self-service group management, Microsoft Identity Manager, and cloud write-back to allow self-service password changes for on-premises users.

- **Azure Active Directory Premium P2:** P2 includes Free and P1 features along with Azure Active Directory Identity Protection for conditional access to apps and critical data, and Privileged Identity Management to discover, monitor, and restrict administrative access to resources.

- **Pay-as-you-go feature licenses:** Add other features to a pay-as-you-go tenant.

Regardless of which Azure AD offering you choose, you do not need to integrate with an on-premises Active Directory to use Azure AD for authentication and authorization. If all your IT resources are in the cloud and you host nothing on-premises, Azure AD can be your sole directory service. However, you can integrate with on-premises AD for hybrid cloud scenarios involving on-premises and cloud services by deploying Active Directory Federation Services (ADFS).

Azure AD supports role-based access control (RBAC) to manage access to cloud resources. With RBAC, you control who has access to specific Azure resources, what actions they can take with those resources, and what areas they can access.

To use RBAC in Azure, you create a role assignment that consists of a security principal, role definition, and scope:

- **Security principal:** Represents a user, group, service principal, or managed identity. A service principal is a representation of an application and is used to define the application's permissions. Managed identities provide services with the ability to authenticate to other Azure services without the need for a developer to create or manage identities or their credentials.

- **Role:** A collection of permissions that determine the actions that the role can perform, such as read, write, and delete. Azure offers built-in roles, and you can create custom roles where needed.

- **Scope:** The set of resources to which the access applies. You can specify scope in Azure at the management group, subscription, resource group, or resource level. A management group is a container for subscriptions, enabling you to organize and control management across multiple subscriptions. Figure 4.4 illustrates management groups.

FIGURE 4.4   Management groups serve as containers for subscriptions and enable you to control management across those subscriptions.

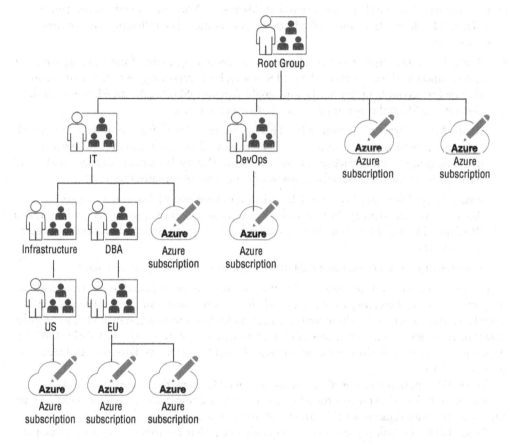

To sum up RBAC, the security principal describes who or what has a set of permissions, the role specifies the permissions that security principal has, and the scope defines where the security principal can use those permissions. So, Security Principal = who, Role = what, and Scope = where.

Authentication and Authorization

There is a difference between *authentication* and *authorization*, and the AZ-900 exam measures your knowledge of that difference. Simply put, authentication identifies a user and authorization determines the actions that an authenticated user can perform. It is a case of "who are you?" and "what can you do?"

In the context of Azure AD or on-premises Active Directory, a user's account identifies the user, providing authentication. So, when you provide a username and password, Azure AD authenticates you against those credentials. When you log into a website, you might submit your email address and a password to go with it. This is another example of authentication. Your debit card uses a form of authentication as well. The card number and numeric PIN that you enter to use the card in an ATM identify (authenticate) you. Presenting your passport to board a flight is another example of authentication because the passport identifies you.

As described earlier, authorization determines the actions you can take *after* you have been authenticated. Using your passport again as an example, the passport authenticates who you are, but it does not by itself allow you to travel to another country. A *travel visa* serves as your authorization to enter the country. Showing your birth certificate to prove that you are eligible for age-based benefits is another example of authorization because it lists your age (authorizing you for benefits) as well as identifying you.

Azure Multifactor Authentication

Multifactor authentication (MFA) is a mechanism that uses more than one *factor* to authenticate you. Assume your organization does not use MFA. To log on to the company intranet, you enter your username and password, and the site grants you access. This is single-factor authentication. The username itself does not authenticate you—providing the appropriate password does.

MFA increases security by requiring a second form of verification. For example, text messages are a common means of MFA. If your organization were using MFA in the previous example, you log on to the website and provide your username and password. The system then sends a text message to the mobile number it has on file for you with an access code. You enter the code into the browser, authenticating your identity. Passwords, voice calls, text messages, and verification emails are examples of methods that can be used to authenticate a user. When you use two or more methods, you are performing multifactor authentication.

Conditional Access

Conditional access is another tool you can use to secure access to Azure resources. Conditional access enables you to use various *identity signals* to allow or deny access to Azure resources in addition to authentication and RBAC (which is covered later in this chapter in the section "Role-Based Access Control"). Examples of identity signals include the user's location, the user's device, or the application the user is trying to access. Azure then uses these signals to determine what action to take. For example, if a user is logging in from a known office location (known network), you can configure conditional access rules to allow access without MFA. If the user tries to access a resource from an external network, MFA is used. Or, you might create a rule to require users to access specific resources only from a managed device.

You implement conditional access by creating conditional access policies that specify the appropriate identity signals and corresponding actions. Azure includes a What If tool that enables you to model conditional access policies and test them against recent login and access attempts from your users to determine what effect the policies would have had in those situations. The tool is therefore useful for testing your conditional access policies before you deploy them into production.

 Conditional access requires an Azure AD Premium P1 or P2 license, or a Microsoft 365 Business Premium license.

Single Sign-On (SSO)

In a typical organization, almost all resources require authentication and authorization. For example, when you log on to an internal company portal, that portal very likely requires you to authenticate and prove not only that you are an employee but that you should have access to the portal. Now, imagine that in the course of your day you use a dozen or more resources, all of which require authentication and authorization. Providing your credentials every time you access a resource would be onerous, to say the least.

Single sign-on (SSO) enables you to use a single set of credentials to access multiple resources. For example, assume your organization has implemented SSO. You connect to a line-of-business application and instead of entering your credentials, the application uses your current user context to authenticate you and grant access automatically. Next, you open the company portal in a web browser. SSO performs the same task, authenticating you without you entering any credentials.

In many organizations, Active Directory on-premises stores user credentials. In order for a user at the office to authenticate in Azure without using a separate set of credentials, there needs to be a synchronization and coordination between AD on-premises and Azure AD. The primary tool that makes that possible is Azure AD Connect, which synchronizes changes between AD and Azure AD, providing a seamless authentication and access experience for the user. Azure AD Connect makes it possible to use not only SSO across both environments, but also MFA and self-service password reset.

Security Tools and Features

Azure includes several services to enable you to employ strong security within your Azure environment. This section explores the security services and features that are covered by the AZ-900 exam.

Azure Security Center

Azure Security Center (Figure 4.5) is a monitoring service that provides a framework for advanced threat protection of your IT workloads both in the cloud and on-premises. Azure Security Center strengthens your security posture by automatically assessing your environment for security risks and providing security-based monitoring, alerts, and recommendations. It can use machine learning to detect and block malware, and you can also create a whitelist of applications that can execute, blocking all others.

Security Center supports Azure-only environments, Azure and on-premises, Azure and other cloud offerings, as well as all three together: Azure, on-premises, and other clouds. Security Center supports both Windows- and Linux-based operating systems.

FIGURE 4.5   You access Security Center from the Azure portal.

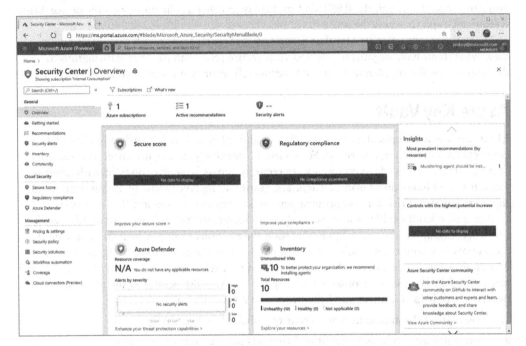

Security Center integrates natively with Microsoft Defender (formerly known as Windows Defender) to provide risk detection and assessment and threat intelligence. Security Center enables automated onboarding for new VMs that you deploy and automatically discovers and assesses resources when you deploy them.

Security Center is offered at two service levels:

- **Free:** This service tier is limited to assessments and recommendations only for Azure resources.

- **Standard:** This service tier provides a broad range of features for continuous monitoring and threat detection.

One feature of Security Center Standard is the capability to perform just-in-time (JIT) access control for ports. For example, assume that you need to occasionally query a database to build a custom report but the necessary ports are blocked. JIT would enable you to request access to those ports for a specified period. Once that period ends, the ports are closed again. JIT dramatically reduces the attack surface by closing ports until they are needed and keeping them open only as long as needed.

Security Center is designed to help you understand your security posture and improve it. A feature that is central to Security Center is *secure score*, which is displayed in a tile in the Security Center portal. The score provides an indication of the overall security posture across your environment, presented as a percentage. The higher your score, the lower the identified risk posture. In addition to viewing your secure score from the Security Center portal, you can access it through the REST API to display in other applications or sites or use Azure Resource Graph to access the score.

Using the secure score reports that Security Center surfaces through the portal, you can view what items have negatively affected your secure score and use that information to develop a remediation plan to improve your overall security posture in Azure.

Azure Key Vault

Many services and applications use certificates and other *secrets* for authentication, data connections, encryption, and so on. For example, imagine your organization has created a custom service that needs to communicate securely across your environment with other services. It would likely do so using credentials. Hard-coding credentials in an application puts those credentials at risk for compromise and makes key management difficult at best.

Azure Key Vault enables you to securely store secrets such as tokens, passwords, certificates, cryptographic keys, and API keys. Using the previous example, instead of storing the credentials in your custom application, you would store the credentials in Azure Key Vault. The application would call Key Vault whenever it needed to use the credentials. The detailed process and mechanisms are outside the scope of the AZ-900 exam, but the following brief overview will help you understand the process in a general way:

1. You register the application as a security principal in Azure AD.

2. You configure a role assignment in Azure AD for that security principal.

3. You configure access policies for that security principal in Key Vault.

4. If needed, you configure firewall access to enable the application to reach the Key Vault.

5. When the application is running and needs to access the credentials, it first authenticates with Azure AD to get an access token and then makes a call to Key Vault.

6. Key Vault calls Azure AD to validate the application's security principal's access token. If the token validates, Key Vault gives the secret to the application. Because the application is only using the secret at runtime, there is no need for the application to store it.

Azure Key Vault also provides a centralized, cloud-based service for creating, storing, and managing keys and certificates. By storing secrets in Key Vault, you gain the capability to easily monitor and audit access. You also gain the capability to easily use those secrets among many Azure services.

Azure Information Protection

Azure Information Protection (AIP) enables you to classify and protect documents and emails by applying labels to them. AIP labels can be created and managed by administrators for use by users, created by users, or created by users based on recommendations created and managed by administrators. The labels identify the information type and can be used to optionally protect the information with Azure Rights Management Service (Azure RMS). Azure RMS can apply policies for encryption, identity, and authorization to the data to control its use and distribution. For example, you might create a policy to prevent email from being forwarded. Applying the appropriate tag to the email would result in recipients of the email being unable to forward it.

The key point to understand about AIP is that it provides a means to classify documents and emails using labels and to optionally protect them with encryption, identity, and authorization.

Azure Advanced Threat Protection

Azure Advanced Threat Protection (ATP) leverages your on-premises Active Directory to detect and identify threats directed at your organization. It enables you to investigate those threats and identify compromised identities and malicious activities. With ATP you can protect identities and credentials stored in Active Directory, monitor users and suspicious activities, report on incidents to help drive protection and remediation measures, and more.

Some of the key threats that ATP will help you detect and deal with are as follows:

- **Reconnaissance attacks:** Attackers scan the network to locate assets and services they can compromise, such as usernames, group membership, and IP addresses. An example of such an attack is probing accounts using an alphabetical list of usernames.

- **Compromised credentials:** Attackers attempt to gain access with compromised credentials, such as a brute-force attack testing multiple passwords against a username.

- **Lateral account movement:** Attackers steal user data on one computer in order to gain access to other computers. Examples include stealing Kerberos tickets (pass-the-token), stealing a key (overpass-the-hash, also a Kerberos attack), and stealing NTLM data (pass-the-hash).

- **Domain dominance:** Attackers compromise the domain through activities such as remote code execution on the domain controller, malicious domain controller replication, and other domain-related attacks.

You can use ATP to notify you of attempts to use decoy accounts, commonly called *honeytoken accounts*. You set up an account that is never used and has no permissions (the decoy), and then configure ATP to alert you when that account shows activity.

Azure Sentinel

Gathering information and managing security events across your environment is critical for protecting your users and data. Systems that provide this broad capability are security information and event management (SIEM) systems. Azure Sentinel is Microsoft's Azure-based SIEM solution.

Azure Sentinel collects data across your enterprise from users, devices, applications, and infrastructure on-premises and in the cloud, including from multiple clouds. It uses a combination of built-in analytics, leveraging information about known threats, machine learning, and other criteria to automatically detect threats. You can also create custom rules to search for specific threat criteria.

Azure Sentinel uses analytics to correlate alerts from across the environment into incidents, enabling you to track and act on possible threats rather than individual alerts. You can then use the orchestration and automation capabilities in Azure Sentinel and through integration with other services, such as Azure Monitor Workbooks and Azure Logic Apps, to not only identify threats but also initiate actions when threats arise. Through Logic Apps, Azure Sentinel supports over 200 connectors to allow you to integrate with ticketing systems, messaging alerts, email alerts, and other systems and services to build automated response strategies for each threat.

To help you avoid threats altogether or mitigate them before they affect your environment, Azure Sentinel enables you to proactively hunt for threats across your entire environment and surface the results for follow-up and further investigation.

Finally, the Azure Sentinel community gives you access to workbooks, playbooks, hunting queries, and other resources that you can use in your own environment. You can also create custom resources to help you tune Azure Sentinel to your environment and specific needs.

Azure Dedicated Hosts

By default, even though your VM workloads are isolated from those deployed and used by other organizations, they are nevertheless potentially hosted on the same hardware. If you have regulatory or other compliance requirements that prevent you from deploying your VMs on shared hardware, or you simply want to add one more layer of isolation, you can deploy your VMs to dedicated hardware. To increase your security posture and reduce your threat profile, you can use Azure Dedicated Hosts for your virtual machines.

An Azure Dedicated Host is an Azure resource mapped to a physical server in Azure that you provision in an Azure region and optionally in an availability zone and fault domain. You create the dedicated host resource within a host group. Once the dedicated host is provisioned, you can deploy your VMs to it and, as indicated earlier, use availability zones and fault domains to provide high availability and fault tolerance. You can also use virtual machine scale sets for additional scalability and management. In the context of the AZ-900 exam, understand that Azure Dedicated Hosts provide the means for you to isolate your VM workloads on dedicated hardware, keeping them physically separate from VMs hosted by other organizations or from other VM resources that you host yourself.

Azure Governance Methodologies

The term *governance* encompasses a wide range of topics but generally describes policies and methods that control how a service is used, roles and responsibilities within the service, and how it should be secured. Azure offers several features to provide those capabilities within Azure, enabling you to build an Azure strategy that is secure, controlled, and manageable. The first of these governance features are *policies* and *initiatives*.

Azure Policies

Azure *policies* define business rules that you can use to assess and ensure compliance with organizational standards in Azure, controlling how Azure resources are deployed and used. The Azure Policy service provides the mechanism to create, manage, and apply those policies. You use functions, parameters, logical operators, conditions, and aliases when creating policies to define matching criteria. The policy service evaluates those criteria and determines what *effect* to apply to resources that match the policy criteria. Each policy applies a single effect, such as *deny*.

An Azure policy alias enables you to restrict the values and conditions permitted for a property of a given resource. Azure offers many pre-defined aliases.

Azure policies are created as JSON files.

Consider an example. Assume you want to ensure that only specific sizes of virtual machines are added to a resource group because you need to control costs. You want to make sure that instead of using a VM with lots of memory and other resources, you allow only VMs with limited resources to meet minimum service requirements. You can always scale as needed if demand increases. In this scenario, you create a policy for the resource group that restricts the types of VMs that can be added to the resource group. If someone attempts to add a VM that does not fit the accepted criteria, the action is denied (because you specify the *deny* effect in the policy).

Azure Policy includes many built-in policies that you can use across a wide range of categories, simplifying and speeding up policy implementation.

As discussed earlier, you specify the scope of a policy by assigning the policy to a specific scope object, such as a resource group or management group. The policy then applies to all child objects within that scope unless you exclude a specific subscope from the policy.

You do not apply permissions with Azure policies. Instead, you specify what actions people can take within a particular management scope using the permissions they already have. For example, a user might be granted permission to create resources in a resource group (using role-based access control, discussed later in this chapter). A policy applied to the resource group could then limit the types of VMs that the user could create in that group.

Azure Initiatives

An Azure *initiative* is a group (collection) of Azure policies. You use the initiative to achieve a collective set of governance goals. For example, perhaps you have an initiative to secure all SQL services in the organization. You would create an initiative for that goal, and then assign policies to that initiative. As with policies, you assign initiatives to specific scopes, so the policies in an initiative then apply to the resources that fall within the specified scope(s).

As with policies, Azure initiatives do not enable you to assign permissions. They simply serve as a container for policies. Since the policies do not apply permissions, neither do the initiatives that contain them.

When you apply an initiative to a scope, the policies contained in the initiative are evaluated and applied to all resources within that scope. You can also apply an initiative to multiple scopes, which means that all the resources in all the assigned scopes will have the policies evaluated and applied. If you need to have a policy evaluated by itself without other policies, either apply the policy outside of an initiative or create an initiative that contains only that policy.

Initiatives can contain only policies in a single subscription. To apply an initiative to resources in multiple subscriptions, create the same initiative within each subscription and apply each initiative as needed within each subscription.

Role-Based Access Control

Role-based access control (RBAC) is a primary authorization mechanism in Azure that enables you to define who has access to Azure resources and what they can do with those resources. For example, if yours is a large organization, you likely have a team responsible for networking, another team for managing VMs, another for databases and database servers, and so on. RBAC enables you to apply that role-based governance to your Azure resources. For example, you could use RBAC to enable the members of your SQL team to manage SQL Server VMs and Azure SQL Databases. Or, you might use RBAC to enable a Linux team to manage your Linux servers but not Windows servers, and vice versa.

You can use RBAC in many ways to control Azure management functions, including managing users, resources, VNets, and so on. Following is a list of some examples of how you might use RBAC:

- Allow your server team to manage VMs in a subscription and your network team to manage the virtual networks.
- Allow your DBA team to manage database VMs and databases in one or more resource groups.
- Allow a user to manage all resources in a particular resource group.
- Allow an application to access specific resources in a resource group.
- Allow a small group of users to manage users in Azure.

To apply RBAC, you first create a role assignment, which consists of three elements that effectively translate to who, what, and where:

- **Security principal:** Specifies the individual user, group, or managed identity to which the role assignment will apply.
- **Role definition:** A collection of permissions that specifies the operations that can be performed, such as read, write, and delete.
- **Scope:** Specifies the resources to which the role assignment applies.

Understanding Roles

Role definitions require some additional discussion to help you understand the actions that RBAC can govern. These roles are divided into three types: classic subscription administrator roles, Azure roles, and Azure AD roles. The classic subscription roles were the initial and only means of managing resources in Azure. Then, RBAC was introduced to provide much more granular control.

Classic subscription administrator roles include the following:

- **Account Administrator:** This is the billing owner. The Account Administrator can manage billing in the Azure portal, manage all subscriptions in an account (including creating new ones), change the billing for a subscription, and change the Service Administrator.
- **Service Administrator:** This role manages the services in the Azure subscription and can cancel the subscription and assign users to the Co-Administrator role.
- **Co-Administrator:** This role has the same privileges as the Service Administrator but cannot change the association of subscriptions to Azure directories. The role can also assign additional users to the Co-Administrator role, but cannot modify the Service Administrator.

Azure RBAC adds more granularity to permission assignment in Azure with over 70 built-in roles, many of which are specific to resource types. For example, the Virtual Machine Administrator Login role can view VMs in the Azure portal and log in as an administrator, but has no permissions to (for example) content delivery networks.

For the purposes of the AZ-900 exam, let's focus on the following four roles:

- **Owner:** This role has full access to all resources and can delegate access to others. The role applies to all resource types. Service Administrator and Co-Administrator roles have Owner permissions as the subscription scope.

- **Contributor:** This role can create and manage all types of Azure resources and create new tenants in Azure AD but cannot grant access to others.

- **Reader:** This role can view (consume) Azure resources. The role applies to all resource types.

- **User Access Administrator:** This role can manage access to Azure resources.

Using RBAC with Management Scopes

RBAC supports four levels of management scope: management group, subscription, resource group, and resource. In many cases, multiple role assignments will apply because a user or group will have overlapping role assignments. RBAC uses an additive model, which means your effective permissions are summed up across all assignments. For example, assume you have a role assignment that grants you Reader permission within a resource group. You also have a role assignment at the subscription level that gives you Contributor permission. Because the resource group is contained in the subscription and inherits permissions as a child, you effectively have Contributor permission on the resources in the resource group. Figure 4.6 illustrates this example.

FIGURE 4.6   RBAC uses an additive model to apply permissions.

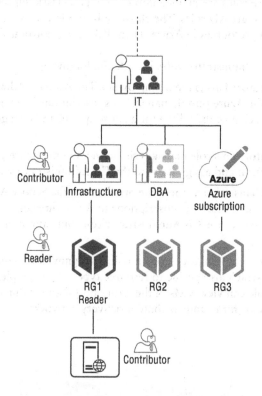

Resource Locks

Creating and managing Azure resources can be a very complex task, particularly in large environments. Azure therefore gives you a means to lock down resources to prevent them from being modified or deleted. Resource locks are the Azure mechanism that enable you to apply that control.

You can apply a ReadOnly or a CanNotDelete lock. The ReadOnly lock enables authorized administrators to read a resource but not delete or update it. The CanNotDelete lock allows authorized administrators to read and modify a resource but not delete it.

Locking a resource does not lock it forever. If you need to delete a resource, you must first remove the lock. Then you can delete the resource. Resource locks are absolute in the sense that RBAC does not override a lock. Even if you own a resource and have full permissions to it, you cannot delete the resource if it is locked. Again, you must remove the lock first and then can delete it.

You cannot apply locks in the context of specific users or roles. Applying a lock to a scope or resource applies the lock to all users, regardless of their RBAC roles and permissions.

Management scope also applies to resource locks, and when you apply a lock to a parent scope, all resources under that scope inherit the lock. For example, if you apply a ReadOnly lock on a resource group, all resources in that group inherit a ReadOnly lock.

If you apply locks for a resource at different scopes, the most restrictive lock applies. So, assume you apply a CanNotDelete lock on a resource group and then apply a ReadOnly lock for a resource in that group. Normally, the CanNotDelete lock would enable you to modify resources in the group but not delete them. Because the resource has a ReadOnly lock, however, you cannot modify the resource, even though the CanNotDelete lock would otherwise allow that.

Locks apply only at the resource management level, not at their functional levels. Assume that you apply a ReadOnly lock on a resource group containing Azure SQL Database instances, which then inherit that lock. You cannot modify or delete one of those database instances without removing the lock, but you can create new databases, as well as update and delete data within databases that exist in that resource group.

Azure Blueprints

Ensuring adherence to standards, patterns, and requirements is a key aspect of governance. For Azure, that means easily and effectively controlling deployment of resources based on resource groups, role assignments, policies, and Azure Resource Manager templates (which define the resources to deploy). Azure Blueprint is the Azure service that gives you this level of governance.

Azure Blueprint lets you define a repeatable group of Azure resources and associated role assignments and policies to meet your organization's standards and practices, and then quickly and easily deploy those resources where needed. Resource groups, role assignments, policies, and ARM templates are the *artifacts* within a blueprint that define its structure and enable a potentially large number of resources to be deployed collectively and in a controlled, standardized way.

Since Azure Resource Manager (ARM) templates also let you easily deploy resources, the capability to keep libraries of ARM templates would seem to offer the same capabilities as blueprints. However, ARM templates retain no connection to the resources they deploy. Blueprints do maintain that connection, so you can track and audit what *was* deployed against what the blueprint specified *should* be deployed. You can also implement changes to all resources and artifacts defined by a blueprint by updating, publishing, and applying a new version of a blueprint. Blueprints do not replace ARM templates. Instead, blueprints can make extensive use of ARM templates to deploy resources.

Blueprint Lifecycle

A blueprint is in draft mode until you publish it using a version designation that you define. Once published, a blueprint is available for assignment. Assigning a blueprint deploys the artifacts defined in the blueprint. So, simply updating and publishing a new version of a blueprint does not affect existing assignments; you must explicitly assign it after publishing it to apply changes.

A published version of a blueprint cannot be altered. If you need to modify the deployment, you create a new version of the blueprint with the appropriate changes, and then publish the new version and apply it. Applying the new version applies changes as defined in the new blueprint version.

You can delete a version of a blueprint only if it is not assigned. Deleting a blueprint version does not delete the other versions of the blueprint. You can also delete a core blueprint, but doing so deletes all versions of the blueprint. These cannot be deleted if they have active assignments, so you must remove assignments for each version of a blueprint before you can delete the core blueprint.

None of the resources defined in a blueprint are deleted when you unassign a blueprint version and delete that version, nor are they deleted when you delete a core blueprint. The resources are simply no longer managed or protected by the blueprint. However, some changes do occur:

- Blueprint resource locks are removed.
- Blueprint assignment object is deleted.
- The system-assigned management identity is deleted if one was used.

When assigning a blueprint, you can choose to use a system-assigned managed identity, which then is granted an Owner role and is used to deploy resources defined by the blueprint.

Blueprint Roles

As you might expect, Azure provides role-based control over who can create, manage, and use blueprints. Azure includes the following built-in blueprint roles:

- **Owner:** Includes all Azure Blueprint permissions.
- **Contributor:** Can create and delete blueprint definitions but cannot assign blueprints.
- **Blueprint Contributor:** Can manage blueprint definitions but not assign them.
- **Blueprint Operator:** Can assign published blueprints but cannot create new blueprints.

 You can create custom blueprint roles if you need permissions that are not provided by the built-in roles.

Microsoft Cloud Adoption Framework for Azure

As you have read through the preceding sections, you have probably realized that moving from an on-premises model to Microsoft Azure is not a trivial task, either in planning or in execution. The Microsoft Cloud Adoption Framework for Azure can help with both planning and execution.

The Cloud Adoption Framework for Azure is a large collection of resources, including documentation, deployment guidance, templates, best practice documentation, and various tools to help with planning, deploying, and assessing your Azure deployment.

The documentation included with the framework needs little explanation other than that it covers all aspects of planning and deploying Azure resources based on best practices. It includes guidance on strategies, governance, migration, innovation, and all other aspects of a successful Azure implementation. The framework documentation alone should be one of your first stops before moving to deploy Azure. But the documentation is just one aspect of the framework.

Of particular note as part of the Cloud Adoption Framework for Azure are the following:

- **Templates:** Within the framework you will find a wealth of templates to help you evaluate your business needs and build an Azure solution to meet them. Some of these templates are documents and others are live, interactive resources that you work through online to generate plans. Some templates work in conjunction with Azure Boards, a rich project workstream tool in Azure.
- **Assessments:** The Cloud Adoption Framework for Azure also provides multiple assessments to help you identify your cloud adoption plan based on business needs, remove blockers and improve processes, implement a sound governance framework, and ensure a well-architected Azure solution.

The framework site also provides information and links to additional resources to help you plan and deploy a sound Azure implementation. These include FastTrack for Azure, a Microsoft service that connects you with Microsoft engineers who help you work through planning and deployment considerations for Azure. The Azure Migration Program provides best practice and other guidance, access to training, Azure engineering support, migration tools, and access to migration partners to help you move your workloads to Azure.

 Visit https://aka.ms/adopt to learn more about the Microsoft Cloud Adoption Framework for Azure.

Azure Monitoring and Reporting Options

Monitoring and reporting are critical components of any IT environment, and Azure is no exception. This section of the chapter explores monitoring and reporting options in Azure.

Azure Monitor

Azure Monitor provides the capability to collect and analyze telemetry from your cloud and on-premises environments and to take appropriate actions based on that analysis. Azure Monitor encompasses several services (see Figure 4.7) that work together to provide a comprehensive monitoring and reporting solution:

- **Application Insights:** This feature enables developers to integrate monitoring for live applications by sending telemetry data to Azure. The data helps developers understand how an app is performing and how it is being used.

- **Azure Monitor for VMs:** This solution provides monitoring for Windows and Linux VMs in Azure, on-premises, and in other cloud environments.

- **Azure Monitor for Containers:** This solution provides monitoring for container workloads deployed to Azure Container Instances, Azure Kubernetes Services, and other container instances both in Azure and on-premises.

- **Log Analytics:** This tool provides the capability to write log queries and analyze query results.

- **Smart Alerts:** This solution automatically groups alerts using machine learning, combining alerts into a single issue to help minimize noise and enable management of related alerts.

- **Automated Actions:** Create actions that execute automatically in response to specific alerts, such as suppressing informational alerts during a planning maintenance window.

- **Dashboards:** Create and share dashboards to visualize the results of log queries.

- **Workbooks:** Create composite reports from multiple data sources to provide insights into performance, availability, resource usage, and more in an interactive report.

FIGURE 4.7 Azure Monitor encompasses multiple services and features to enable you to collect, analyze, and visualize events and metrics.

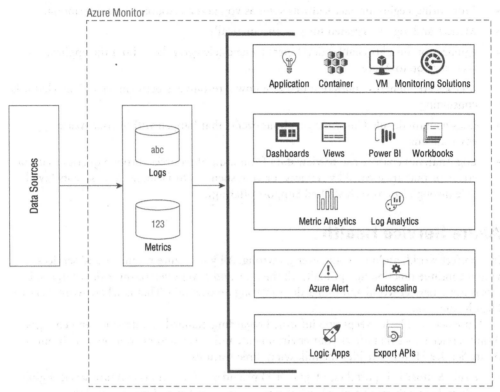

It is important to understand the types of data that Azure Monitor uses to learn how Azure Monitor functions and the roles it can play. These two data types are *metrics* and *logs*.

Metrics describe some aspect of a system at a given time using numerical values. As such, metrics are a snapshot in time of a specific characteristic of a resource. Two examples are the number of requests processed by Web Application Firewall and the amount of storage in bytes used by a storage account's file service.

Logs contain a record of events that happen within a system. Whereas metrics can only use numeric data to store information, logs can store a variety of data types in different structures, enabling logs to store more complex information. Logs are stored in tables within a Log Analytics workspace. You can build, edit, and run queries in Log Analytics to analyze log data.

Azure Monitor begins collecting data as soon as you add a resource to a subscription. You do not need to start the monitoring manually or configure any monitoring settings within the resource itself.

The key points to understand about monitoring and alerting in Azure, and about Azure Monitor in particular, in the context of the AZ-900 exam are as follows:

- Monitoring begins automatically as soon as you add a resource to a subscription.

- Metrics and logs are created for you automatically.

- Application Insights enables developers to send telemetry data about the applications they develop to Azure.

- Metrics are numeric values that describe how a resource is performing and/or what it is consuming.

- Logs contain detailed information about events that happen within your Azure environment.

- Log Analytics enables you to view data from multiple sources through queries that you create or that are created by services for you, such as On-Demand Assessments (available through Microsoft's Unified Support offering).

Azure Service Health

In a perfect world, nothing would ever go wrong. All your Azure resources and services would continue functioning optimally all the time and never overconsume their targets. But this is not a perfect world and things do go wrong on occasion. That is where Azure Service Health comes in.

Azure Service Health keeps you informed regarding planned maintenance and changes, Azure service issues that affect your environment, and issues within your own environment. Azure Service Health provides the following three features:

- **Azure Status:** This portal (see Figure 4.8) provides information on Azure services globally to help you see at a glance what services are affected and in what regions.

- **Service Health:** This service tracks the state of your Azure services by region and gives you access to information about service issues, planned maintenance, health advisories, and security advisories in a customizable dashboard (see Figure 4.9).

- **Resource Health:** This service, which is part of Service Health, tracks the state of the resources you have deployed to Azure to give you visibility to any ongoing or historical issues with those resources.

In addition to giving you a customizable dashboard to track the health of Azure services in the regions where your resources are located and get more information about issues, Service Health enables you to set up service health alerts. Service Health works with Azure Monitor to provide alerts through emails, text messages, and webhook notifications (to display alert information on your websites). You can use action groups, which are collections of notification preferences, to define actions and recipients who are notified when an alert is triggered. Action groups provide a means for building governance and consistency in how you deploy alerts in your organization and simplify creating your alerting process. You can create up to 2,000 action groups in a subscription.

FIGURE 4.8 Azure Status provides status information about Azure services worldwide.

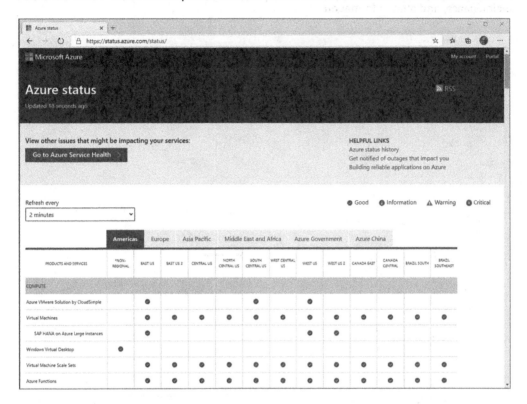

The last component of Azure Service Health to explore is Resource Health, which offers information about Azure issues that are affecting your resources or that have affected them in the past. You can use Resource Health to diagnose issues with your Azure resources to determine an appropriate course of action. For example, you can see if a resource is available or unavailable, view recent events such as an unplanned reboot of a system, or see whether a resource has experienced a degradation in performance. To view the Resource Health dashboard, open the Service Health portal and click Resource Health in the left navigation pane (Figure 4.10).

Azure Advisor

Azure Advisor is another resource you can use in Azure to improve the security posture of your environment. Azure Advisor, which you access through the Azure portal, provides a web-based report intended to help you optimize your Azure environment. The tool captures a wide range of data points across the environment, evaluating performance criteria, cost-effectiveness, reliability, security, and operational excellence. Azure Advisor offers guidance on ways to improve your deployments in those areas.

FIGURE 4.9 Service Health provides information on Azure service health, planned maintenance, and other information.

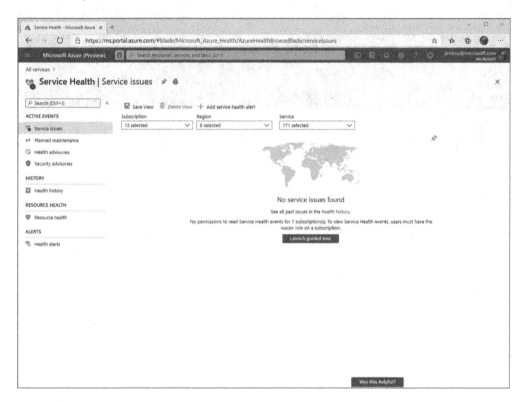

Azure Advisor Score is a feature in preview as of this writing that provides a score based on the analysis that Azure Advisor performs, similar to the secure score offered by Security Center. Addressing items identified by Azure Advisor in a positive way drives your score higher.

FIGURE 4.10   You can view health data for resources in your Azure environment in the
Resource Health dashboard.

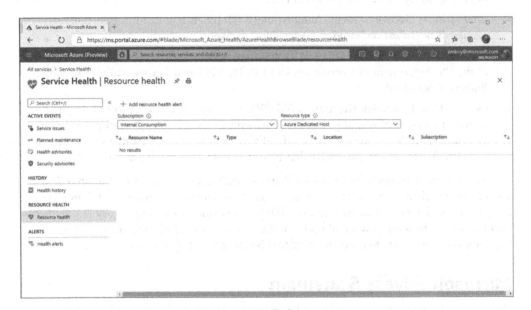

Compliance and Data Protection Standards

Key factors for many organizations when choosing a cloud solution are compliance, privacy, and adherence to data protection standards. This section explores these factors and the Azure services that support them. A good grasp of these topics begins with an understanding of common compliance standards and terms.

Industry Compliance Standards and Terms

Azure supports a broad range of compliance offerings. The following list describes the most common:

- **Health Insurance Portability and Accountability Act (HIPAA):** This is a US federal law that regulates protected health information (PHI) with a goal of protecting privacy surrounding individuals' health care.

- **International Organization for Standards (ISO):** ISO is a standards-based, nonregulatory organization located in the United States.

- **International Electrotechnical Commission (IEC):** IEC is a nonprofit, nonregulatory standards organization based in Geneva, Switzerland.

- **National Institute of Standards and Technology (NIST):** NIST is a nonregulatory agency of the US Department of Commerce. Until 1998, NIST was known as the National Bureau of Standards.

- **General Data Protection Regulation (GDPR):** The General Data Protection Regulation defines data protection and privacy requirements as a regulation in European Union (EU) law. It applies to personal data of individuals who are in the European Economic Area (EAA) and to any enterprise that processes data of individuals in the EAA.

Some of these standards are discussed in more detail in the context of Azure in following sections of this chapter. For now, understand that these compliance offerings fall into two categories: regulatory and nonregulatory. GDPR is an example of a regulatory requirement that is enforced by a governmental body (in this case, the EU). ISO, IEC, and NIST are non-regulatory organizations that define standards but do not regulate or enforce them.

Microsoft Privacy Statement

The Microsoft Privacy Statement located at `https://privacy.microsoft.com/priva-cystatement` describes not only what personal data processes, but also how and why.

Anything other than anonymous access requires a login account, and this includes Microsoft 365, Azure, and other resources like the Windows Store, Volume Licensing Service Center, support portals, and other resources provided by Microsoft. With Azure, your user login will reside in Azure AD. The same is true with Microsoft 365. Whether you use a personal email or work email to establish that user account is situation specific. In an enterprise, your account will be tied to your work email address. You might also be using a Microsoft account to access some services, such as the Windows Store or Xbox Live. Microsoft accounts can be tied to a personal email account, a work or school account, or an account set up for you by a third party, such as your Internet provider.

Regardless of the account type, some Microsoft products and services require that you provide a user account. In that sense, those products and services require you to provide your personal information, and without that, you are unable to use the product or service. This is required in some cases by law and in others is required to establish a contract between you and Microsoft. Using a service such as Xbox Live is an example of the latter.

There are multiple levels of privacy protection for you defined within the Microsoft Privacy Statement, but privacy is not absolute. Microsoft can share your personal information with vendors working on Microsoft's behalf, Microsoft-controlled subsidiaries and affiliates, and others when required by law or in response to a legal process. Obtaining support for a product is an example. Microsoft might contract with a vendor to provide support for a product to supplement its own support resources. Without some personal information, the vendor would be unable to provide support.

Online Service Terms

The Azure Online Service Terms (OST), which is a legal agreement between an Azure customer and Microsoft, details the obligations for the organization and Microsoft in the processing and security of personal and customer data. The OST covers not only Azure, but also Office 365, Dynamics 365, and Bing Maps. You will find the OST at www.microsoft.com/licensing/terms/product/ForallOnlineServices.

Data Protection Addendum

The Data Protection Addendum (DPA) adds to the definition of obligations detailed in the OST. It defines the terms for legal compliance, disclosure of processed data, data security practices and policies, data encryption, data access, and audit compliance. The DPA also defines terms for data transfer, retention, and deletion. You can find the DTA by navigating to www.microsoftvolumelicensing.com/DocumentSearch.aspx and searching for DPA.

 The Microsoft Privacy Statement, the Online Service Terms, and the Data Protection Addendum encompass Microsoft's terms for protecting customer data and privacy across its cloud offerings.

Trust Center

Microsoft Trust Center is a website that provides information about how Microsoft implements and supports compliance, security, privacy, and transparency across its cloud products and services. The site is located at www.microsoft.com/trustcenter. Trust Center is intended to help you design and implement a secure Azure solution.

Understanding that Trust Center contains a wide range of security information is a key certification topic, but understanding what Trust Center is *not* is also important. Trust Center does not provide any type of risk assessment for your Azure resources and services—Compliance Manager fulfills that function. Nor does Trust Center offer best practice recommendations for hybrid Azure implementations—Azure Security Center provides those recommendations. Last, Trust Center does not enable you to configure or enforce compliance settings or define policies—that is a function of Azure Policies.

In summary, Trust Center is a website containing information about security, privacy, compliance, transparency, and related products and services.

Service Trust Portal

Service Trust Portal is a public site through which Microsoft publishes audit reports and other compliance-related information for its cloud services, including Azure. You can use Service Trust Portal to download audit reports required by your organization or by third-party auditors and access reports that describe how Microsoft builds and manages Azure, Microsoft 365, and Dynamics 365. Service Trust Portal also offers information to help you understand how Azure can help you meet standards and regulations defined by ISO, NIST, GDPR, and others.

> The Service Trust Portal is located at `https://servicetrust` `.microsoft.com`.

Service Trust Portal also hosts the Compliance Manager, which is described in the following section.

Compliance Manager

Compliance Manager is a dashboard published through the Service Trust Portal that enables you to view compliance information and track compliance-related activities, including the following:

- View information provided by Microsoft to third-party auditors and regulators detailing compliance for various standards.

- View information compiled by Microsoft to demonstrate Microsoft's compliance with various regulations.

- View your organization's compliance self-assessment and score.

- Assign and track compliance-related activities within your organization.

- Maintain a secure repository for your compliance audits and related evidence for compliance activities and outcomes.

- Access detailed compliance report documents to provide to internal stakeholders and third-party auditors and regulators.

Compliance Manager uses a workflow-based risk assessment to develop your organization's assessment score. As described briefly in the previous list, Compliance Manager enables you to build a compliance framework where you can create and assign compliance-related tasks to individuals in your organization and track progress toward completion of those activities.

> Compliance Manager can offer recommendations for helping you achieve compliance goals and requirements, but it cannot guarantee compliance. Responsibility for compliance ultimately falls to your organization.

Azure Government

The US government has strict requirements for data privacy, isolation, compliance, and security. Microsoft created Azure Government to meet those requirements. Azure Government is a separate instance of Azure with data centers only in the United States to support US federal agencies, state and local governments, and solution providers that support these governmental entities. Azure Government is physically isolated from commercial Azure and is supported and managed by screened US personnel. Deployments to Azure Government are subject to validation of eligibility.

> Azure Government and Azure China are referred to as Azure Sovereign Regions because they are specific to the United States and China, respectively.

Services in Azure Government and in commercial Azure are mostly the same, and the user experience is also generally the same. For example, the Azure portal offers the same user experience in both environments, but they are accessed through different URLs.

Hosting resources in Azure Government does not in itself meet specific governmental compliance requirements. Although Azure Government does meet broad compliance requirements and Level 5 Department of Defense (DoD) approval, you must ensure that your organization's implementation of Azure meets all compliance requirements.

> As with commercial Azure, Microsoft deploys Azure Government in regions. A region can be a commercial region or a government region, but not both. Data centers located in a government region host only government resources.

Azure China

Chapter 1, "Cloud Concepts," briefly described Azure China, a physically isolated instance of Azure located in China and designed to meet strict Chinese regulations. Azure China is independently operated by Shanghai Blue Cloud Technology Co., Ltd. (commonly known as 21Vianet). Azure China must be hosted and managed by 21Vianet due to a Chinese requirement that providers of cloud services must have a value-added telecom permit. To qualify for a permit, a company must have less than 50 percent foreign investment. 21Vianet therefore licenses Azure technologies from Microsoft.

Azure China is available to any organization that needs to host resources and services in China. Azure China is not restricted to Chinese government agencies or companies. Instead, it is intended for any organization doing business in China that needs to meet Chinese regulations.

Connectivity is another consideration. Assume that your organization needs to establish a presence in Azure China but also needs interconnectivity with your on-premises network in China or with Azure. The following list summarizes the two possible scenarios:

- **Within China:** You can use ExpressRoute to establish a secure connection between Azure China and your on-premises data center or private cloud located within China. ExpressRoute is not supported for direct network connectivity to sites outside of China or to Azure outside of China.

- **Outside of China:** Establish a site-to-site VPN between Azure China to a location outside of China.

Regardless of which scenario applies, you must acquire the VPN or ExpressRoute service from telecom providers licensed by the Chinese Ministry of Industry and Information Technology (MIIT).

Portability is a final consideration for Azure China. Because of differences in services, pricing, and regulations, you cannot move Azure accounts from Azure to Azure China. You must create a separate Azure China account. Cross-border data transfer is also subject to security assessment and government approval.

Summary

This chapter explored several topics related to network security, authentication and authorization, governance methodologies, and data protection and compliance standards in Azure. All of these resources and services help ensure your Azure environment is not only secure from threats, but also designed with an appropriate governance model to protect resources from modification, whether intended or unintended, and ensure that resources are deployed and managed using the standards and requirements established by your organization. Governance is an extremely important aspect of planning and deploying an Azure solution and should be considered early and often.

Azure offers many tools and features to help you both implement and assess security. These include Security Center, Key Vault, Azure Information Protection (AIP), and Advanced Threat Protection (ATP). Azure also offers tools for ensuring adherence to compliance and data protection standards through Trust Center, Service Trust Portal, and Compliance Manager.

You also learned a bit more about Azure Government and Azure China, both of which are designed to meet stringent government regulations and requirements in the United States and China, respectively.

Exam Essentials

Describe securing network connectivity in Azure.   Azure Firewall provides broad-based firewall coverage for networks and resources in Azure and are often deployed in concert with other network security services. Use Azure Firewall when you need to filter traffic based on IP address, port, and/or protocol.

Web Application Firewall (WAF) works in concert with Application Gateway, Front Door, and CDN and is specific to web application scenarios. For services other than web applications, turn to Azure Firewall and network security groups.

Network security groups (NSGs) are deployed at the subnet or VM level to provide traffic filtering at those levels. NSGs filter traffic based on protocol, source address, source port, destination address, and destination port. You will often use NSGs in concert with application security groups.

Application security groups (ASGs) enable you to group servers based on the applications running on them and manage security for them as a group. An ASG is an object reference within an NSG, making it easy to apply rules to the VMs contained within an ASG.

User-defined routes (UDRs) enable you to create custom routes to direct traffic through non-default routes.

Azure DDoS Protection provides a means of protecting against distributed denial-of-service attacks. DDoS Basic offers active traffic monitoring and automatic attack mitigation. DDoS Standard adds an SLA, mitigation policies, metrics and alerts, and reporting.

Describe core Azure identify services.   Azure AD provides identify management for Azure, enabling users to log into cloud services such as Office 365 and access resources in Azure. Azure AD Free provides management of users and groups, synchronization with on-premises AD, basic reporting, and self-service password change for Azure AD accounts, along with single sign-on (SSO) for Azure, Microsoft 365, and Dynamics 365. Azure AD Premium includes additional features such as the ability to authenticate to on-premises resources, self-serve password reset for on-premises users, dynamic groups, and more.

Authorization goes hand in hand with authentication. Whereas authentication identifies the user, authorization determines whether an identified user is authorized to use a resource.

Describe security tools and features of Azure.   Azure offers many tools and resources for ensuring security. Azure Security Center provides monitoring, alerts, and recommendations for security risks for both Windows and Linux systems. Security Center integrates with Microsoft Defender to provide risk detection and assessment. Security Center automatically discovers and assesses resources when you deploy them.

Azure Key Vault provides a secure repository for certificates, keys, and other secrets, along with the capability for applications to call Key Vault to access stored secrets when needed. You can also create and manage secrets with Key Vault.

Azure Information Protection (AIP) uses rights management and labels to classify and optionally protect documents and emails with encryption, identity, and authorization.

Advanced Threat Protection (ATP) leverages on-premises Active Directory to detect and identify threats directed at your organization. ATP protects against reconnaissance attacks, compromised credentials, lateral account movement, and domain dominance attacks.

Describe Azure governance methodologies.   Azure offers several features to help you design and enforce a governance model. Azure policies define business rules that you use to control how Azure resources are deployed and used, providing a mechanism to create, manage, and apply policies. An Azure initiative is a group of policies that you create and deploy to meet a collective governance goal.

Role-based access control (RBAC) is a primary authorization mechanism in Azure that enables you to define who has access to Azure resources and what they can do with those resources. You apply RBAC by creating a security principal if one does not already exist, assigning a role definition, and defining the scope to which the role assignment applies. Azure includes many predefined roles, with the most common being Owner, Contributor, Reader, and User Access Administrator. Permissions granted through RBAC are additive.

Resource locks enable you to control what actions can be performed on resources. You can apply a ReadOnly lock that enables authorized administrators to read a resource but not delete or update it. CanNotDelete enables authorized administrators to read and modify a resource but not delete it. The most restrictive lock applies when locks are applied at different scopes.

Azure Blueprints enables you to define a repeatable group of Azure resources and associated role assignments and policies, and then quickly and easily deploy those resources where needed. A blueprint is in draft until published and must then be assigned to a resource group to apply it to those resources. Although removing an assigned blueprint does not delete resources, doing so does impose some changes, including removing resources locks, deleting the blueprint assignment object, and deleting the system-assigned management identify if one was used.

Describe monitoring and reporting options in Azure.   Azure Monitor is a group of services and features that work in concert to provide a robust reporting, analysis, and alerting capability in Azure. Azure Monitor uses logs and metrics to capture data. Metrics are numeric values that describe how a resource is performing or what it is consuming. Logs capture data about events that happen in Azure. Monitoring begins automatically when you add a resource to a subscription; you do not need to configure logs or metrics manually. You can view reports with Azure Log Analytics. You can create custom queries and use dashboards to visualize the results of your queries.

Application Insights enables developers to send telemetry data from your custom applications to Azure, where that data can be consumed for monitoring and reporting.

The Azure Status portal provides a view of the global health state for Azure services by geography and region. Azure Service Health provides information on the health of Azure globally and of your resources deployed in Azure. Resource Health is a component of Service Health and shows information about resources you host in Azure.

Describe privacy, compliance, and data protection standards in Azure. Azure provides many features to enable organizations to meet standards, both regulatory and nonregulatory, in their Azure environments. Nonregulatory organizations such as ISO, IEC, and NIST produce and publish standards but do not enforce them through regulations. HIPAA and GDPR are examples of regulations that are enforced by government agencies or governmental bodies.

The Microsoft Privacy Statement describes the personal data that Microsoft processes, as well as how and why they process it. Using some Microsoft services requires providing personal data. Microsoft can and does share some personal data with its vendors, subsidiaries, and affiliates, and with others when required by law or in response to a legal process.

Trust Center is a Microsoft website containing information about security, privacy, compliance, transparency, and related products and services. Trust Center does not provide any type of risk assessment for your Azure resources and services, nor does it offer risk assessments or enable you to configure or apply compliance settings or policies.

Service Trust Portal is a public site that you use to access audit and compliance reports for Azure. You can also access information to help you understand how to meet standards and regulations. Service Trust Portal also hosts Compliance Manager.

Compliance Manager enables you to view information that Microsoft provides to third-party auditors to demonstrate compliance. You can also use Compliance Manager to build a compliance framework and assign and track compliance tasks for your organization. Compliance Manager also uses a workflow-based risk assessment to develop your organization's compliance score.

Azure Government is an isolated instance of Azure supporting US federal agencies, state and local governments, and solution providers that serve these governmental entities. Azure Government is supported and managed by screened US personnel.

Azure China is an isolated instance of Azure supporting organizations that need to host Azure resources within China. Azure China is hosted and supported by 21Vianet under license from Microsoft. Azure China is not restricted to Chinese government entities or Chinese companies. Data connections between Azure China and other sites inside China require ExpressRoute. Connections between Azure China and sites outside of China require a site-to-site VPN. In both cases, the connection must be made by a telecom provider licensed by the Chinese Ministry of Industry and Information Technology.

Review Questions

1. You are setting up resources in Azure and need to filter traffic based on source IP address and port, destination IP address and port, and protocol between your on-premises network and Azure. Which of the following meets these minimum requirements?

   A. ExpressRoute

   B. Azure Firewall

   C. Application security groups

   D. User-defined routes

2. Is the underlined portion of the following statement true, or does it need to be replaced with one of the other fragments that appear below?

   You are evaluating moving a web application that you host on-premises to Azure. The solution comprises three VMs—a web front end, an application server, and a database server. You need to ensure that your administrators can access all of the VMs for remote management on port 3389, but only the web front end should be accessible over port 80. You decide to deploy an application security group to protect the web server and enable access to the other servers.

   A. deploy Web Application Firewall to filter and route traffic to the web server and deploy network security groups to enable RDP to all three VMs.

   B. deploy Web Application Firewall to filter the traffic and meet both requirements.

   C. deploy a network security group to filter traffic and meet both requirements.

   D. No change is needed.

3. You have deployed a VM to a subnet in Azure and need to ensure that only your and one other individual can connect to the VM using RDP on port 3389 to manage it. No other access from outside the subnet should be allowed at this time on any other ports. Which of the following should you use? (Choose all that apply.)

   A. Use a network security group to filter traffic and only allow port 3389 to the VM.

   B. Apply an Azure policy to the subnet to limit access on port 3389 to only your and your peer's accounts.

   C. Create a policy initiative that restricts access to the server based on your and your peer's roles, and to port 3389 for the IP address of the VM.

   D. Use role-based access control (RBAC) to ensure that only you and your peer can access the server.

4. You are considering deploying a key web application to Azure. You decide to deploy Web Application Firewall with Application Gateway as part of the project. Which of the following correctly describes the function of Web Application Firewall in this scenario?

   A. When properly configured, it ensures that traffic reaches the application only on port 80 for HTTP traffic.

   B. It protects the web application from common web-based attacks.

C. It ensures that users can reach the web service on port 80 and administrators can RDP to the VMs on port 3389.

D. None of the above.

5. Your organization hosts a VM that performs a security-related function. For both security and auditing purposes, you need to ensure that all traffic reaches the VM from a single IP address in another subnet, regardless of source. Which of the following solutions meets this requirement?

A. Create a network security group (NSG) that directs all traffic for the VM to the designated IP address and then apply the NSG to all subnets as required.

B. Create an application security group (ASG) that directs all traffic for the VM to the designated IP address and apply the ASG to all subnets in the virtual network.

C. Create a user-defined route as a custom routing table and apply the table to all subnets in the virtual network.

D. Use rules in Azure Firewall to route traffic to the target VM based on source and target IP addresses.

6. Which of the following describes Azure DDoS Protection Standard? Choose all that apply.

A. It protects against volumetric, protocol, and resource layer attacks.

B. It alerts you when an attack is happening.

C. DDoS Standard protects all resources on a virtual network as soon as the service is enabled.

D. It provides mitigation reports.

7. Your organization has made the decision to move workloads into Azure. As the Directory Services administrator, you need to explain authentication and authorization in Azure to the program managers leading the project. Which of the following are correct statements?

A. Identifying a user by a username and password is a form of authorization.

B. Validating that a user account has the necessary permissions to access a resource is an example of authorization.

C. Authentication identifies a user but does not provide access to resources.

D. Providing a password to access a shared resource is a form of authorization.

8. Which of the following is the least expensive option that enables Azure AD users to change their passwords online?

A. Azure Active Directory Base

B. Azure Active Directory Free

C. Azure Active Directory Premium P1

D. Azure Active Directory Premium P3

9. Which of the following correctly describe Azure Active Directory? (Choose all that apply.)

A. Azure AD is a key component of role-based access control (RBAC) in Azure.

B. You must register an Azure web application with Azure AD to enable that application to authenticate and authorize users.

  C. All editions of Azure AD enable management of users and groups.

  D. You must use on-premises Active Directory along with Azure AD to enable on-premises users to authenticate in Azure.

10. Which of the following capabilities require an Azure AD Premium edition? (Choose all that apply.)

  A. Self-service password management for on-premises users, enabling them to change their own passwords

  B. Enabling users to access on-premises resources such as an on-premises website using an Azure AD account

  C. Managing Azure AD groups

  D. Using RBAC to control access to resources with policies and initiatives

11. Is the underlined portion of the following statement true, or does it need to be replaced with one of the other fragments that appear below?

  Entering your PIN after you insert a debit card into an ATM is an example of multifactor authentication (MFA).

  A. Providing a username and password to log into Windows.

  B. Entering a PIN code on a keypad to enter a building.

  C. Providing an email address and password to log into a website.

  D. No change is needed.

12. Which of the following are correct statements regarding Azure Security Center? (Choose all that apply.)

  A. Security Center integrates natively with Microsoft Defender to provide risk detection and assessment.

  B. Security Center supports Linux operating systems.

  C. You must add resources to Security Center to begin monitoring those resources.

  D. Security Center provides monitoring and threat protection for VMs in Azure as well as on-premises.

13. You are tasked with explaining some of the security options in Azure to your CIO, who has asked about how Azure will improve security over your on-premises environment. Which Azure service provides security recommendations for securing your Azure resources?

  A. Advanced Threat Protection (ATP)

  B. Azure DDoS Protection

  C. Security Center

  D. Azure Service Health

14. You are moving a SQL Server Analysis Services (SSAS) solution from on-premises to Azure to support custom reporting through Power BI. You want to enable access only when a report creator needs to query for data. Which Azure service supports just-in-time (JIT) access control, enabling users to gain access to the server for only a specified period of time?

    A. Advanced Threat Protection

    B. Security Center

    C. Azure Key Vault

    D. Azure Service Health

15. Which of the following accurately describe Azure Key Vault? (Choose all that apply.)

    A. Provides the capability to create, manage, and store certificates and other secrets.

    B. Provides highly secure storage for certificates and other keys but not the capability to create them.

    C. Works in conjunction with Azure Threat Protection (ATP) to secure and contain certificate-based threats.

    D. Enables application developers to avoid storing credentials in an application.

16. Is the underlined portion of the following statement true, or does it need to be replaced with one of the other fragments that appear below?

    Azure Information Protection (AIP) enables organizations to protect emails and documents using encryption, identity, and authorization policies.

    A. encrypts data stored in Azure Premium storage.

    B. provides secure storage for certificates, cryptographic keys, and other secrets.

    C. is a mechanism in Azure Active Directory for encrypting and securing administrator credentials.

    D. No change is needed.

17. Which of the following Azure services can identify suspicious activities such as pass-the-hash attacks?

    A. Security Center

    B. Azure Information Protection (AIP)

    C. Azure Advanced Threat Protection (ATP)

    D. Microsoft Defender

18. Which of the following threats can ATP help you detect?

    A. Reconnaissance attacks

    B. Pass-the-hash

    C. Pass-the-token

    D. All of the above

19. Which of the following is an example of a honeytoken attack?

    A. Testing multiple passwords against a username

    B. Authentication attempts against an alphabetical list of usernames

    C. Login to a fake account that you created

    D. None of the above

20. You want to ensure that the VMs created in a resource group do not exceed certain limits for cores and other resources to reduce costs. Which of the following Azure features enables you to control this?

    A. Resource locks

    B. Azure policies

    C. Azure Resource Manager

    D. Azure initiatives

21. Is the underlined portion of the following statement true, or does it need to be replaced with one of the other fragments that appear below?

Azure initiatives enable you to build blueprints to define how resources should be created and deployed in your Azure environment.

    A. control how blueprints are published and assigned to resources.

    B. enable you to manage and implement policies as a group to achieve governance goals.

    C. define security policies that you apply using Azure Security Center.

    D. No change is needed.

22. Which of the following are correct statements describing Azure policies? (Choose all that apply.)

    A. You can apply policies individually to a resource or within an Azure initiative.

    B. You can apply permissions using policies to determine what actions a user can take against a resource.

    C. Applying a policy to resource group causes the policy to apply to all resources within that resource group.

    D. Azure policies are a component of Security Center that enables you to define security-related policies to protect resources.

23. Which of the following enable you to assign permissions to enable users to create and/or use resources in Azure?

    A. Azure policies

    B. Resource groups

    C. Role-based access control (RBAC)

    D. Security Center

24. You need to delegate the capability to add users in Azure to another individual at your organization. Which of the following RBAC roles should you apply to the user to provide this capability to manage management groups with the least privilege?

- **A.** Owner
- **B.** User Access Administrator
- **C.** Contributor
- **D.** Account Administrator

25. What is the role you should use to grant users the capability to create and manage resources in Azure while ensuring they have the fewest permissions needed?

- **A.** Creator
- **B.** Reader
- **C.** Owner
- **D.** Contributor

26. Which of the following statements accurately describe Azure locks? (Choose all that apply.)

- **A.** An administrator with sufficient permissions in an RBAC role can override locks.
- **B.** If you apply a lock to a resource group, the lock applies to all resources in the group, including any new resources that you create in the resource group.
- **C.** The most restrictive lock applies in a situation where multiple locks are applied at different scopes.
- **D.** You can delete a locked resource only after removing the lock, unless you have been assigned the Owner role.

27. Is the underlined portion of the following statement true, or does it need to be replaced with one of the other fragments that appear below?

The CanNotDelete lock is more restrictive than the ReadOnly lock.

- **A.** prevents administrators from modifying a resource.
- **B.** enables administrators to read but not modify a resource.
- **C.** is less restrictive than the ReadOnly lock.
- **D.** No change is needed.

28. Which of the following statements are correct regarding Azure Blueprints? (Choose all that apply.)

- **A.** Azure Blueprints use Azure Resource Manager (ARM) templates to deploy resources.
- **B.** Azure Blueprints let you define a repeatable group of Azure resources and associated role assignments and policies.
- **C.** A blueprint does not take effect until you publish the blueprint.
- **D.** Azure provides multiple roles for creating and managing blueprints.

29. Is the underlined portion of the following statement true, or does it need to be replaced with one of the other fragments that appear below?

    When you delete a blueprint, <u>all of the resources defined in the blueprint are deleted.</u>

    A. all versions of the blueprint are deleted.

    B. none of the resources defined in the blueprint are deleted.

    C. you must publish the change for it to take effect.

    D. No change is needed.

30. Which of the following statements regarding blueprints are accurate? (Choose all that apply.)

    A. All assignments of a blueprint are updated when you publish a new version of the blueprint.

    B. When you unassign a blueprint, no resources defined in the blueprint are deleted but resource locking is removed.

    C. A user with the Blueprint Contributor role can manage and publish blueprints.

    D. You can delete a blueprint only if you unassign it first.

31. Which of the following statements about Azure Monitor is not correct?

    A. Azure Monitor begins monitoring resources as soon as you create a resource.

    B. Azure Monitor begins monitoring resources as soon as you create metrics and logs for them.

    C. Application Insights enables developers to send telemetry data about the applications they develop in Azure.

    D. Azure Monitor supports Windows and Linux operating systems.

32. You are an Azure administrator and want to view status information for the resources that you host in Azure, by region. Which of the following resources should you use for that purpose?

    A. Azure Status

    B. Azure Service Health

    C. Resource Health

    D. Azure Portal

33. Which of the following would you use to view information about planned maintenance in Azure?

    A. Azure Monitor

    B. Azure Security Center

    C. Azure Advisor

    D. Azure Service Health

34. Which of the following statements are correct about Azure Service Health? (Choose all that apply.)

    A. Azure Service Health includes Azure Status, Service Health, and Resource Health.

    B. You can set up service health alerts to send email and text notifications regarding items collected by Azure Monitoring.

    C. You can use Service Health to publish Azure alerts to a website using webhooks.

    D. You can create customizable dashboards in Azure Service Health to track the health of your resources.

35. Which of the following are standards-based, nonregulatory organizations or agencies? (Choose all that apply.)

    A. NIST

    B. ISO

    C. GDPR

    D. HIPAA

36. Which of the following statements is true? (Choose all that apply.)

    A. You must provide personal information to use some Microsoft products.

    B. Microsoft cannot share your personal information with any third party.

    C. You cannot use a work email when setting up a Microsoft account that you will use to access Microsoft services.

    D. You must use a personal email account when setting up a Microsoft account.

37. Is the underlined portion of the following statement true, or does it need to be replaced with one of the other fragments that appear below?

The Microsoft Trust Center <u>enables you to view a broad range of security information about Azure and access risk assessments for your Azure resources.</u>

    A. enables you to establish high-level initiatives and policies to drive security and compliance.

    B. enables you to view audit and compliance reports published by Microsoft.

    C. is a website that provides information about how Microsoft implements and supports compliance, security, privacy, and transparency across its cloud offerings.

    D. No change is needed.

38. You are a compliance manager for your organization, which has decided to move several services from your on-premises data center into Azure. Which of the following should you use to view audit reports published by Microsoft to assure your CIO that Azure offers a secure and compliant platform?

    A. Trust Center

    B. Compliance Manager

    C. Service Trust Portal

    D. Azure Compliance Portal

39. Is the underlined portion of the following statement true, or does it need to be replaced with one of the other fragments that appear below?

Compliance <u>is the sole responsibility of Microsoft.</u>

    A. is the sole responsibility of organizations that host their services in Azure.

    B. is a shared responsibility between your organization and Microsoft.

    C. is guaranteed by SLAs in Azure.

    D. No change is needed.

40. Which of the following statements are correct regarding Azure Government? (Choose all that apply.)

    A. Azure Government is an isolated instance of Azure in the United States.

    B. Azure Government is only available to governmental entities in the United States.

    C. Hosting in Azure Government meets all governmental compliance requirements.

    D. Resources deployed to Azure Government are hosted in data centers that are separate from nongovernment resources.

41. Which of the following statements are correct regarding Azure China?

    A. Azure China is available only to Chinese governmental agencies and solution providers that support them.

    B. Azure China is an isolated instance of Azure managed by Microsoft.

    C. You can easily move resources and Azure accounts from Azure to Azure China, and vice versa.

    D. A Chinese company, 21Vianet, manages Azure China.

42. Which of the following provides broad guidance, tools, and assessments to help with a migration of workloads to Azure?

    A. FastTrack for Azure

    B. Azure Advisor

    C. Cloud Adoption Framework for Azure

    D. Azure Migration Planning Service

Chapter

5

Azure Solutions

MICROSOFT EXAM OBJECTIVES COVERED IN THIS CHAPTER:

DESCRIBE CORE SOLUTIONS AND MANAGEMENT TOOLS ON AZURE

✓ **Describe core solutions available in Azure**

- Describe the benefits and usage of Internet of Things (IoT) Hub, IoT Central, and Azure Sphere

- Describe the benefits and usage of Azure Synapse Analytics, HDInsight, and Azure Databricks

- Describe the benefits and usage of Azure Machine Learning, Cognitive Services, and Azure Bot Service

- Describe the benefits and usage of serverless computing solutions that include Azure Functions and Logic Apps

- Describe the benefits and usage of Azure DevOps, GitHub, GitHub Actions, and Azure DevTest Labs

Chapter 2, "Azure Core Services," introduced primary services available in Azure, including core data services such as Azure SQL Database and Cosmos DB. Subsequent chapters explored Azure networking and security-related services. This chapter continues your exploration with a look at Azure solutions in the areas of Internet of Things (IoT), artificial intelligence (AI), and serverless computing.

Internet of Things (IoT)

Loosely defined, the Internet of Things (IoT) describes connected devices equipped with sensors that collect data and send that data to an endpoint for logging, processing, and/or other actions. Consider a manufacturing floor where sensors track the manufacturing process and send data back to a centralized system that operators and engineers use to monitor and control the manufacturing process. Or, imagine a connected house where the refrigerator, oven, microwave, lighting systems, garage door, thermostat, and security system all collect and send data to a central app or service to enable the homeowner to monitor and potentially control the function of all of these systems. Finally, consider an automobile manufacturer that builds sensors into its vehicles to monitor performance and sends that data to Azure for real-time analytics. These scenarios are examples of IoT.

Consolidating sensor data is just one aspect of IoT. Controlling and managing the distributed devices is another aspect. For example, you might need to update firmware in devices that you manage in addition to collecting data from them.

Azure includes several services that enable organizations to integrate IoT devices quickly and easily and deploy solutions based on IoT. The following sections explore these services.

Azure IoT Hub

Azure IoT Hub is an Azure-hosted service that functions as a message hub for bidirectional communication between your deployed IoT devices and Azure services. IoT Hub supports multiple protocols and open source software development kits (SDKs), enabling it to integrate most IoT devices. IoT Hub is highly scalable, which means it can integrate billions of devices.

IoT Hub supports multiple communication and control functions, including the following:

- Device-to-cloud telemetry to collect data
- Device-to-cloud file upload to collect and transfer data

- Request/reply methods for controlling devices from the cloud
- Monitoring

Communication with IoT Hub is not limited to devices and IoT Hub. IoT Hub can route messages received from devices to other Azure services as needed. In summary, IoT Hub is the service that integrates your IoT devices and other Azure services. However, IoT Hub does not provide analysis services or dashboards for viewing device state or analyzing data. That is where IoT Central comes in.

Azure IoT Central

Azure IoT Central (Figure 5.1) builds on the functions provided by IoT Hub to provide visualization, control, and management features for IoT devices. Through IoT Central's interface, you can easily connect new devices, view telemetry, view overall device performance, create and manage alerts that notify you when a device needs maintenance, and push updates to devices when needed.

FIGURE 5.1 IoT Central provides a visual interface for viewing and managing IoT devices and telemetry.

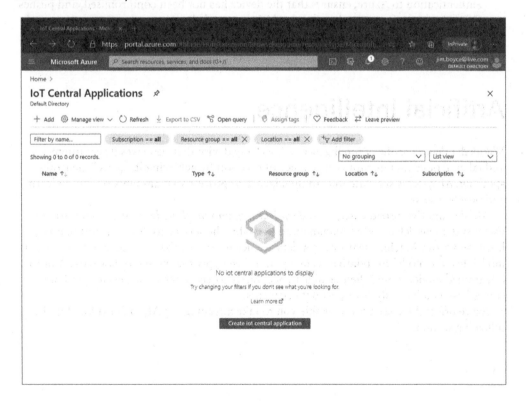

You can imagine that managing 1,000 discrete devices would be challenging, and millions of devices would be almost impossible to manage without a simplified means of deployment. IoT Central provides that simplification through *device templates*, which allow you to connect to new devices without any coding in IoT Central. IoT Central creates the dashboards, alerts, and other visualization and management elements based on the template. The device just needs to be compatible with the device template specifications. So, if you deploy 1,000 Model RG12 Gold Widgets, you use the corresponding template—which already "knows" how to connect to that device type—to connect to and begin managing those 1,000 devices, all without writing a single line of code.

Azure Sphere

Azure Sphere is an integrated IoT solution that consists of three key parts:

- **Azure Sphere micro-controller units (MCUs):** The MCU is a hardware component built into the IoT device that processes the OS and signals from attached sensors.
- **Management software:** A custom Linux operating system that manages communication with the security service and runs the vendor's device software.
- **Azure Sphere Security Service (AS3):** This Azure service handles certificate-based device authentication to Azure, ensures that the device has not been compromised, and pushes OS and other software updates to the device as needed.

Although you can build a complete IoT solution using just IoT Hub and IoT Central, Azure Sphere gives you the ability to create a custom, highly secure IoT solution.

Artificial Intelligence

Wikipedia defines artificial intelligence (AI) as "any device that perceives its environment and takes actions that maximize its chance of successfully achieving its goals." Generally speaking, AI systems simulate human intelligence to process vast amounts of data to learn and problem solve.

AI falls into two broad categories: *deep learning* and *machine learning*. Deep learning uses a system modeled on the human mind to enable the service to discover information, learn, and grow. Machine learning is a data science technique that uses data to train a data model, test the model for relative accuracy, and then apply the model to new data. A properly trained model should then be able to accurately forecast behaviors, events, and outcomes based on its analysis of past data elements.

Azure offers three services to enable you to take advantage of AI, each explored in the following sections.

Azure Machine Learning

Azure Machine Learning consists of a collection of Azure services and tools that enable you to use data to train and validate models. Through testing, you determine the model that provides the most accurate predictions. Then you can deploy the model for use through a web API endpoint. Azure Machine Learning provides a number of features that enable you to define how to obtain and manage data, train and validate predictive models, manage the process and resources for scoring your algorithms, and deploy the final model to an API endpoint, where it can be used in real time by other applications.

Azure Machine Learning encompasses multiple services and features to support your AI development efforts. For example, Azure Machine Learning Studio (Figure 5.2) is a web portal through which developers can create no-code and code-first solutions using a selection of tools, including drag-and-drop model design. You can also use Machine Learning Studio to manage assets and resources, publish your models as web services, and more.

FIGURE 5.2   Azure Machine Learning Studio provides a rich portal-based experience for creating, managing, and publishing machine learning models.

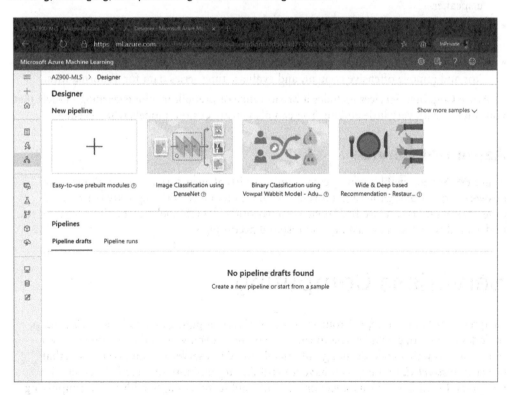

The legacy ML Studio (classic) tool for creating and managing machine learning models is still available but lacks many of the features included in Machine Learning Studio. ML Studio does not interoperate with Azure Machine Learning.

Azure Cognitive Services

Azure Cognitive Services provides machine learning models designed to interact with humans and execute cognitive functions that humans would normally do, such as recognizing images. The following list summarizes the services available within Azure Cognitive Services:

- **Language:** Use Azure Cognitive Services to process natural language to determine, for example, the user's sentiment or what the user is requesting or asking.

- **Speech:** Use Cognitive Services to convert speech into text or text into speech. Speech services can also translate from one language to another, as well as recognize and verify a speaker.

- **Vision:** This service provides identification and recognition services for analyzing images, videos, and similar visual data.

- **Decision:** Use this service to personalize a user experience with recommendations, monitor and remove offensive content, and evaluate time-series data for abnormalities.

Azure Cognitive Services includes a broad range of prebuilt machine learning models that you can use with very little coding. You can also create custom models when needed.

Azure Bot Service

Azure Bot Service enables you to create and use virtual agents to interact with users by answering questions, gathering information, and potentially initiating activities through other Azure services. Azure Bot Service can use other services such as Cognitive Services to understand what users are asking and respond accordingly.

Serverless Computing

Chapter 1, "Cloud Concepts," touched on serverless computing and its benefits. To recap, serverless computing enables you to run code without deploying and managing a server to host and run that code. Although ultimately there is a server running your code, that server is *abstracted*, meaning you have no visibility to or ability to directly interact with the server. Instead, you focus solely on the code and its function. In addition to simplifying management of the solution, Azure handles scaling when needed. In addition, you pay only for the resources used by the code.

Azure offers two primary serverless computing services, Azure Functions and Azure Logic Apps, which are explored in the following sections.

Azure Functions

The Azure Functions service enables you to host a single method or function that runs in response to an event such as a queued message, HTTP request, or timer event. You can use any of several programming languages, such as Python, Java, JavaScript, C#, and PowerShell, to create functions. Like many other services, the Azure Functions service scales automatically, enabling your function to scale to meet changes in demand without any interaction or configuration by your developers. Perhaps best of all, you pay only for the time and resources needed while a function is running.

Generally, an Azure function is *stateless*, meaning it does not store its state from execution to execution. Instead, it executes the same every time it responds to an event. You can configure a function to maintain state by connecting an Azure storage account to the function, enabling it to store its state between executions. You can also use an extension called Durable Functions to chain together functions and maintain their state while the functions are executing.

Azure Functions is an excellent solution for building small blocks of code that run for a very short period in response to a triggering event, as described earlier.

Azure Logic Apps

Functions are great for very discrete processing tasks, but when you need something much more complex, like a workflow or a process, Azure Logic Apps is a good solution. Logic Apps enables you to create no-code and low-code solutions hosted in Azure to automate and orchestrate tasks, business processes, and workflows. Like Functions, Logic Apps are serverless in that you focus on the app rather than the underlying server or resources needed to maintain and run the app.

You build Logic Apps using a web-based design environment. Like many workflow solutions, Logic Apps lets you build the app by connecting *triggers* to *actions* with various *connections*. For example, a message arriving in a queue is a trigger. The event you associate with that trigger might be passing the message to another Azure service through that service's connection. Whatever the situation, simply understand that Logic Apps gives you the ability to graphically create low-code and no-code complex workflows using a web-based design environment.

Azure Functions and Azure Logic Apps can integrate, allowing you to call one from the other. For example, you might create a function that passes data to a logic app for processing. Or you might call a function from a logic app.

Functions and Logic Apps are both priced based on consumption, like most Azure services. However, the Azure Functions service is priced based on the number of function executions and running time for each. The Azure Logic Apps feature is priced based on the number of executions and the type of connectors that the app uses.

DevOps

Software development can be a complex and time-consuming process that uses IT services but is not always well integrated into IT. The term *DevOps* describes process, practices, and services designed to integrate development and IT with the end goal of simplifying and streamlining development efforts while maintaining high quality. For example, assume your development team needs to develop and deploy a new application that will require 20 virtual machines of various types. DevOps services help simplify and automate that deployment process.

Azure includes a handful of services targeted at DevOps. The following sections describe these services.

Azure DevOps Services

Azure DevOps is not a single service but rather a group of services designed to enable and support development at multiple stages in the development process. The services include the following:

- **Azure Artifacts:** Provides a repository for storing development artifacts such as compiled source code. Artifacts can be used by other services for testing or deployment.

- **Azure Boards:** Provides capabilities for managing development projects and individual items, including user stories, backlog items, tasks, features, and bugs.

- **Azure Pipelines:** Enables you to automatically build and test code projects.

- **Azure Repos:** A source-code repository for publishing and collaborating on development projects.

- **Azure Test Plans:** Provides an automated testing tool for testing code.

GitHub and GitHub Actions

GitHub is a popular code repository for open source software that enables code sharing, development collaboration, review and discussion, documentation, and other collaboration mechanisms for sharing and collaborating on open source code projects. GitHub Actions provides workflow automation services.

GitHub and GitHub Actions offer many of the same functions as Azure DevOps, and these services can integrate. In general, GitHub is the appropriate choice for collaborating on open source projects and DevOps is the appropriate choice for enterprise/internal projects.

Azure DevTest Labs

Azure DevTest Labs automates the deployment, configuration, and decommissioning of virtual machines and other Azure resources. For example, let's assume you need to deploy 20 virtual machines of various types in a test subnet with specific network security groups and other resources. You can use DevTest Labs to automate that deployment, and when testing is complete, you can decommission all of those services so that you pay only for the resources you need for testing while you are actually testing them. All of this can be largely automated, greatly simplifying the development testing process.

DevTest Labs can use Azure Resource Manager (ARM) templates to deploy nearly any type of Azure resource, enabling your development team to model application environments and quickly provision and decommission not only the servers but support resources as well. However, DevTest Labs does not provide monitoring, alerting, or telemetry services to monitor those resources.

Summary

This chapter covered the core solutions in Azure that support IoT development and implementation, including IoT Hub, IoT Central, and Sphere. These services allow you to deploy IoT solutions incorporating standard and custom IoT devices, manage those devices, and gather and report on data sent from the devices.

The chapter also covered AI services, including Azure Machine Learning, Azure Cognitive Services, and Azure Bot Service. These services enable you to build complex and powerful solutions for analyzing data and interacting with users in an automated way.

Finally, this chapter explored many of the development-related services and solutions in Azure that allow you to more easily and effectively deploy custom solutions with minimal expense. Azure Functions and Azure Logic Apps let you build simple functions and more complex workflow processes without worrying about the underlying servers and services. Azure DevOps provides a broad range of services and solutions for developing, managing, collaborating on, and deploying code.

Exam Essentials

Internet of Things   The IoT-related services in Azure enable you to build complex IoT solutions. Azure IoT Hub functions as a hub for bidirectional communication between IoT devices and Azure services. IoT Central builds on IoT Hub to provide visualization, control, and management features for IoT devices. Azure Sphere enables you to deploy and manage IoT solutions through custom devices using a combination of integrated microcontroller units, management software, and certificate-based security services, ensuring a secure IoT solution tailored to your organization's needs.

Machine Learning and AI   Azure Machine Learning consists of a collection of Azure services and tools that you use to train and validate AI models. Azure Cognitive Services provides a comprehensive set of machine learning models to execute cognitive functions that humans would normally do, such as recognizing images, performing speech-to-text and text-to-speech functions, and translating languages. Azure Bot Service enables you to create and use virtual agents to interact with users, answering questions, gathering information, and initiating corresponding activities.

Development and Serverless Computing   With Azure Functions, you can create simple, typically stateless bits of code that execute in response to events. With the addition of a storage account, you can make functions stateful, maintaining their state between executions. Azure Logic Apps, also a serverless computing solution, enables you to build low-code and no-code workflow and process solutions using a web-based design interface.

DevOps features in Azure are designed to simplify code development and collaboration. Azure DevOps Services consists of several services for code management, testing, and deployment. GitHub and GitHub Actions provide many of the same types of features but are targeted and open source projects. Finally, Azure DevTest Labs provides the means for development teams to easily deploy virtual machines and other Azure services for code testing, then quickly and easily decommission those resources when testing is completed.

Review Questions

1. Is the underlined portion of the following statement true, or does it need to be replaced with one of the other fragments that appear below?

    IoT Hub is an Azure service that <u>enables you to view telemetry from IoT devices and view a dashboard showing device state.</u>

    A. supports secure communication between devices and controls applications using custom microcontrollers and certificate-based authentication of devices.

    B. provides bidirectional communication between IoT devices and other Azure services and/ or an IoT application.

    C. enables you to easily manage deployed IoT devices with dashboards and reports.

    D. No change is needed.

2. Your organization is building an IoT solution that enables you to monitor and control thousands of sensors deployed in your manufacturing facilities. You need to be able to analyze the telemetry data coming from the devices. Which of the following is the appropriate Azure solution?

    A. IoT Hub

    B. IoT Central

    C. Sphere

    D. None of the above

3. Is the underlined portion of the following statement true, or does it need to be replaced with one of the other fragments that appear below?

    Azure Machine Learning <u>consists of multiple services that enable you to use data to train and validate AI models.</u>

    A. enables you to create virtual machine agents that learn from user interaction and provide corresponding services such as answering questions.

    B. can be used to analyze photos and videos for content.

    C. enables you to deploy AI models as stand-alone applications in Azure or on premises.

    D. No change is needed.

4. Which of the following describe Azure Machine Learning Studio? (Choose all that apply.)

    A. It provides the ability for developers to create no-code and code-first machine learning solutions.

    B. It provides a web portal through which developers can use drag-and-drop to create machine learning solutions.

    C. It enables you to deploy machine learning models as web services.

    D. None of the above

5. Which of the following are capabilities of Azure Cognitive Services? (Choose all that apply.)

    A. Processes natural language to determine what a user is asking.

    B. Performs translation from one language to another.

    C. Acts as a virtual agent to interact with users in a humanlike way.

    D. Analyzes photos to identify content within them.

6. Is the underlined portion of the following statement true, or does it need to be replaced with one of the other fragments that appear below?

    Azure Bot Services provides the capability to analyze photos and other data types to identify specific content.

    A. is a stand-alone Azure service that cannot interact with other Azure services.

    B. provides natural language translation services.

    C. enables you to build virtual agents that interact with users in a humanlike way.

    D. No change is needed.

7. Which of the following Azure services provides the ability to create workflow-based processes?

    A. Functions

    B. Bot Service

    C. Logic Apps

    D. None of the above

8. Which of the following correctly describe Azure Functions? (Choose all that apply.)

    A. Functions are typically stateless but can be made stateful with the addition of a storage account.

    B. Functions operate independently and cannot be integrated with Logic Apps.

    C. You can use drag-and-drop features to create functions that automate processes.

    D. Functions can be developed with any of several programming languages.

9. Is the underlined portion of the following statement true, or does it need to be replaced with one of the other fragments that appear below?

    Azure Artifacts is a component service of Azure DevOps that provides a repository for storing development artifacts such as compiled source code.

    A. provides a means for managing development projects and individual items such as features and bugs.

    B. is intended for open source code development projects.

    C. works in conjunction with Azure Blueprints to provide a means of storing information about Azure resources.

    D. No change is needed.

10. Which of the following is intended primarily for collaborating on open source development efforts?

    A. Azure Repos

    B. Azure Boards

    C. GitHub

    D. Azure DevTest Labs

11. Is the underlined portion of the following statement true, or does it need to be replaced with one of the other fragments that appear below?

Azure DevTest Labs <u>provides a customizable development environment in which your developers can collaborate on code projects.</u>

    A. provides alerting and monitoring tools to analyze telemetry from servers in an application test.

    B. enables your development team to quickly and easily deploy virtual machines and other Azure resources to test an application, then decommission those resources.

    C. can provision Windows servers but not Linux servers.

    D. No change is needed.

Chapter

6

Azure Pricing, Service Levels, and Lifecycle

MICROSOFT EXAM OBJECTIVES COVERED IN THIS CHAPTER:

DESCRIBE AZURE COST MANAGEMENT AND SERVICE LEVEL AGREEMENTS

✓ **Describe methods for planning and managing costs**

  - Identify factors that can affect costs (resource types, services, locations, ingress and egress traffic)

  - Identify factors that can reduce costs (reserved instances, reserved capacity, hybrid use benefit, spot pricing)

  - Describe the functionality and usage of the Pricing Calculator and the Total Cost of Ownership (TCO) Calculator

  - Describe the functionality and usage of Azure Cost Management

DESCRIBE AZURE COST MANAGEMENT AND SERVICE LEVEL AGREEMENTS

✓ **Describe Azure service level agreements (SLAs) and service lifecycles**

  - Identify the purpose of an Azure service level agreement (SLA)

  - Identify actions that can impact an SLA (e.g., Availability Zones)

  - Describe the service lifecycle in Azure (Public Preview and General Availability)

Previous chapters have explored the fundamentals of services and solutions in Microsoft Azure. This chapter explores the mechanisms by which you purchase Azure services and manage costs, take advantage of service level agreements, and work within the Azure services lifecycle.

First, let's explore how you purchase Azure services.

Purchasing Azure Services

As you learned in Chapter 2, "Azure Core Services," Azure subscriptions are the mechanism that gives you access to Azure services. Various types of subscriptions offer different capabilities for purchasing Azure services. The following section explains these options.

Azure Subscriptions

Microsoft provides free and paid subscriptions for Azure services. These include the following:

- **Free trial:** This type of subscription provides 12 months of select free services and credit to use any Azure service for 30 days. These services are disabled when the 12-month period ends or when your 30-day credit expires. You can convert the free subscription to a paid subscription.
- **Pay-as-you-go:** With this type of subscription, you pay for services as you consume them. The subscription can be tied to a credit card or debit card, or you can use prepaid invoicing to gain access to volume discounts.
- **Member offers:** Some Microsoft products and services, such as Visual Studio and Microsoft Partner Network, provide credits toward Azure services.

Which subscription type you choose depends on your consumption scenario and other factors. For example, you might start with a free subscription to test Azure features and gain an understanding of Azure, and then convert it to a pay-as-you-go subscription when you are ready to start deploying Azure resources in earnest.

Keep in mind that you are not limited to a single subscription. You can have any number of Azure subscriptions, each containing various resources and services as needed. Using multiple subscriptions can be useful for helping allocate costs across your organization.

Purchasing Services

Subscriptions enable you to access Azure services, but they do not in themselves provide the means to purchase Azure services. You have three options for purchasing Azure services:

- **Enterprise Agreement:** Enterprise customers often purchase Microsoft licensing and services through an enterprise agreement (EA). EAs are generally three years in length and invoiced annually, although customers can purchase multiyear agreements and pay for them up front. An EA offers the flexibility to "true up" licensing annually and generally includes incentives to help reduce costs. EAs are negotiated with Microsoft and fulfilled through a third-party licensing partner.

- **Web Direct:** With this method you purchase Azure services directly through the Azure portal. Services are billed monthly to a credit card or through invoicing, depending on which method you establish when you create the subscription.

- **Cloud Solution Provider (CSP):** CSPs are Microsoft partners that specialize in helping their clients deploy and manage cloud services.

Choosing the right mechanism to purchase Azure services is an important consideration. For example, if your organization already has an EA, then it likely makes sense to include your Azure expenses in your EA through incentives and other potential discounts or investments that Microsoft agrees to make for your EA term.

Purchasing through a CSP also adds points for consideration. When you use a CSP, the CSP is responsible for your Azure support. If you have a break-fix issue, rather than contact Microsoft you contact your CSP. The CSP is then responsible for working to resolve the issue either directly or through Microsoft support channels. If you currently have a Premier or Unified Support agreement with Microsoft and are used to getting your support directly from Microsoft, the CSP's required involvement will be an operational change for you. However, even if you purchase Azure services through a CSP, you can still purchase a Premier or Unified Support agreement with Microsoft and use that for your on-premises and hybrid issues. Work with your Microsoft Customer Success Account Manager (formerly known as Technical Account Managers, or TAMs) to determine what support options you have directly with Microsoft when you also have a CSP in place.

Factors Affecting Cost

Many factors influence the cost of Azure services, and understanding these factors can help you reduce and control costs. For example, some services offer different tiers of service, with storage being a good example. The type of storage, performance tier, and access tier all affect cost. Moving from one type of storage to another can cause a significant increase in cost. Before deploying an Azure service, make sure you understand the service tiers and other factors that affect that service's cost.

Regardless of which services you deploy in Azure, you can track service usage with usage meters that Azure creates automatically when you deploy a resource. Azure uses the data generated by the usage meter to determine what to bill you at the end of each billing period. For example, assume you stand up a virtual machine in Azure. Azure tracks CPU time, incoming and outgoing network traffic, disk usage and read/write operations, and the time a public IP address is associated with the virtual machine. All of these are billable items that determine the overall cost in that billing period for the VM. If you turn off the VM, it generates no resource usage and therefore no cost other than for storage. Because the storage persists, you will continue to incur storage costs, even when the VM is off.

Usage captured by each usage meter results in a certain number of billable units, and those billable units are converted to charges based on resource type. One billable unit for a particular service will be different in value from the value of a billable unit for another service.

Resource allocation and uptime are key aspects of Azure cost management. If you are using a resource, you are getting billed for it (unless you are using a free subscription). As described earlier, VMs are a good example of where shutting down resources when not needed will have a major effect on cost. Likewise, leveraging serverless offerings such as Azure Functions that incur costs only when they are running and using resources is a great way to minimize costs.

Another potential way you will incur costs in Azure is by purchasing solutions or services from the Azure Marketplace. These services and solutions are provided by third-party vendors and billed by those vendors. Before you purchase a service or solution from the Azure Marketplace, be sure to investigate and understand the recurring cost associated with the offering.

Where you deploy Azure resources also affects costs. You must specify a region when you create a resource, and although regions enable you to locate resources nearest to where your users will consume them, the regions potentially have different costs. So, where you deploy a resource can determine the costs for that resource.

Network traffic is also a consideration for cost. Network traffic flowing into an Azure data center is free. Network traffic flowing out, however, has a cost associated with it. For example, assume that to save on expenditure you place Azure resources in a region that has a lower cost. However, you need to perform data transfers on a periodic basis from that region to another. The cost associated with that outgoing traffic could offset the cost savings you achieved by placing the resources where you did.

Data transfer cost between regions depends on the region and location. There is one cost within a region and a higher cost when going from a region on one continent to a region on another continent. Data transferred through Internet egress routed through the Microsoft Premium Global Network or through the Routing Preference Standard Tier also have differing costs. The bottom line is that you need to carefully consider ingress and egress traffic costs when determining where to place your Azure resources.

Billing Zones

A billing zone is a geographical grouping of Azure regions for billing Azure resources. For example, Zone 1 includes (among other regions) Australia Central, West US, East US, Canada West, West Europe, and France Central.

The key point to understand about billing zones is that network traffic flowing between regions and across billing zones has a different billing rate depending on the source and destination of the traffic. As you work to determine where to place your Azure resources, keep this factor in mind to minimize costs where possible.

You will find more information about billing zones at https://azure. microsoft.com/en-us/pricing/details/bandwidth.

Now that you have some background in how to purchase Azure services and how they are billed, let's look at how you can plan and manage costs in Azure.

Planning and Managing Azure Costs

Microsoft offers several resources to help you plan your Azure implementation and minimize costs as much as possible. The following sections explore these resources.

TCO Calculator

The Total Cost of Ownership (TCO) Calculator for Azure enables you to estimate the cost of operating your IT services and solutions in Azure over time compared to your current on-premises costs. Total cost of ownership seeks to include obvious costs as well as sometimes less tangible costs. These include, for example, electricity, cooling, and other facilities costs, as well as licensing, hardware, and labor, among others. Figure 6.1 shows the TCO Calculator.

Visit https://azure.microsoft.com/en-us/pricing/tco/calculator to access the TCO Calculator.

FIGURE 6.1   Estimate Azure costs with the TCO Calculator.

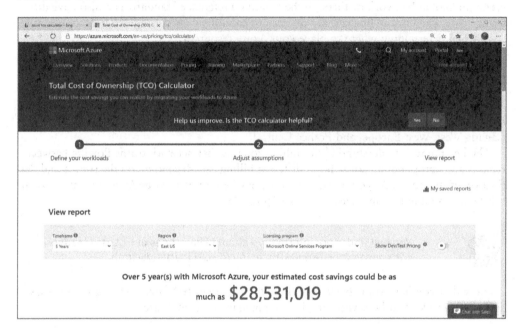

The first step in estimating costs with the TCO Calculator is to define your on-premises workloads in the categories of servers, databases, storage, and networking. Next, you provide information about your current on-premises licenses and whether they are enrolled in Software Assurance (SA), which is a benefit of a Microsoft Enterprise agreement. If they are enrolled in SA, you can potentially save money by reusing those licenses in Azure.

With your workloads and licensing defined, the next step is to adjust assumptions in the calculator. For example, you adjust the rate you pay for electricity per kilowatt hour, the hourly rate for IT staff, maintenance costs, and other factors. The TCO Calculator applies those adjustments and gives you a suggested cost savings. You can then download, share, or save the report.

The TCO Calculator obviously cannot provide exact costs because your assumptions are just that—assumptions. However, the TCO Calculator can provide a "directionally correct" estimate of how moving workloads to Azure can affect the costs of deploying and maintaining those workloads in Azure compared to your current solution. The TCO Calculator will not give you an exact cost for all your workloads, but it will give you a first look at Azure pricing overall and help you decide what magnitude of cost savings you will experience by moving to Azure.

   You do not need an Azure subscription to use the TCO Calculator.

Pricing Calculator

When you need a more refined cost estimate for specific workloads, you can turn to the Pricing Calculator. With the Pricing Calculator, you specify the Azure products that you want to include in a pricing estimate. For example, assume you want to price a simple web application that requires six VMs, storage, and two Azure SQL Database instances. The Pricing Calculator can give you the operational costs for all of those resources to help you understand the cost of standing up that specific solution in Azure.

When you first open the Pricing Calculator, you will see a list of products, as shown in Figure 6.2. Begin building your estimate by selecting the resources that comprise the solution. Using the earlier example, click Virtual Machines to add VMs to the solution. Then add Azure SQL Database and Storage Accounts in the same way. The Pricing Calculator adds them below, as shown in Figure 6.3.

FIGURE 6.2   Begin in the Pricing Calculator by selecting the products to include in your solution.

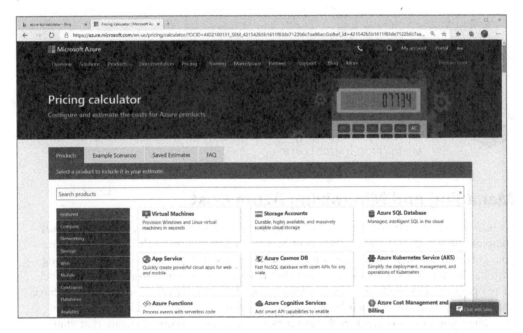

You now need to specify parameters for each resource. With the VMs, for example, you specify parameters such as the region, OS type, tier, number, and other values. As you modify parameters, the Pricing Calculator updates estimated costs for each resource. At the bottom of the page you choose support options, special programs and offers, and additional information to adjust the pricing. You can then export, save, or share the price for the solution.

FIGURE 6.3   Specify the options for each resource.

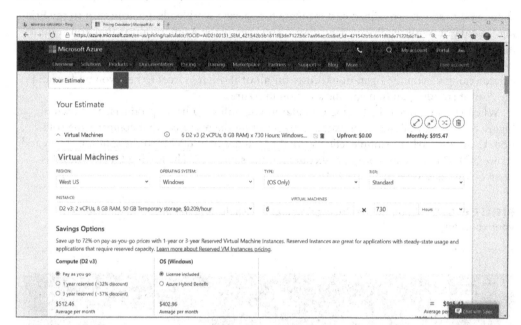

   As with the TCO Calculator, you do not need an Azure subscription to use the Pricing Calculator. You will find it at `https://azure.microsoft.com/en-us/pricing/calculator`.

Managing and Minimizing Azure Cost

It is easy to manage costs when you have only a few resources in Azure, but imagine how complex cost estimation and management becomes when you make the decision to move your entire data center into Azure and build a new disaster recovery solution to go along with it. Moving to Azure requires a mind shift from a capital expenditure (CapEx) model to an operational expenditure model. CapEx costs are relatively easy to calculate as a fixed asset, whereas operational costs based on consumption are more difficult. There are several things you can do to track and manage your expenses in Azure to ensure that your investment in Azure continues to result in cost savings for your organization. The following sections explore these topics.

Estimating Costs

As discussed previously in this chapter, Azure offers pricing tools that enable you to not only get an estimate of a large-scale deployment to Azure, but also get fairly accurate estimates for specific workloads or solutions. It is easy to deploy resources and solutions in Azure, to the point where you might get into the mindset of simply deploying a solution without fully determining the cost beforehand. Even if you are working with a free subscription to test Azure, understanding the potential costs of a resource or solution is critical. So, turn to the TCO Calculator when you are considering a move to Azure, but be sure to use the Pricing Calculator before you deploy a new resource or solution, entering the values for a worst-case consumption scenario to make sure you understand the effect of deploying the service.

Monitoring Consumption with Azure Advisor

Estimating usage is certainly an important first step, but monitoring your Azure consumption is equally important to managing costs. Azure Advisor provides a means for you to track Azure consumption and offers recommendations not only for cost savings but also for performance, reliability, and security. Figure 6.4 shows an example of Azure Advisor, which you access through the Azure portal.

FIGURE 6.4   Use Azure Advisor to help manage costs.

You can choose which subscription you want to view in Advisor, which then provides recommendations across several categories, including Cost. You can then click a category to view specific recommendations that Advisor offers based on usage telemetry and other factors.

Implementing Spending Limits

If you have a free trial subscription or credit-based subscription, Azure imposes limits automatically. If you have a credit-based subscription that gives you a certain value of services you can consume in a month, Azure shuts off your subscription when you reach the limit, then turns it back on at the beginning of the next billing cycle. For credit-based subscriptions with credits applied over multiple months, you can turn off the spending limit through the Cost Management + Billing service, discussed later in the section "Azure Cost Management + Billing." If you need to turn off limits for a free trial account, convert the account to a pay-as-you-go subscription.

Managing Subscription Limits (Quotas)

Many services in Azure have adjustable limits with a default limit that can be adjusted up to a maximum limit (also called a *hard limit*). These limits are also sometimes called *quotas*. If you are attempting to create a resource and receive a message that you must increase your subscription limits, this means you have hit the limit for that resource. With many resources you can increase the limit, not to exceed the hard limit. To increase a subscription limit, simply open a case online.

Prepaying with Azure Reservations

Azure Reservations enables you to save on Azure costs by reserving (prepaying) for resources. The cost savings can be significant, up to 70 percent or more. For example, you might prepay for an entire year on the VMs that you will be using to reduce cost or commit to an even longer period for greater savings. You can pay for a reservation up front for the specified period (such as a year) or pay the reservation monthly. The latter enables you to enjoy the cost savings of the reservation without a lump sum payment up front. There is no additional cost to pay monthly rather than lump sum.

You can use Azure Reservations with enterprise agreements, CSP subscriptions, and pay-as-you-go subscriptions. You will typically use the Azure portal to purchase a reservation, but you can also do so through Azure APIs, PowerShell, and CLI.

Choosing Less Expensive Regions

Regions potentially have different costs for the same resources compared to other regions. You can often save costs by placing resources in a less expensive region. However, you do need to consider factors such as closeness to your users, varying regulatory requirements, and network egress bandwidth. In general, you should place connected resources with metered bandwidth within the same region to avoid additional network egress charges.

Managing Resources and Billing for Cost Efficiency

Several other design and operational factors can have a significant effect on the overall costs of your IT services. For example, actively managing the number, size, and state of your VMs is a key mechanism for managing your VM costs:

- **Resize:** Periodically review VM sizing based on consumption, performance, and costs to determine if you can reduce the size of your VMs to save additional operational costs.

- **Turn off:** Ensure that VMs are turned off when not in use to avoid consumption charges when you do not need the VMs.

- **Delete:** If you are no longer using a VM, make any appropriate backups and then delete the VM.

Effectively managing your VMs can have a significant impact on your Azure consumption costs, particularly if you use several VMs.

Moving from an IaaS model to a PaaS model can also have a major effect on your Azure operational costs. For example, if you are using SQL Server VMs today to provide SQL services for an application, moving to SQL Server for Azure or SQL Server Managed Instance could reduce costs because you are charged for your consumption of the database service, not the VMs that support it. Many other scenarios exist where moving from IaaS to PaaS can reduce costs, but consumption charges are just one aspect of these scenarios. Hosting services on VMs that could otherwise be moved to a PaaS offering means you must manage the VM operating systems, patching, and so on, which imposes an operational overhead that you eliminate by moving to a PaaS solution.

One final option for managing costs is using tags to identify resource owners for billing purposes. Assume, for example, that the marketing department has a set of resources deployed in Azure that your team manages for them. The marketing department is responsible for the operational costs associated with those resources. So, tagging their resources to identify them as marketing resources enables you to not only identify what their costs are but also use that information to cross-bill them or allocate costs to their cost center.

You can apply tags when you create a resource or edit the tags after the fact. Use Azure Cost Management + Billing to view billing information, including tags.

Azure Hybrid Benefit

If your Windows Server or SQL Server licenses are covered by Software Assurance (SA), you might be able to reduce Azure costs when you move those workloads to Azure VMs. Azure Hybrid Benefit enables you to repurpose your perpetual licenses for these products for use in Azure VMs and gain a corresponding costs savings.

Spot Pricing

Another way to save on Azure costs is through spot pricing. Spot pricing enables you to take advantage of discounted pricing for resources that are not being used. With this model, you purchase VMs with the understanding that those VMs can be evicted from Azure with 30 seconds' notice when Azure needs those resources for other, non-spot workloads. You can configure the VMs to be either deallocated or deleted. If deallocated, the VMs are placed in a stopped-deallocated state and can be redeployed later. However, there is no guarantee that the reallocation will be successful, considering that the VMs are subject to resource availability. Deallocated VMs continue to incur any storage costs associated with the VMs. If you configure the eviction policy to delete the VMs, those VMs are stopped and deleted and incur no additional costs. Spot VMs do not have SLAs.

Spot VMs offer a significant cost savings but are not appropriate for workloads requiring continuous operation or SLAs. Nevertheless, spot VMs can be particularly useful for dev/test systems or production systems running processes that can be interrupted.

> You have the option to set a maximum price for a spot VM, which gives you some flexibility to retain the VM until it essentially prices itself off the service and is evicted. You can also set the maximum price to –1, which prevents it from being evicted but also means it then potentially runs at standard cost rates. The VM's price is the current spot price or the standard VM price, whichever is less, provided resources are available to accommodate the VM.

Reserved Capacity

Another way to reduce costs in Azure is to use reserved capacity for Azure SQL Database and SQL Managed Instance. With reserved capacity, you make a commitment to either of these SQL services for a period of up to three years and receive a corresponding reduction in price. You specify the Azure region, deployment type, performance tier, and term for the reservation and receive pricing based on those factors. Once the reservation is in place, Azure SQL Database or SQL Managed Instances that you have running automatically receive the reserved pricing instead of pay-as-you-go pricing. Reservations do not automatically renew, however, and pricing reverts to pay-as-you-go pricing when the reservation term expires. You can then establish a new reservation.

Azure Cost Management + Billing

Azure Cost Management + Billing, as its name implies, combines cost management functions with billing functions to provide a single place where you can manage both in Azure. You access it through the Azure portal. Click Cost Management in the navigation pane to access the Cost Management tools.

Azure Cost Management uses analytics to report on costs and usage patterns in Azure. You can define budgets for your subscriptions and receive notifications related to expenses against budgets, schedule automated report distribution, and manage other features that enable you to understand consumption and spending in Azure.

Setting budgets on your subscriptions allows you to track expenses against those budgets and receive alerts as spending crosses thresholds that you set. This helps you identify changes, such as resizing resources or turning off unused resources, that you might need to make to avoid exceeding your budget.

Cost Management also provides cost analysis and forecasting to help you not only manage costs but also plan. You can view recommendations offered by Azure Advisor through Cost Management to further help you manage costs.

Service Level Agreements

A service level agreement (SLA) is an agreement between a service provider and a consumer that generally guarantees that the SLA-backed service will be available for a specific period during the month. SLAs are typically binding, financially backed agreements in which the provider either pays a penalty or provides a credit to the consumer for the period in which the SLA is not met. For example, if a provider offers a 99.9 percent SLA for a service, they are guaranteeing that the service will be unavailable no more than 43.2 minutes during the month, corresponding to downtime of no more than about 8.76 hours a year. For those Azure services for which Microsoft offers an SLA, Microsoft will provide a credit in any billing period in which a service fails its SLA.

Microsoft does not issue SLA credits automatically. You must open a billing case to request an SLA or work with your CSP to obtain a credit.

SLAs are often referred to based on the number of digits in the SLA. An SLA of 99.9 percent is often referred to as "three nines." Likewise, a 99.99 percent SLA is referred to as "four nines" and corresponds to downtime of no more than 52.56 minutes per year.

Understanding and designing around Azure SLAs is important to ensure you receive appropriate credits when the SLAs are not met, but is equally important for designing your Azure solutions to meet your own business requirements. If you need a specific web app to be down no more than an hour per month, you should design the solution for the appropriate SLA (in this case, 99.9 percent). As you will learn in the section "Composite SLAs" later in this chapter, you must consider the individual SLAs for each component in your solution.

A key point to understand is the difference between *available* and *available at degraded performance*. If an Azure service is available but with degraded performance, it still meets the SLA. The service must be completely unavailable to fail the SLA and qualify for a service credit. For example, assume that identity services are affected and logon times for your users to Azure resources is significantly affected, but users are not prevented from logging in. This would not qualify as an SLA failure because the service is still available.

Different Azure resources have not only different SLAs, but also different *service credits*. The service credits associated with the SLA for a given service determine the credit you will receive when you or your CSP submits a credit request. Generally the higher the SLA, the lower the service credit will be. For example, a 99.99 percent SLA might have a service credit of 10 (equating to 10 percent), whereas a 99 percent SLA for the same service might have a service credit of 25 percent.

Free Azure products generally do not have any SLA associated with
them.

The Azure Status portal is a great place to get information about ongoing incidents or
outages and access status history. You can also set up notifications so that you receive alerts
when a service-impacting event (SIE) occurs. As mentioned earlier, you need to submit a
billing case with Microsoft to receive a credit, or if you work through a CSP, the CSP will
typically manage the credit process for you.

Composite SLAs

Most Azure resources and services have a set SLA. Many solutions that you build in Azure,
however, are composites of multiple Azure services. A *composite SLA* is the SLA that results
from combining services with potentially differing SLAs. For example, assume that your
solution includes two VMs, one Azure SQL Database instance, and one Azure Load Balancer
instance. The VMs have an SLA of 99.9 percent, Azure SQL Database 99.99 percent, and
Azure Load Balancer 99.99 percent. To determine the composite SLA, you simply multiply
the SLA values for each resource:

$$0.999 \times 0.999 \times 0.9999 \times 0.9999 = 0.9978$$

The resulting composite SLA in this example is 99.78 percent. Why include the VMs
twice when they have the same SLA? Both are points of failure with the possibility of
affecting performance or availability, so both need to be factored into the equation.

When you are planning an Azure deployment, you should always do the math to understand the resulting composite SLA. If the composite SLA does not meet your business needs,
either review the design to determine if the reduced SLA is sufficient or redesign the solution
with appropriate resources that do have the SLAs needed to meet the requirement.

Multiple factors can affect composite SLA. The disk type you choose for
a VM, for example, changes the resulting SLA for the VM. For services
that offer different tiers, choosing a higher tier will result in an SLA where
none would otherwise apply or in an increased SLA.

Availability Zones

Another way to raise the SLA for a given solution in Azure is to design it with high availability in mind. This can sometimes be counterintuitive, however. For example, adding VMs
to a solution to balance the load would add a measure of high availability to the solution.
If one VM fails, the others can continue functioning, resulting in availability of the service
but potentially with reduced performance. Because each VM's SLA gets factored into the

composite SLA, adding more VMs actually *lowers* the composite SLA. This is where availability zones come into play.

As explained in Chapter 2, an availability zone is a distinct physical location within an Azure region consisting of one or more physical data centers. Each zone has its own independent power, cooling, networking, and related services. If one zone goes down because of a localized event, other zones can continue to operate. Deploying instances of a VM across two or more availability zones raises the SLA for the VM from 99.9 percent to 99.99 percent. Factoring that into your composite SLA equation results in a higher composite SLA.

You should not design your solutions for unrealistically high SLAs. You will never achieve 100 percent availability, at least not over a long period of time. Consider the business needs for the solution, determine the resulting *reasonable* availability expected, and design to that number. Do not make your solution more complex than it has to be to meet the business need.

Service Lifecycles

A *service lifecycle* determines how a product is released and supported. Azure provides two lifecycle phases: *preview* and *general availability (GA)*, explained in the following sections.

Preview

Azure features in the preview phase of their lifecycle are essentially in beta testing. Using preview features enables you to test out new Azure functionality. Features in preview are not guaranteed to be deployed to general availability (discussed in the next section). Preview features are also not subject to SLAs and the limited warranty outlined in the Online Service Terms. They may not be covered by support and might be subject to different security, compliance, and privacy commitments from Microsoft.

Most previews are *public previews* that are available to everyone who uses Azure. In some cases, Microsoft offers *private previews* to selected organizations by invitation.

General Availability

The next step after the preview phase for an Azure service is *general availability*. These services are subject to the published SLAs and other service terms and warranties defined by the Online Service Terms.

Moving the GA does not guarantee that a service will always be offered by Microsoft. Microsoft can and does deprecate and sunset services. The modern lifecycle policy governing Azure provides for a minimum of 12 months' notice before a GA feature is retired.

Summary

Previous chapters have focused mainly on explaining how Azure works and the various resources and services available in Azure. This chapter turned to lifecycle and cost management topics to help you understand how to plan your long-term Azure strategy, adapt to changing requirements and resource offerings, and plan and manage costs.

Before you deploy your solutions to Azure, ensure that you use the TCO Calculator to estimate the cost savings you will realize by moving your on-premises workloads and workloads hosted in other cloud services to Azure. Then, use the Pricing Calculator to estimate the cost more closely for each resource or solution that you intend to deploy.

Once you have deployed resources to Azure, use Azure Advisor to discover opportunities to reduce costs. Implementing spending limits, prepaying for services with Azure Reservations, deploying resources into different regions, and leveraging your existing licenses with Azure Hybrid Benefit can all result in cost savings.

Also, take the time to understand SLAs in Azure and the SLA associated with each resource or service. Consider the business need for each solution and the acceptable downtime, and then design the solution for an appropriate composite SLA. Consider using different service tiers and availability zones to improve composite SLAs for your solutions.

Finally, take into account the lifecycle of each service that you deploy in Azure. Monitor lifecycles of your solutions to determine if and when a service will be retired so that you can implement changes as needed.

Exam Essentials

Identify factors that can affect costs (resource types, services, locations, ingress and egress traffic).   Many factors can affect Azure costs. Each resource or service has specific costs that can vary according to its size, tier, or other factors. The location of a resource also potentially affects its cost. For example, network traffic between regions can incur additional charges that must be factored in when designing a deployment.

Identify factors that can reduce costs (Reserved instances, Reserved capacity, Hybrid use benefit, Spot pricing).   Azure provides several methods for reducing overall cost. Reserved instances enable you to prepay for services and receive a discount corresponding to the length of the commitment. Payment flexibility enables you to spread the commitment across the agreement to help shift from lump-sum payment to recurring operational cost. The Hybrid Use Benefit lets you bring your Windows Server and SQL Server licenses covered by Software Assurance into Azure to lower licensing costs. Other offers such as spot pricing and promotional offers can also help you reduce Azure costs.

Describe the functionality and usage of the Pricing Calculator and the Total Cost of Ownership (TCO) Calculator.   The TCO Calculator is intended to help you estimate the cost of moving workloads into Azure at a large scale. The TCO Calculator not only takes into account the resources (such as VMs) but also factors in facilities and staffing cost to estimate the total cost to move a solution to Azure. When it comes time to move specific workloads into Azure, use the Pricing Calculator to estimate the costs associated with the specific resources that will comprise the solution.

Identify the purpose of an Azure service level agreement (SLA). SLAs are agreements between Microsoft and you in regard to the availability of an Azure service. Many but not all Azure services have SLAs. When designing a solution, you must consider the composite SLA that results from the individual SLAs for each resource in the solution. Multiply the individual SLAs to determine the composite SLA for the solution.

Identify actions that can impact an SLA (for example, availability zones). Choosing higher tiers or service levels for a given service can improve its SLA. For example, the type of storage you choose for a VM affects its SLA. Deploying VMs into two or more availability zones can increase the SLA for a VM or for the solution using those VMs. Consider these factors when planning for high availability.

Describe the service lifecycle in Azure (public preview and general availability). The service lifecycle in Azure includes two phases: preview and general availability. Services in either public or private preview are not subject to SLAs or other terms in the Azure Online Service Terms. Services in general availability are subject to those terms. Microsoft provides a minimum of 12 months' notice before retiring a GA service.

Review Questions

1. Which of the following is the first step in deploying services to Azure?

   A. Choosing a storage tier

   B. Purchasing the appropriate Azure resources

   C. Creating an Azure subscription

   D. None of the above

2. You are deploying a new solution that requires four instances of Azure SQL Server in an existing subscription, and you receive a message that you need to increase the subscription limit to create these resources. Which option correctly describes how to increase the limit?

   A. Modify the policy that is restricting you from creating the resource.

   B. Use Azure Resource Manager to increase the limits.

   C. You must create a new subscription and deploy the resources to it.

   D. Open an online support case to have Microsoft increase the limit for you.

3. Which of the following is *not* an option for purchasing Azure services?

   A. Enterprise agreement

   B. Cloud solution provider

   C. Web Direct

   D. Unified Support

4. Which two of the following would potentially increase operational costs for an Azure solution that you have deployed?

   A. The region in which the resources are deployed

   B. The subscription in which the resources are deployed

   C. The billing account used for the target subscription

   D. Deploying resources across multiple regions

5. You are the Director of Infrastructure for your organization, which currently has no Azure subscriptions. Your CIO has requested an estimate of how much your organization can save by moving its entire data center to Azure. Which of the following should you use for an initial overall estimate?

   A. Azure Advisor

   B. Pricing Calculator

   C. TCO Calculator

   D. Create an Azure subscription and use the Azure Estimator tool to model costs.

6. Is the underlined portion of the following statement true, or does it need to be replaced with one of the other fragments that appear below?

   The Azure Pricing Calculator <u>enables you to estimate the cost of a specific Azure solution based on the resources and services in that solution.</u>

A. can calculate the estimated cost of moving a data center to Azure.

B. factors facilities costs such as power and cooling into an estimate.

C. is a downloadable tool that can help you calculate the costs of deploying an Azure solution.

D. No change is needed.

7. Which of the following use scenarios are appropriate for Azure Advisor? (Choose all that apply.)

A. Determining ways to reduce costs

B. Deploying security policies and initiatives based on recommendations from Microsoft

C. Getting recommendations for improving security

D. Viewing service health

8. Your organization completed a sizable Azure deployment over the past year encompassing compute, storage, big data, and serverless computing, with a relatively small DevOps component. As the IT Director, you have been tasked by the CIO with reducing Azure expenditures. You cannot reduce the resources you have deployed in Azure. Which option could provide the most significant cost savings?

A. Reviewing and resizing VMs

B. Moving resources to less expensive regions

C. Using Azure reservations to prepay for services

D. Moving from Azure SQL Database to Azure SQL Managed Instance

9. Which of the following is most likely to increase Azure operational costs?

A. Adding another subscription

B. Moving storage from the hot access tier to the archive tier

C. Deploying connected resources across multiple regions

D. None of the above

10. Is the underlined portion of the following statement true, or does it need to be replaced with one of the other fragments that appear below?

Azure Hybrid Benefit <u>is a cost-saving option offered by Microsoft for all Azure hybrid deployments</u>.

A. enables you to leverage your existing Windows Server and SQL Server licenses that are covered by Software Assurance for deployments in Azure.

B. reduces pricing for network ingress traffic from your on-premises data center to Azure in a hybrid deployment.

C. enables you to leverage all your Microsoft perpetual licenses in Azure if those licenses are decommissioned in your on-premises data center.

D. No change is needed.

11. Which of the following enables you to define budgets for your subscriptions and receive notifications when spending crosses alert thresholds that you have set?

   A. Azure Quota Management

   B. Azure Budget Management

   C. Azure Cost Management

   D. Azure Monitor

12. You are planning to deploy a solution in Azure that comprises two VMs, each of which has a 99.5 percent SLA, and one Azure SQL Database with a 99.99 percent SLA. Which of the following is the resulting composite SLA for this scenario?

   A. The lowest SLA value, 99.5 percent

   B. The highest SLA value, 99.99 percent

   C. The average of the three SLAs, or 99.97 percent

   D. The product of the three SLAs, or 98.99 percent

13. You have deployed several VMs into Azure and need to increase the SLA for the VMs to meet mandated business requirements. Which of the following would achieve that requirement?

   A. Adding more storage for the VMs

   B. Deploying additional instances of the VMs to two or more availability zones

   C. Increasing the number of VMs

   D. None of the above

14. Is the underlined portion of the following statement true, or does it need to be replaced with one of the other fragments that appear below?

   An Azure service that is in public preview is <u>available to public customers by invitation from Microsoft</u>.

   A. available to all Azure customers.

   B. available only with an enterprise agreement.

   C. subject to SLAs.

   D. No change is needed.

15. Which of the following accurately describe Azure Services that are in private preview? (Choose all that apply.)

   A. They are available for all customers in the United States only.

   B. They are available for customers by invitation from Microsoft.

   C. They are generally not subject to SLAs.

   D. They are not guaranteed to move to general availability.

16. How much notice does Microsoft provide before it retires an Azure service?

   A. 30 days

   B. 6 months

   C. 12 months

   D. 5 years

Chapter

7

Creating and Managing Azure Resources

MICROSOFT EXAM OBJECTIVES COVERED IN THIS CHAPTER:

DESCRIBE CORE SOLUTIONS AND MANAGEMENT TOOLS ON AZURE

✓ **Describe Azure management tools**

- Describe the functionality and usage of the Azure Portal, Azure PowerShell, Azure CLI, Cloud Shell, and Azure Mobile App

Azure is a very rich, complex offering. As the number of services and resources rises, so does the complexity of deploying and managing resources. Fortunately, Azure offers multiple methods for managing the resources in your Azure environment. In most cases, you can use one of several management tools for the same task, enabling you to choose a tool that offers the appropriate balance between ease and functionality.

This chapter explores the management tools available in Azure and helps you put them to use to gain some experience in creating and managing your own Azure resources.

Azure Management Tools

It is easy to deploy a single VM using the Azure portal. You choose some options from a few controls on a web page and soon your VM is up and running. But what if you need to deploy 50 VMs? What if you have internal line-of-business apps that you have to integrate into the deployment process? In those scenarios, a web portal is far from optimal. That's why it is important to choose the right management option for each scenario. Let's examine these options, starting with the Azure portal.

Azure Portal

The Azure portal is a web interface that enables you to view, create, and manage Azure resources and services. The Azure portal provides access to almost every aspect of Azure, but as hinted at earlier, it is not always the best management solution for a given scenario. Nevertheless, the Azure portal offers the simplest solution for managing individual resources and services. Figure 7.1 shows the Azure portal.

When choosing a management tool for Azure, the most important considerations for the Azure portal are ease of use and visualization. The Azure portal is easy to use because it offers a familiar web-based user experience. It also provides a wealth of visualization tools and reports for understanding your Azure environment and managing it. One benefit of the Azure portal is that, as a web-based tool, it is available on most devices with a browser. So, if you need to create a VM from an Android laptop or tablet, doing so is as easy as on a Windows device.

FIGURE 7.1   You can use the Azure portal to manage most Azure resources.

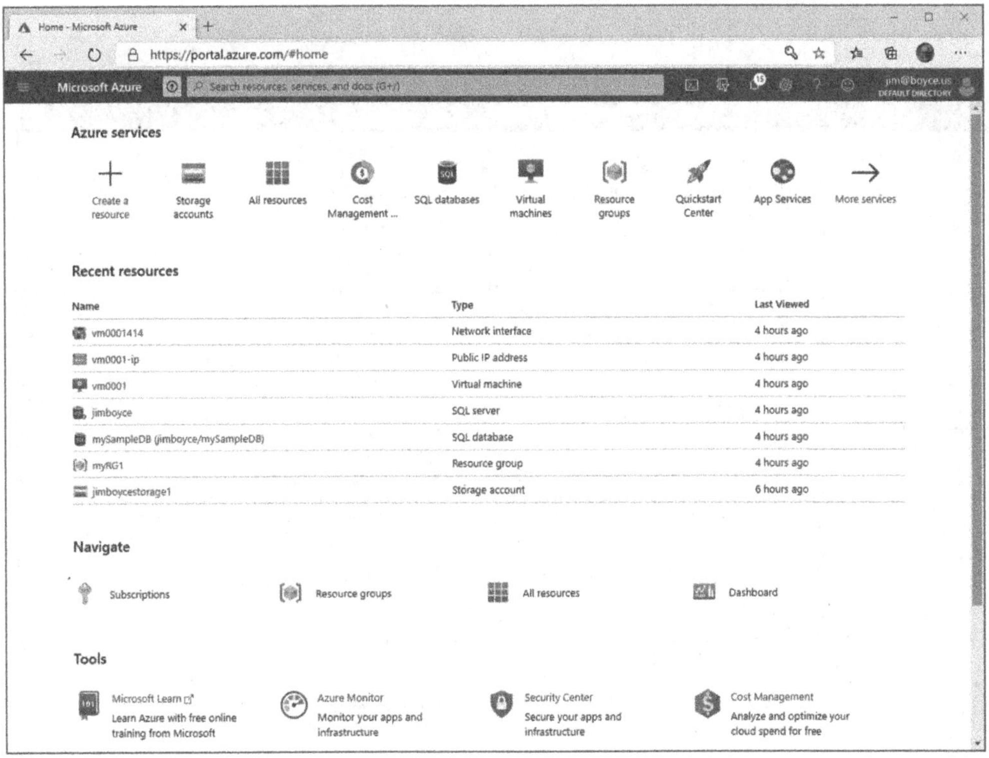

	With changes happening in Azure all the time, the Azure portal might look somewhat different for you compared to the images in this book. The overall functionality is the same.

The home page of the Azure portal is simple, with common services shown at the top and recent resources listed below, along with navigation options and tools. Clicking a service in the Azure Services list at the top opens a page for that service. Clicking More Services opens a navigation pane at the left that lists service categories. If you want to work with VMs and related resources, for example, click Compute. The Azure portal then shows a list of all the Compute resources and services, as shown in Figure 7.2.

You might encounter several questions on the AZ-900 exam that ask what Azure portal *blade* you should use to manage specific Azure resources or access specific services, such as the Security Center. The Azure portal design has changed over time, but the items in the Azure portal menu have long been referred to as blades. The best way to prepare for these questions is to spend some time in the Azure portal, getting familiar with it and understanding which items in the Azure portal menu (navigation pane) give you access to which services.

FIGURE 7.2   The Compute category is selected in the Azure portal with all Compute resources and services listed.

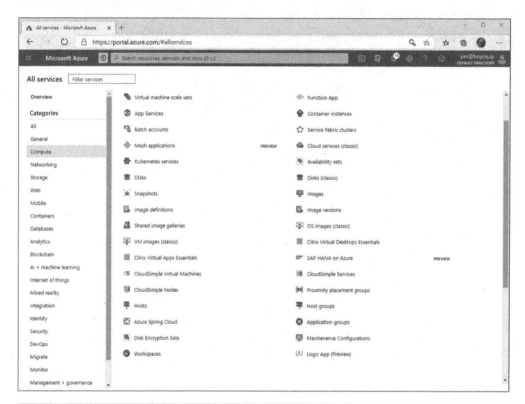

 You can configure the Azure portal to either dock the Azure portal menu or use it as a flyout menu. Click the Settings button in the portal to open the Portal Settings menu, where you can choose between Flyout and Docked.

Azure PowerShell

Azure PowerShell is a scripting environment that you can use to execute commands (called cmdlets, pronounced *command-lets*) that perform management tasks in Azure through the Azure REST API. You can perform essentially any task in Azure using Azure PowerShell. You can also combine cmdlets into scripts to execute multiple commands to orchestrate more complex tasks. These scripts can be quite simple or very complex, potentially deploying hundreds of resources and supporting services in a very short period.

Using Azure PowerShell scripts provides a repeatable method for auto-mating specific tasks in Azure.

Azure PowerShell is available on Windows, Linux, Mac, and ARM. You can also access Azure PowerShell through the Azure Cloud Shell, discussed later in this chapter in the section "Azure Cloud Shell." This is a key point to remember for the AZ-900 exam—in scenarios where it is not possible or feasible to run Azure PowerShell natively, you can use the Azure Cloud Shell to run Azure PowerShell.

You must install Azure PowerShell to use the tool natively on a device. Azure PowerShell Core is available as an open source project on GitHub. For more information, see https://docs.microsoft.com/en-us/powershell/scripting/install/installing-powershell.

Azure CLI

If you are experienced with Linux and proficient with the Bash shell and command language, you might prefer to use the Azure command-line interface (Azure CLI) instead of Azure PowerShell. Like Azure PowerShell, the Azure CLI is a command-driven scripting environment that also uses the Azure REST API to execute management tasks in Azure. It is nearly identical to Azure PowerShell in capability and function, running on Windows, Linux, and Mac. It simply uses a different command syntax with which you might be more familiar as a Bash shell user. Also, as with Azure PowerShell, you can run the Azure CLI in a web browser through the Azure Cloud Shell, giving you the capability to run the Azure CLI in scenarios where running it natively might not be possible or feasible.

Azure Cloud Shell

As described briefly earlier, Azure Cloud Shell is a web-based interface that enables you to run Azure PowerShell and Azure CLI commands and scripts. You can access Azure Cloud Shell at https://shell.azure.com (which redirects to https://portal.azure.com/#cloudshell, but shell.azure.com is easier to remember and type). On the resulting page you click either Bash or PowerShell depending on which environment you want to use. Figure 7.3 shows the Cloud Shell running PowerShell.

You can also access the Azure Cloud Shell through the Azure portal by clicking the Cloud Shell icon in the group of icons to the left of your username in the upper right corner of the browser. Figure 7.4 shows an example.

FIGURE 7.3   The Azure Cloud Shell running Azure PowerShell

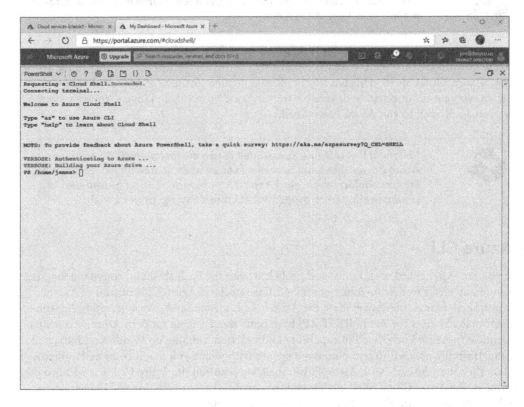

FIGURE 7.4   You can quickly access the Cloud Shell from the Azure portal.

Open Azure Cloud Shell

The key point to understand about the Azure Cloud Shell is that it enables you to run either Azure PowerShell or the Azure CLI in a web browser.

Azure Mobile App

The Azure Mobile App is available for Android and iOS devices and enables you to manage Azure resources from your mobile device. You can use the Azure Mobile App for one-off tasks such as monitoring health and status of resources, checking alerts, restarting web apps or VMs, and running Azure CLI or Azure PowerShell commands. Naturally, the Azure Mobile App isn't a great management solution when you need to perform more complex tasks, but it nevertheless enables you to perform many Azure management functions from your mobile device. For example, if you need to reset a web app, you can open the Azure Mobile App and run the appropriate Azure CLI command to perform the reset.

Using ARM Templates

Azure Resource Manager (ARM) templates are discussed in earlier chapters, so you should have some understanding by now of their function. To summarize, ARM templates are JSON files that declare infrastructure and configuration for Azure resources, enabling you to deploy resources in a well-defined, repeatable way. Rather than use ARM templates by themselves as a management tool, you will use them in conjunction with other management tools, such as the Azure portal.

Bringing It All Together

All the Azure management options available to you can be confusing when you first start working with Azure. You can clear up the confusion by understanding some key concepts, which will also help you be successful in answering management tool questions in the AZ-900 exam. These concepts are as follows:

- Azure PowerShell and the Azure CLI both provide essentially the same capabilities and enable you to manage most aspects of Azure through scripting. The difference is in syntax. If you are already familiar with PowerShell, then Azure PowerShell is the best solution for you. If you are most comfortable in the Linux Bash shell, the Azure CLI is the best solution for you.

- Azure PowerShell and the Azure CLI can both be run natively when installed on a device. These include Windows, Linux, and Mac devices.

- Azure PowerShell and the Azure CLI can both be run in a web interface through the Azure Cloud Shell. So, think of the Cloud Shell as just a web-based means to run either PowerShell or the Azure CLI when running them natively isn't possible or feasible, such as from a device that doesn't support them natively.

- The Azure Mobile App gives you quick access to many Azure management functions on your Android or iOS mobile device but is generally not as useful for complex management tasks. If you are out to dinner at a restaurant and need to reset a VM, the Azure Mobile App is the right solution. If you need to script the deployment of several resources, then Azure PowerShell or the Azure CLI running either natively or through the Azure Cloud Shell is the appropriate solution.

Creating and Managing Resources

Now that you have some understanding of the tools you can use to create and manage Azure resources, let's put that knowledge to work and create some. As you have learned in other chapters, you cannot create Azure resources without an Azure subscription. So, if you do not already have one, the first step is to create a free subscription. The following section explains how to do so.

Although you could use Azure PowerShell or the Azure CLI to create resources, doing so requires some skill with those command environments. The following sections focus on using the Azure portal to create and manage resources.

Creating a Free Subscription

Creating a free Azure subscription is very easy. However, free subscriptions are available only to new users and limited to one per person, so you will need to sign in with an account that is not already associated to an Azure subscription. Start by navigating to `https://azure.microsoft.com/en-us/free` in a web browser. Then, click Start Free. You will need to log in with a Microsoft account. If you don't already have one, visit `https://account.live.com` to create one.

The Azure website will step you through the process of signing up for your free subscription. You will provide contact information and enter a credit card number. Microsoft won't charge anything on the card unless you eventually upgrade to a paid subscription later. You will see the Quickstart Center (see Figure 7.5) after you complete the sign-up process. You can get started with the options shown on the page or click the button in the upper-left corner of the browser (three horizontal lines, sometimes called the hamburger button) to view the Azure portal navigation options. The resulting menu is also referred to as the Azure portal menu.

FIGURE 7.5   The first thing you see after creating a free subscription is the Quickstart Center.

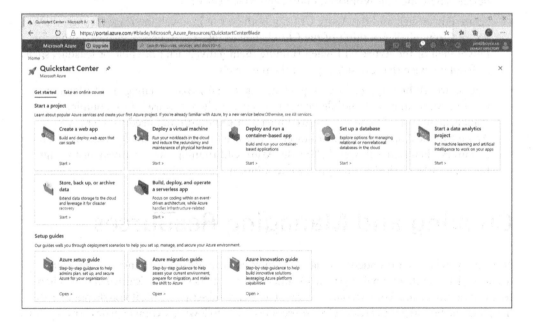

Creating Resource Groups

Before you create some Azure resources, you should create a resource group to contain them. Follow these steps to create a resource group:

1. Log into `portal.azure.com` with the account you used to create your free subscription.

2. In the Azure portal, click Resource Groups in the Navigate group to open the page shown in Figure 7.6.

FIGURE 7.6 Use the Resource Groups page to create and manage resource groups.

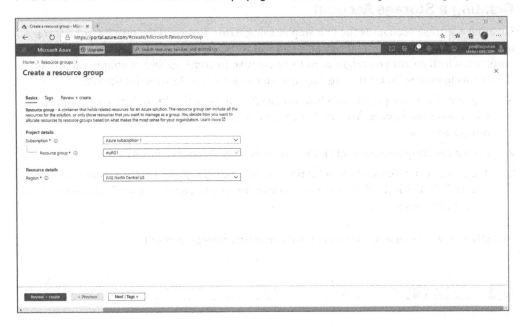

3. Click Create.

4. On the Create A Resource Group page, enter the name **myRG1** for the resource group.

5. Choose the region in which to create the resource.

6. Click Next.

7. On the Tags page, enter **RGType** as the name of the tag and **TestRG** as the value.

8. Click Review And Create.

9. If all is correct, you should see a message on the resulting page that validation passed. If not, navigate back in the browser to correct any issues.

10. Click Create to create the resource group.

Now when you navigate to the Resource Groups page you will see the group myRG1 that you just created. Next, let's add some resources to the resource group. The following section takes you through the process for creating a small number of different Azure resource types to familiarize you with the process and concepts.

Creating Azure Resources and Services

In this section you will create a handful of Azure resources of different types. Let's start with a virtual machine.

Creating a Storage Account

Creating a storage account is the first step in using Azure storage. One property of a storage account is its name. The storage account name must be unique across all Azure storage accounts, which means you might need to be creative to come up with a unique value. Use the following process to create a storage account in your free Azure subscription:

1. Log into the Azure portal and click Storage Accounts in the Azure Services group, or if you don't see Storage Accounts as an option, click in the search box and search for **storage account**.

2. On the resulting web page, click the Create Storage Account button.

3. Azure asks you to choose the subscription and resource group for the storage account (Figure 7.7). Click the Resource Group drop-down and choose the myRG1 resource you created previously.

FIGURE 7.7   Enter information to create your first storage account.

4. Enter a unique storage account name. You can use only lowercase letters and numbers.

5. For this example, choose Premium.

6. From the Account Kind list, select FileStorage.

7. From the Replication list, choose Locally-Redundant Storage (LRS).

8. Click Next.

At this point in the process, you must decide on the networking options for your storage account. Because this is a sample account you will use for testing, let's assume you won't put any information in Azure storage that poses any security or data privacy concerns. We will use the default options:

1. Keep the default settings of Public Endpoint and Microsoft Network Routing, then click Next.

2. Review the options for information but leave all of them unselected and click Next.

3. Again, review the options for informational purposes but leave them as is and click Next to add a tag to your storage account.

4. Enter **Storage** as the tag Name and **FileStorage** as the Value, and then click Review + Create.

5. If validation doesn't pass, correct any issues. Then click Create to create the storage account.

The Azure portal displays some status information as it creates the storage account. When the portal indicates that the deployment is complete, click Go To Resource. You should see something similar to Figure 7.8.

FIGURE 7.8   A storage account created in Azure called jimboycestorage1

In this example, you can work with the storage as if it were local storage. First, however, you must download and install the Azure Storage Explorer. Click the download link on the page to download and install the version appropriate to your operating system. The first time you run the Azure Storage Explorer it prompts you to add storage (Figure 7.9). In this case we will add an Azure account. With Add An Azure Account selected, choose the environment where your Azure account resides (likely, Azure). Then click Next. When prompted, log in with the appropriate account. The Azure Storage Explorer adds the account.

FIGURE 7.9   Use the Azure Storage Explorer to view storage in Azure.

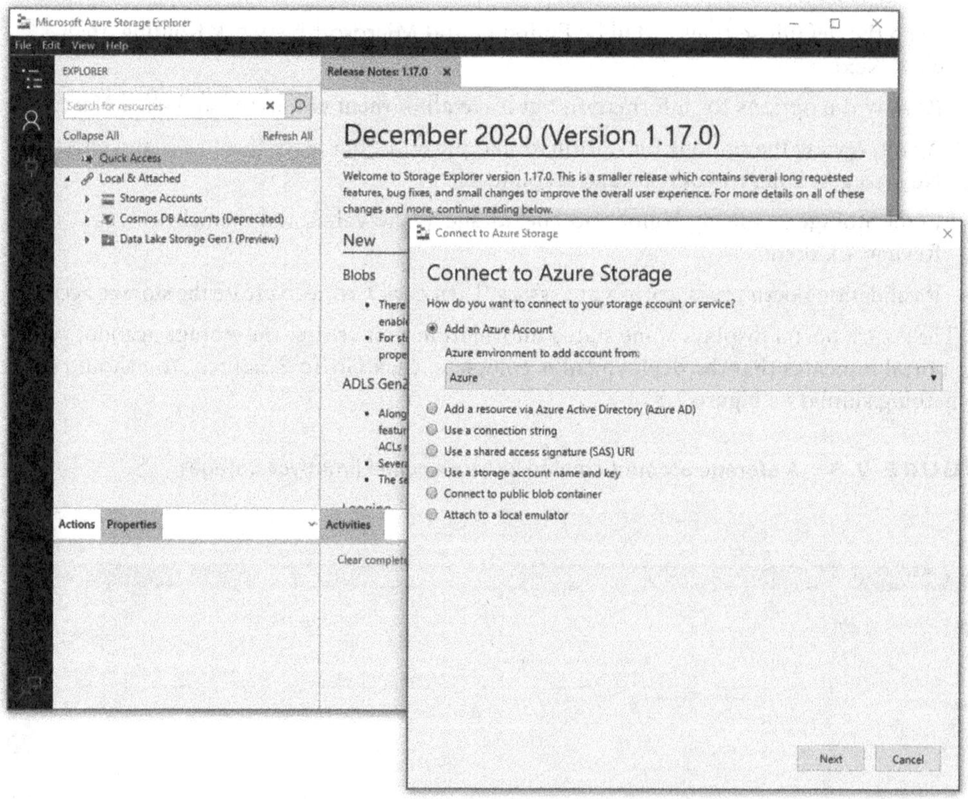

With your Azure account added, let's add a file share:

1. In the Azure Storage Explorer, select File Shares, as shown in Figure 7.10, and then click Actions, Create File Share.

2. Enter **test1** for the file share name and press Enter.

3. Click New Folder and create a folder called **Documents**.

4. Click New Folder and create another folder named **PowerShell**. Figure 7.11 shows the results.

FIGURE 7.10   An Azure account added to the Azure Storage Explorer

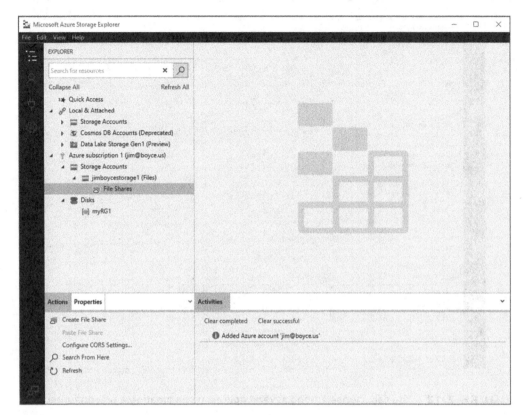

Although we won't walk through the process now, you can now upload files to the folders that you create. Just click Upload to select a file and upload it to Azure.

Creating a VM

One of the resource types you will probably use quite a bit in Azure is virtual machines. As with many Azure resource types, it's relatively easy to create a VM. Follow these steps to create a VM:

1. In the Azure portal, choose Virtual Machines from the navigation menu.

2. On the resulting Virtual Machines page, click Add. At this point you can either create a customized VM or start from a preset configuration. For simplicity at this point, choose Start With A Preset Configuration.

3. The Azure portal then offers several options, as shown in Figure 7.12. You can choose between Dev/Test and Production (the default option). Leave Production selected and choose General Purpose (D-Series).

FIGURE 7.11 Two folders created in a file share called test1

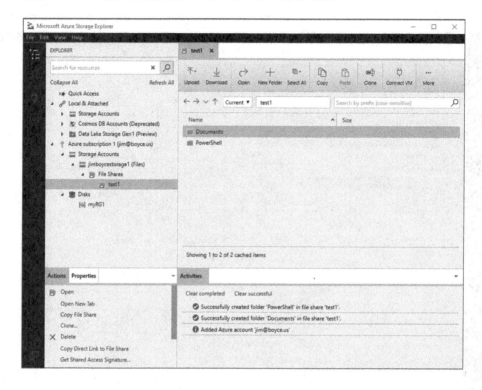

FIGURE 7.12 You can choose among several options when creating a preconfigured VM.

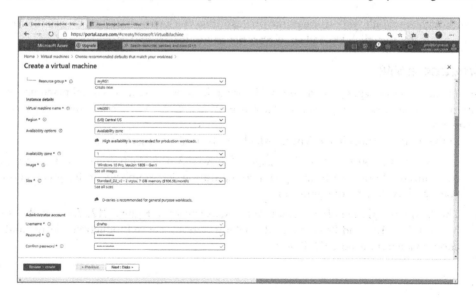

4. Click the button labeled Continue To Create A VM.

5. You could create a separate resource group for the VM, but in this case, select your previously created myRG1 group.

6. Enter **vm0001** as the VM name.

7. Choose an appropriate region (some regions do not provide the option to specify an availability zone).

8. If desired, choose an availability zone.

9. Choose the desired OS from the Image list.

10. Choose the VM size from the Size list, noting the monthly cost associated with the selection.

Although this is a free subscription, resources count against the subscription limits. For example, a VM might have a monthly cost of $160 or so, which if it were running constantly would generate that amount in consumption cost. In this situation, however, you will create the VM, use it for a little while, and then delete it, which will stop any consumption costs for the VM.

1. Enter an admin account name and password and click Next.

2. Review the default options on the Disks page and then click Next to use the defaults.

3. Review the default options on the Networking page and click Next to use the defaults.

4. Click through the Management and Advanced pages, accepting the defaults.

5. On the Tags page, add the name tag **VMType** with a value of **Test**. Note that the tag will be applied to 12 resource types used by the VM, and then click Review + Create.

At this point you might receive a validation error. For example, if you selected Windows 10 Pro as the OS image, there is a check box on the Basics page that you must select to confirm that you have an appropriate license for Windows 10 that you can use in Azure. Clear up any validation issues and then click Create to create the VM.

After the VM is created, you can click Go To Resource in the Azure portal to view its status. Figure 7.13 shows an example. Creating the VM is really just the first step in most cases. As Figure 7.13 indicates, for example, you can configure a DNS name for the VM and set other properties. You can also connect to the VM, restart it, stop it, and so on. If you would like to experiment with the VM, click Connect and follow the prompts to connect to and log into the VM. When you're finished experimenting, come back to the Azure portal and stop the VM by clicking Stop in the menu at the top of the page.

Why stop the VM? If you aren't using it, stopping the VM will pause most consumption charges associated with the VM. Even though this is a free Azure subscription, you don't want to use any more of your monthly credit than necessary.

FIGURE 7.13   Viewing status of a VM in the Azure portal

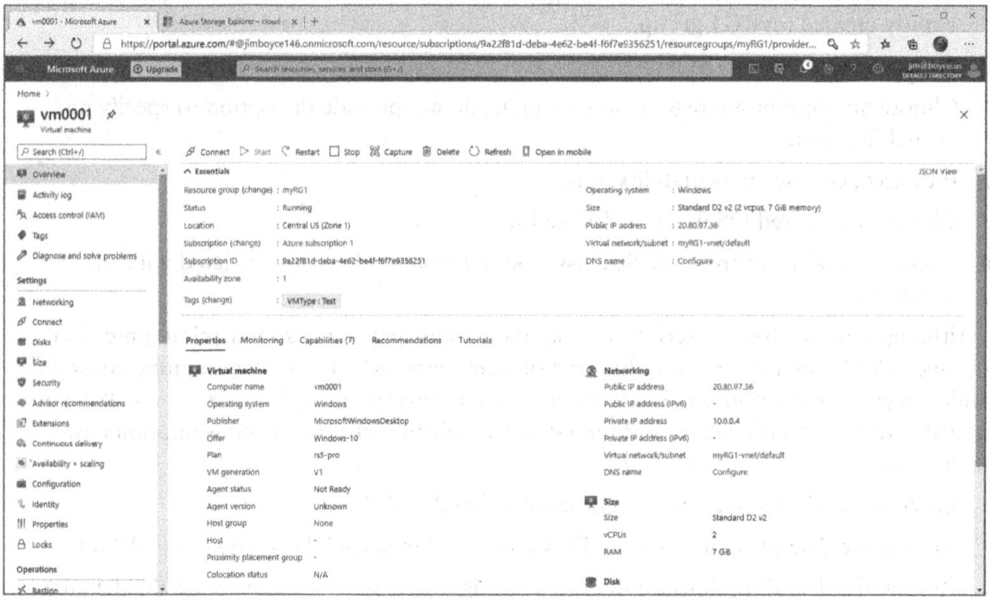

Creating a SLQ Database

Next, create a SQL Database instance to see how easy it is to create one. You do not need to be a SQL expert here. To start the process, open the Azure portal and then click SQL Database in the navigation pane. On the resulting SQL Databases page, click Add to view the Create SQL Database page.

Follow these steps to complete the process of setting up a SQL database instance:

1. Choose the resource group you created earlier.

2. Enter **mySampleDB** in the Database Name field.

3. From the Select A Server drop-down, select Create New.

4. Enter a unique server name, admin credentials, and region, as shown in Figure 7.14, and then click OK.

5. Click Next to view the Networking page.

6. Since you won't be putting any data in the database for this example, choose No Access and click Next.

7. Review the default options for information and then click Next to add tags.

8. Choose **RGType** as the tag name and enter **SQL** as the value, and then click Review + Create.

9. Note the estimated operation cost for the resource and then click Create.

After Azure deploys the database, you can click Go To Resource to view the status. Figure 7.15 shows an example.

FIGURE 7.14   Use the Create SQL Database page to create an instance of a SQL database.

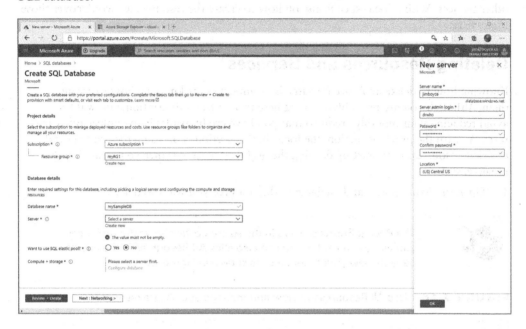

FIGURE 7.15   The Azure portal shows the status of a newly created SQL Database instance.

Obviously, additional considerations are involved in creating a SQL Database instance. For example, you will likely need access to it for management purposes and to connect it to other services. With a focus specifically on how to create the resource, we won't cover those topics here.

Deleting Resources and Services

Knowing how to delete an Azure resource is as important as knowing how to create them. Although you are probably working here from a free subscription, you want to avoid reducing your monthly credit so that you have credit available to explore other features. As with the previous section, the focus in this section is on using the Azure portal to delete resources. Let's start by deleting the SQL Database instance you created in the previous section.

1. Open the Azure portal and navigate to the resource you want to delete.

The Recent Sources group in the Azure portal shows the resources you've used recently. You can also click All Resources in the navigation pane to view your resources, as shown in Figure 7.16.

FIGURE 7.16 Use All Resources to view and manage your Azure resources.

2. In All Resources, click the check box beside the mySampleDB that you created earlier and then click Delete in the top menu.

3. The Azure portal displays a warning message indicating that deleting the resource is irreversible. Click in the Confirm Delete box and type **yes,** then click Delete. Azure then deletes the database.

 If you have problems finding a specific resource in All Resources, try sorting the view by Type.

Next, let's delete the VM that you created earlier:

1. In the Azure portal, click All Resources in the navigation pane and click vm0001. The Azure portal displays a page showing the VM's properties and status.

2. Click Delete. The Azure portal displays, indicating that the VM will be deleted but associated resources will not be.

3. Click Yes to delete the VM.

4. Delete the other resources with names starting with vm0001 to remove them as well, starting with the virtual network interface. You will then be able to delete the NSG and IP address associated with the VM.

5. Delete the virtual disk associated with the VM.

Summary

This chapter explored the tools available for managing Azure resources. You learned about Azure PowerShell and the Azure CLI, and how they can be installed natively or used within the Azure Cloud Shell. The chapter also explored the Azure Mobile App and how ARM templates fit into the bigger Azure management picture.

This chapter also introduced you to creating and deleting Azure resources so that you can begin experimenting more deeply with Azure. As you add resources, just keep in mind that even if you are using a free subscription, those resources will reduce your monthly credit. As explained throughout this book—particularly in Chapter 6, "Azure Pricing, Service Levels, and Lifecycle"—use best practices to turn off Azure resources you aren't using. This is particularly true for VMs that will incur consumption costs as long as they are running, even if you aren't using them.

Exam Essentials

Describe the functionality and use of the Azure portal, Azure PowerShell, the Azure CLI, the Cloud Shell, and the Azure Mobile App. Although the Azure management tools can seem confusing at first glance, once you understand some basic concepts the relationship between the tools makes sense. Azure PowerShell and the Azure CLI provide essentially the same management capabilities, with both providing command-line, scripted management of all Azure resources and functions. The main difference between the two is in syntax. Both can run natively after you install them on a device, or you can run either one in the Azure Cloud Shell.

The Azure Cloud Shell is a web-based environment specifically for running either Azure PowerShell or Azure CLI command sessions.

The Azure Mobile App gives you some management capabilities on Android and iOS mobile devices but naturally doesn't provide the same management capabilities as the Azure portal, Azure PowerShell, or the Azure CLI.

If you need to perform relatively simple, one-off management tasks, the Azure portal is often the simplest choice. If you need that capability from a mobile device, then the Azure Mobile App is a good solution. For anything requiring complex actions, Azure PowerShell or the Azure CLI are most appropriate. When you need to build out repeatable processes for deploying and managing resources with related resources, ARM templates are the appropriate choice.

Review Questions

1. You are a developer and need to deploy a single VM to test some code overnight. Which of the following management options is the best choice?

    A. Azure PowerShell

    B. Azure CLI

    C. Azure portal

    D. ARM templates

2. You are an infrastructure management engineer for your organization. You work most with Linux servers and are therefore very familiar with Bash and know what command you would use to retrieve specific properties of a VM. Which of the following management solutions should you use to retrieve a property of one of the VMs that you manage?

    A. Azure PowerShell

    B. Azure CLI

    C. Azure portal

    D. Azure Monitor

3. You are the Director of IT for your organization. Your CIO has asked you what methods or processes your organization should consider using to build out the capability to deploy large numbers of Azure resources with connected services and policies in a controlled way. Which of the following solutions should you recommend?

    A. Azure PowerShell

    B. Azure CLI

    C. Azure portal

    D. ARM templates

4. You want to use the Azure CLI to perform management functions in Azure. Which of the following configurations does not suit this requirement?

    A. You install the Azure CLI on a Windows 10 PC.

    B. You install the Azure CLI on a Mac.

    C. You open the Azure portal in a browser and then run the Azure CLI in the Azure Cloud Shell.

    D. You run the Azure CLI from PowerShell on a Windows 10 device.

5. You are out of the office at an appointment and one of your team members sends you an urgent request to reset a web app because the only other people with the appropriate access are not available. All you have is your mobile device. Which two options can you use to reset the web app?

    A. Azure portal

    B. Azure CLI

C. Azure Cloud Shell

D. Azure PowerShell

6. Which blade in the Azure portal should you use to view security alerts and recommendations?

A. All Services

B. App Security

C. Security Center

D. Monitor

Appendix

Answers to Review Questions

Chapter 1: Cloud Concepts

1. A. Azure enables your organization to pay for only those services it uses, which enables you to budget your IT infrastructure costs as an operational expenditure based on the services you consume in each month. Operational expenditures are generally those that you consume on a pay-as-you-go basis. By contrast, purchasing hardware and software would require a capital expenditure, which is an acquisition of fixed assets.

2. C. Microsoft acquires large amounts of hardware and other infrastructure resources to support Azure, enabling it to purchase at a reduced cost, which represents an economy of scale. In addition, distributing those resources among multiple customers also drives economy of scale and reduces the end cost to consumers of Azure.

3. B. This scenario represents an example of horizontal scaling (scalability) because you are adding servers. If you were adding memory to the web server instead of adding servers, it would represent an example of vertical scaling. There is no restriction on moving the database cluster to Azure along with the web server. Finally, though Azure can perform both horizontal and vertical scaling, you must configure autoscaling—it does not happen by default.

4. B. Moving to a public cloud enables you to easily scale your infrastructure as needed. In a public cloud, you do not have full control over all resources since many of the resources are managed by the cloud provider. Your operational expenditures will increase but capital expenditures will decrease. Contoso will still need to manage the infrastructure, so a reduction in IT staff is not guaranteed.

5. B, D. A hybrid cloud scenario exists where services hosted in Azure interact with services hosted outside of Azure, whether in a third-party data center, your own data center, or a private cloud. Options A and C both represent a public cloud scenario because all services are hosted within Azure.

6. A. This scenario represents a consumption-based model where you pay for only those Azure resources that you consume. It does not involve Azure services for developing web applications, and therefore does not represent a PaaS solution. IT staffing is not necessarily reduced because you must still manage the virtual machines, operating systems, and applications running on them. Although you can use several firewall-related services in Azure, you could deploy those same or similar solutions in your own data center.

7. B. This scenario does not leverage virtual machines or infrastructure that you manage and therefore does not represent IaaS. You are developing custom applications rather than using applications provided by Microsoft, so this scenario does not represent an SaaS solution. There is no DaaS service category in Azure.

8. C. With Microsoft 365, Microsoft manages the Office applications that your users consume through an assigned subscription. Microsoft manages the applications and updates. Although you determine who has access through subscription assignment, Microsoft manages all other aspects of the software. This represents SaaS. Development services are not part of the solution, so PaaS is not correct. Virtual machines and other infrastructure are not involved, so IaaS is not correct.

9. B. You are replacing your on-premises servers with VMs hosted in Azure, which represents an IaaS solution. You are not using any development services to redesign the application (Paas) or moving to Dynamics 365 (SaaS) at this time. This scenario does not describe integration between services hosted on-premises and in Azure, so it is not a hybrid cloud scenario.

10. B. The third-party provider manages the hardware, networking, and other resources for you, but you maintain control over the VMs, applications, and data. Because no other organizations are using those resources and there is no stated integration between the cloud and your on-premises services, this scenario represents a private cloud model.

11. C, D. When the CPU becomes overtaxed, a fault occurs, making the application temporarily unavailable. Scaling out in this situation enabled the service to handle the fault and remain operational, resulting in improved fault tolerance. Scaling out also reduced the amount of time it was unavailable, resulting in higher availability. The service did not crash due to a major failure or disaster and therefore require restoration, so disaster recovery is incorrect. Agility is the characteristic of Azure that enabled you to quickly deploy a new VM, but adding the VM did not improve agility.

12. A. The capability to automatically expand resources when needed describes elasticity. This scenario does not describe resources used to quickly develop and deploy applications, so PaaS is incorrect. Fault tolerance describes the capability of a system to endure a fault in one of its resources. No fault occurs in this scenario, so fault tolerance is incorrect. High availability is generally achieved by deploying multiple resources to guard against failures, so high availability is not a correct answer.

Chapter 2: Azure Core Services

1. A. Although an Azure geography often aligns to a specific country, a geography can also align to a market, such as Europe or Asia. You can host resources in any region, so geographies by themselves do not determine where you can place resources. Geographies also do not correspond to physical data centers, but instead contain regions in which data centers reside.

2. B, D. A region encompasses multiple data centers, so option A is not correct. Regions are paired within an Azure geography to ensure high availability for resources in the primary region. Although a geography might span more than one country (Europe as an example), regions are defined within a single country, so option C is incorrect. When you deploy resources, you must specify the target region for the resources, so in that sense regions do specify the location of Azure resources.

3. B. Azure China is a physically isolated instance of Azure designed to meet very strict Chinese regulatory requirements. The services available in Azure China are available in other Azure regions (although not all services are available in all regions).

4. D. All the answers correctly describe Azure regions. When you create a resource, you must specify the region in which it will reside. Regions are always paired with another at least

300 miles away in the same geography for high availability and fault tolerance. An Azure region contains at least one data center.

5. C. Availability zones are deployed across different data centers in a region, with each zone as a separate update and fault domain. Because they are in the same region, latency is minimized. Using replication across different regions is not correct because of the additional latency introduced across regions and the overhead needed to manage the replication and failover process. Resource groups are not an appropriate solution because they only provide logical organization to your resources; they have no effect on availability or performance. Availability sets are not an appropriate solution because the availability sets exist within the same data center and are subject to power or other outages at that data center.

6. A. Achieving a 99.99 percent SLA requires that you deploy at least two instances in different availability zones within the same region.

7. D. Resource groups are a logical container for Azure resources. They do not provide any high availability features and only serve as a container. Although you can apply locks to a resource group to prevent the resources in it from being deleted, locks are not created automatically, so option B is incorrect. The resource group can contain resources from multiple regions, making option C incorrect as well.

8. C. Tags provide a means to help identify a resource group and apply only to the resource group itself, not to the resources in the group, making option C the correct answer. Locks prevent resource deletion, not tags, so option A is not correct. Tags do not control permissions in any way, so option B is not correct.

9. B. Azure Resource Manager supports the use of declarative templates to define resources for deployment, enabling you to create a template based on existing resources, making option B the correct answer. The new resources will be deployed to resource groups, but the resource groups are simply logical containers used to organize your resources, making option A incorrect. Azure Resource Templates is not an Azure service, so option C is not correct.

10. A, C, and D. Azure subscriptions act as a logical container similar to a resource group but at a higher level. As such, you can have multiple subscriptions aligned to a billing account, which makes answer A correct. Answer B is incorrect because a subscription can contain resources from multiple regions. The subscriptions serve as a billing node under the billing account, which enables you to segregate Azure resources and services into separate sections of your invoice, making answer C correct. You can move a subscription to a new tenant, making answer D correct. Moving a subscription does have potential consequences, however, and these are discussed in Chapter 6.

11. D. Option A is incorrect because, even though the specified process would work, it does not present the easiest option. The location of a resource group does not define the location of the resources contained within the group, so option B is incorrect. Azure Resource Manager enables resource management but does not provide migration or replication features, making option C incorrect.

12. C. Azure App Service provides a framework for developing and deploying web apps with support for many languages, including Java and Python. It supports both Windows and Linux platforms, as well as containers. Azure App Service does not provide firewall services by itself, but instead requires you to use the Application Gateway service for firewall protection.

13. D. Containers support Windows and Linux. They contain the dependencies needed to run the application. They also all share the same operating system. The only option that is not correct is D. The primary benefit to using containers is the ease with which you can deploy them without setup and configuration of a VM to host the app and dependencies.

14. B. The only storage option that you can use within a container to persist data is Azure Files.

15. D. Azure Kubernetes Service (AKS) is the container orchestration service offered in Azure and meets the requirements of simplified management and scalability. ACI does not provide orchestration services and is only appropriate for individual container deployments, making option A incorrect. Scale sets do not provide container management capabilities, so option B is incorrect. Option C is incorrect because there is no Docker Management Portal in Azure.

16. B. Azure SQL Database enables you to host SQL databases in Azure without standing up and managing a virtual machine or the SQL Server application. Cosmos DB is a NoSQL solution designed to store and manage nonstructured data, making option A incorrect. Although you could deploy a VM with SQL Server and host the data, doing so increases consumption cost and management overhead, making option C incorrect.

17. D. Azure Cosmos DB supports NoSQL and is designed to store and retrieve data in non-relational databases, making option D the correct answer. Azure SQL Database is designed specifically to store relational SQL databases, making option A incorrect. HDInsight is Microsoft's cloud distribution of Hadoop that is designed for processing massive amounts of data, making option B incorrect. Azure Database for MySQL supports MySQL relational databases, so option D is incorrect.

18. C. Windows Virtual Desktop provides a virtualized Windows client experience through a client installed on the user's device or through an HTLM 5–compliant web browser, which provides a consistent experience across the enterprise. There is no Azure Client Emulator service, and Windows 10 Enterprise and Microsoft 365 do not provide client OS support for macOS, iOS, or Android devices.

19. D. The archive access storage tier is intended for scenarios in which you must maintain data that is seldom, if ever, accessed. It provides the most cost-effective storage solution in this scenario. File storage and disk storage are both active storage types that are not intended for archival purposes. Cool access storage is intended for scenarios where you need to access data, but not frequently and only for a relatively short period of time.

20. B. The first step in adding storage in Azure is to create a storage account, making option B the correct answer. You do not need to enable storage at the subscription level, and you must create a storage account before choosing a storage type or access tier, making options A and C incorrect. VMs do not include hot access tier blob storage by default, making option D incorrect.

21. D. SQL Managed Instance provides many of the same features as Azure SQL Database but with enhanced features, including easier migration capabilities between your on-premises SQL instances and Azure. Azure Database for MySQL is an open source alternative to SQL and does not provide the needed migration capabilities in this scenario. There is no Azure SQL Database Premium offer from Microsoft, making option C incorrect.

22. A. MySQL is a component of LAMP (it is the "M" in LAMP) and therefore Azure Database for MySQL is the appropriate solution to consider for LAMP-based development.

Chapter 3: Azure Core Networking Services

1. C. Azure Load Balancer distributes traffic based on IP address and is the appropriate solution for this scenario. Azure Application Gateway and Azure Traffic Manager do not route based on IP address, making both of these options incorrect. Azure Front Door is designed for global routing scenarios.

2. B. Although Azure Application Gateway supports URL path–based routing to accommodate your need to optimize processing of images and video, it does not provide the global routing capabilities offered by Front Door. Traffic Manager is intended for non-HTTP(S) traffic and uses DNS-based routing, making it an incorrect choice where URL-based routing is required.

3. A. Azure Application Gateway supports URL path–based routing and is intended for regional load balancing, making option A correct. Neither Traffic Manager nor Azure Load Balancer supports URL path–based routing, making options B and C incorrect. Although Front Door supports URL path–based routing, it is intended for global deployments, so option D is incorrect.

4. D. Azure ExpressRoute provides a secure VPN tunnel across the Internet between your on-premises network and Azure, and is managed by a third-party communications provider, making option D the correct answer. ExpressRoute Direct connects directly to the Microsoft network, bypassing the Internet, making option C incorrect. Azure Client VPN is not an Azure service. Azure VPN Gateway makes it possible to create a VPN connection from your on-premises network to Azure but offers lower speeds than ExpressRoute and is managed by your organization, not a third-party provider.

5. D. Your requirement is to provide a connection from only vmtest01 to Azure, and creating a point-to-site VPN connection involves the least effort and cost. ExpressRoute would connect your entire Alpha data center to Azure, not just vmtest01. A multi-site VPN connection would connect both data centers to Azure, not just vmtest01. Option C is incorrect because a site-to-site VPN connects an entire site to Azure, not just a single server (point).

6. B. Azure ExpressRoute Direct provides site-to-site connectivity from your data center to Azure and connects directly to the Microsoft network, bypassing the Internet. Azure VPN Gateway and Azure ExpressRoute both connect through the Internet to Azure.

7.   A. Azure Content Delivery Network provides caching and other features for hosting content in a geographically dispersed way, placing content near the users who consume it. Although options B and C might be part of your Azure solution, they do not directly affect your ability to place content closer to your users.

Chapter 4: Security, Compliance, Privacy, and Trust

1.   B. Azure Firewall provides traffic filtering based on the specified criteria and can filter traffic between Azure subnets and between Azure and your on-premises network. ExpressRoute is a VPN solution that does not provide traffic filtering. Application security groups enable you to group applications and apply network security as a group using network security groups. They do not provide the required filtering. User-defined routes enable you to create custom routes but not to filter traffic.

2.   C. Web Application Firewall protects web applications from common attacks and does not provide traffic filtering, making options A and B incorrect. A network security group filters traffic between subnets based on the specified criteria, making option C the correct answer.

3.   A, D. A network security group is the appropriate means for filtering traffic into the target subnet based on destination port but cannot restrict access to the VM, making option A part of the answer. Policies do not enable you to define permissions, and initiatives are collections of policies, so by themselves neither policies nor initiatives meet the dual requirement of IP filtering and role-based access. RBAC can be used to restrict access to the VM to specific users, making option D the second part of the correct answer.

4.   B. Web Application Firewall does not provide traffic filtering, making options A and C incorrect. Web Application Firewall protects web applications against common web-based attacks.

5.   C. Network security groups, application security groups, and Azure Firewall do not give you the capability to create custom routes, making option C the only correct answer.

6.   A, B, C, and D. DDoS Protect Standard provides all the features described. DDoS Protection Basic provides only active traffic monitoring, detection, and mitigation.

7.   B and C. Identifying a user by username and password is a form of authentication, not authorization. Providing a password identifies a user; it does not authorize the user to access resources.

8.   B. Azure Active Directory Free includes password self-serve, enabling users to change their passwords online. Azure AD Premium P1 and P2 also offer this capability but are not free. There is no offering called Azure Active Directory Base.

9.   A, B, C. Azure AD provides the authentication mechanism for RBAC in Azure. Before an Azure web application can use Azure AD to authenticate and authorize users, you must register the web app with Azure AD. User and group management is available in all editions of

Azure AD. On-premises users with accounts in Azure AD can authenticate using only Azure AD, making option D incorrect.

10. **A, B.** The capability to manage groups is included in Azure AD Free. Using RBAC with policies and initiatives is not restricted to a specific edition of Azure AD.

11. **D.** Multifactor authentication requires more than one piece of data to authenticate a user. The debit card and the PIN provide two data points for authentication, making option D correct. A PIN code by itself on a device that you do not possess (such as a door security panel) represents a single point of identification, making option B incorrect. The password associated with an email address represents only one form of authentication.

12. **A, B, D.** Security Center automatically begins monitoring resources when you create them, so option C is incorrect.

13. **C.** Security Center provides monitoring and threat protection and also offers recommendations for remediating threats. ATP, Azure DDoS, and Azure Service Health do not offer recommendations for remediation.

14. **B.** Security Center supports JIT access control for ports, enabling you to open ports only when needed, making option B correct. The other Azure services listed do not provide this capability.

15. **A, D.** Azure Key Vault enables you to create, store, and manage keys and other secrets, including credentials used by applications to authenticate, making options A and D correct. Key Vault can create as well as store and manage secrets, making option B incorrect. Key Vault does not work in conjunction with ATP to secure against certificate-based threats.

16. **D.** Azure Information Protection provides a means to classify documents and emails using labels, and to optionally protect those items with encryption, identity, and authorization, making option A correct. AIP does not provide secure storage for secrets; Key Vault serves that function. AIP is not a mechanism in Azure AD.

17. **C.** Azure Threat Protection (ATP) can detect and identify a variety of threats and provides reporting and other resources to help secure your environment, making option C the correct answer. Security Center, AIP, and Microsoft Defender do not provide that threat detection and reporting capability.

18. **D.** ATP can help you detect all these types of attacks, as well as brute-force attacks, overpass-the-hash, and domain dominance attacks.

19. **C.** Testing multiple passwords against a username is an example of a brute-force attack. Making authentication attempts against an alphabetical list of usernames is an example of a reconnaissance attack.

20. **B.** Azure policies enable you to create JSON-based rules that apply effects to resources, such as limiting the types of VMs that can be created in a resource group. Resource locks apply restrictions on actions that you can take with resources but do not control the types of resources you can create. Azure Resource Manager is the template-based service that enables

you to create resources but does not apply restrictions on resources. Azure initiatives enable you to create and manage a group of policies but do not apply restrictions themselves.

21. B. An initiative is a group of policies, enabling you to create, manage, and deploy policies as a group to support governance goals and organizational standards. Blueprints represent a different service called Azure Blueprints that enable you to create repeatable groups of Azure resources, role assignments, and policies. You do not assign security policies using Azure Security Center.

22. A, C. You can apply policies individually or within an initiative, which is a group of policies. You cannot apply permissions using permissions with a policy; instead, you specify what actions are allowed with a specified scope based on the RBAC permissions a user already has. A policy applies to all resources within the scope at which it is applied, making option C correct. Azure policies are not a component of Security Center.

23. C. RBAC is the mechanism that enables you to specify permissions for Azure. Azure policies, resource groups, and Security Center do not provide any capability to create or assign permissions.

24. B. Although the Owner role has the capability to manage management groups, using the User Access Administrator role grants the least privileges. The Account Administrator role is intended for managing subscriptions and billing.

25. D. There is no Creator role in RBAC. Reader enables a user to access resources but not create or modify them. The Owner role enables creating and managing resources but does not fit the requirement for least privilege. Contributor enables the required permission while maintaining least privilege.

26. B, C. RBAC roles do not override or take precedence over resource locks. Applying a lock to a resource group applies the lock to all resources contained in the resource group, including new resources that you later add. The most restrictive lock applies where more than one lock applies at different scopes. You cannot delete a resource without removing the lock, regardless of your role assignment.

27. C. The CanNotDelete lock enables read and modify rights for authorized administrators but not delete rights for a resource. The ReadOnly lock allows only read access but not modification or deletion. The CanNotDelete lock is therefore less restrictive than the ReadOnly lock. CanNotDelete does not prevent modification, making option A incorrect.

28. A, B, D. Azure Blueprints can use ARM templates to deploy resources. They also provide a means to create repeatable groups of Azure resources with role assignments and policies. Blueprints must be assigned after publishing to apply them and have them take effect. Azure Blueprints supports multiple roles to control the actions users can take regarding blueprints.

29. B. Deleting a blueprint does not delete the resources defined in the blueprint. Deleting a blueprint only affects that version of the blueprint, not all versions. You must publish a blueprint before you can assign it, but not to delete it.

30. B, D. Publishing a blueprint does not assign the blueprint, making option A incorrect. When you delete a blueprint, resource locking is removed but the resources are not deleted. A user with the Blueprint Contributor role can manage blueprints but not publish them. You must unassign a blueprint before you can delete it.

31. B. Azure Monitor does not require you to create logs or metrics for it to start capturing data.

32. B. Azure Status provides information about Azure services globally and not information specific to your resources. Azure Service Health provides information about your resources by region. Resource Health provides information about resources but does not do so by region.

33. D. Of the available options, only Azure Service Health provides information on planned maintenance in Azure.

34. A, B, C, D. The options all describe features that are part of Azure Service Health.

35. A, B. NIST and ISO are both standards-based, nonregulatory entities. GDPR defines data protection and privacy requirements as a regulation in European Union law and therefore is regulatory. HIPAA is a U.S. federal law and therefore also regulatory in nature.

36. A. Some Microsoft applications or services require that you provide personal information such as an email address in order to use the application or service. Microsoft can share your personal information with vendors and affiliates, and when required by law or a legal process. You can use a personal email, work email, or email account created by a third party such as an Internet service provider (ISP) to set up a Microsoft account, making options C and D both incorrect.

37. C. Trust Center does not provide any capability to perform risk assessments, establish policies or initiatives, or view audit and compliance reports. Trust Center is a public website that offers a broad range of information about compliance, security, privacy, and transparency.

38. C. Service Trust Portal is the website where Microsoft publishes audit reports and other compliance-related information to help your organization meet regulatory and compliance requirements. Trust Center and Compliance Manager do not provide audit reporting, and Azure Compliance Portal does not exist.

39. B. Microsoft provides a compliance framework and the ability to meet compliance requirements, but each organization must also ensure that their Azure implementations are compliant. Compliance is therefore a shared responsibility. There are no SLAs associated with compliance in Azure.

40. A, D. Azure Government is an isolated instance of Azure with data centers that are separate from commercial, nongovernment Azure data centers. Azure Government is available to U.S. governmental entities and to solution providers that support them. Although Azure Government offers a high level of compliance with government requirements, including Department of Defense (DoD) requirements, entities hosting services in Azure Government must ensure compliance.

41. D. Azure China is available to any entity needing to host Azure resources within China; it is not restricted to governmental agencies or solution providers. Although Azure China is an isolated instance of Azure, it is not managed by Microsoft, making option B an incorrect answer. Because of differences in services and pricing, you cannot easily move resources and accounts between Azure and Azure China. Azure China is managed by 21Vianet based on technology licensed from Microsoft, making D the only correct option.

42. C. Option C is correct. The Cloud Adoption Framework for Azure provides a large library of documentation built on best practices, planning templates and tools, and assessments to help you deploy Azure workloads. FastTrack for Azure can assist you with deploying Azure but does not offer the breadth of information, guidance, and tools included in the framework. Azure Advisor provides guidance around security of your existing Azure environment. There is no service called Azure Migration Planning Service.

Chapter 5: Azure Solutions

1.   B. IoT Hub provides bidirectional communication services for IoT devices and IoT applications and services. Dashboards for viewing and managing devices is a function of IoT Central, not IoT Hub. Option A describes the function of Azure Sphere.

2.   B. IoT Central provides the means to receive data from IoT devices and analyze telemetry data. IoT Hub enables you to gather data from IoT devices but does not provide analysis capabilities, making option A incorrect. Sphere is appropriate for developing highly secure IoT solutions and is not the best solution in this scenario.

3.   D. Azure Machine Learning consists of multiple services for building, training, and validating AI models that can then be deployed as web services in Azure. Cognitive Services is used to analyze photos, videos, and other content, not Azure Machine Learning, making option B incorrect. With Azure Machine Learning, you can deploy models as web services, not as standalone applications.

4.   A, B, C. Azure Machine Learning Studio provides all of features and functions described in options A, B, and C.

5.   A, B, D. Azure Cognitive Services offers the capabilities described in options A, B, and D. Azure Bot Service gives you the ability to act as a virtual agent, not Cognitive Services, making option C incorrect.

6.   C. Azure Bot Service can interact with other Azure services, making option A incorrect. Azure Cognitive Services provides natural language translation capabilities and the ability to analyze data content, not Azure Bot Service.

7.   C. Logic Apps is the workflow creation and orchestration solution in Azure. Functions enables you to create serverless application functions but does not provide workflow creation and orchestration. You use Bot Service to create virtual agents.

8. A, D. Azure Functions and Azure Logic Apps can integrate with one another, making option B incorrect. Drag-and-drop workflow creation is an aspect of Logic Apps, not Functions.

9. D. Azure Boards provides the means for managing development projects and items, making option A incorrect. GitHub and GitHub Actions are intended for open source projects and collaboration, not Azure Artifacts. Azure Artifacts does not store information about Azure resources for use with Blueprints.

10. C. Azure Repos and Boards are components of Azure DevOps Services intended primarily for enterprise and custom development, not open source projects. Azure DevTest Labs provides features for easily deploying and decommissioning Azure resources such as virtual machines, network security groups, and other resources to support app testing.

11. B. Azure DevTest Labs does not provide a development environment, making the sample statement incorrect. Azure DevTest Labs does not provide alerting and monitoring tools, making option B incorrect. Azure DevTest Labs can deploy Windows and Linux servers, as well as other Azure resources, through ARM templates.

Chapter 6: Azure Pricing, Service Levels, and Lifecycle

1. C. Although considerable planning needs to take place beforehand, the first step in deploying a service in Azure is creating the subscription that will contain the resource(s). You would choose a storage tier only after the subscription exists and when you are deploying storage. Whether you purchase services or use free services, you must still have a subscription, making option B incorrect.

2. D. You must open a support case with Microsoft to increase subscription limits, making option D correct. Azure Resource Manager enables you to create resources but does not enable you to modify limits. Although you could create a new subscription, doing so does not suit the requirements of this scenario.

3. D. Options A, B, and C are all methods for purchasing Azure services. Unified Support is a Microsoft support offering that provides as-needed support for all of your Microsoft on-premises and cloud technologies, but it does not provide a means for purchasing Azure services.

4. A, D. One region might have different resources costs than another region, and you might incur costs for data transfers between regions, making options A and D correct in this scenario. The target subscription and billing account have no effect on cost.

5. C. The TCO Calculator factors in workload types, facilities and staffing costs, and other assumptions to provide an overall cost for an Azure deployment. You would use Azure Advisor after you have a subscription and deploy resources to help manage cost, so option A is incorrect for this scenario. The Pricing Calculator estimates costs for specific workloads without factoring in facilities and other costs, making option B incorrect. There is no Azure Estimator tool.

6. D. The TCO Calculator is the appropriate tool when you need to estimate an entire data center move to Azure and factor in corresponding facilities costs, making options A and B incorrect. The Pricing Calculator is a web-based tool available outside of Azure; it is not a downloadable tool.

7. A, C. Azure Advisor provides recommendations for cost management, security, operational excellence, reliability, and performance, making options A and C correct. You cannot deploy policies or initiatives through Azure Advisor. Service Health is the appropriate service to view service health, making option D incorrect.

8. C. Prepaying for Azure services through Azure reservations could result in as much as 70 percent savings on many of your Azure resources, making C the option with the potential for greatest cost savings. Although resizing VMs can reduce costs, this scenario encompasses much more than just VMs. Moving resources to a less expensive region could reduce some costs but could also result in added cost for network traffic. Moving from Azure SQL Database to Azure SQL Managed Instance would not likely result in a significant savings.

9. C. Adding another subscription does not in itself increase Azure costs, because you could be simply moving existing resources from an existing subscription to the new one. Moving storage from the hot access tier to archive should reduce costs. Deploying connected resources across multiple regions will generate egress traffic that will increase operational costs.

10. A. Azure Hybrid Benefit enables you to use Windows Server and SQL Server licenses that are covered by Software Assurance in Azure, thus reducing costs. Azure Hybrid Benefit does not apply to all hybrid deployments, nor does it affect network pricing. It is specific to Windows Server and SQL Server, not to all Microsoft licenses that your organization owns.

11. C. Azure Cost Management is the service that enables you to establish budgets on your Azure subscriptions and receive alerts, making C the correct option. Azure Quota Management and Azure Budget Management are not services in Azure. Azure Monitor enables you to establish alerts but is not specific to spending or cost management.

12. D. A composite SLA is always the product of the individual SLAs for the resources in the solution, making D the correct option.

13. B. Adding more storage for the VMs increases costs but does not improve the SLA. Simply increasing the number of VMs also increases costs without improving the SLA and in fact can actually reduce the SLA depending on how they are deployed. Using availability zones can improve the SLA in this scenario.

14. A. Features and services in public preview are available to all Azure customers, regardless of how they purchase Azure, making option B incorrect. Preview features are not subject to SLAs, making option C incorrect.

15. B, C, D. Features in private preview are available to organizations by invitation from Microsoft regardless of where the customer is located. Like features in public preview, they are not subject to SLAs and are not guaranteed to move to general availability.

16. C. Microsoft provides 12 months' notice before retiring an Azure service.

Chapter 7: Creating and Managing Azure Resources

1. C. Creating a single VM is a one-off management task most easily accomplished through the Azure portal. Azure PowerShell and the Azure CLI require familiarity with the respective syntax and would be more appropriate for more complex management tasks or scripting deployment of many resources.

2. B. The Azure CLI is an implementation of Bash, making it the appropriate choice in this scenario. Azure PowerShell could be used as well but requires familiarity with PowerShell syntax. The Azure portal could also be used, but entering an Azure CLI command would generally be quicker than navigating to the resource in the Azure portal to view its properties. Azure Monitor is not an appropriate solution for viewing the properties of resources in this scenario.

3. D. Although you can script the deployment of resources using scripts with Azure PowerShell and the Azure CLI, the appropriate approach in this scenario is to use ARM templates. The templates can incorporate related resources such as networking, storage, and other resources. Resource Manager also orchestrates the deployment of resources in the proper order so you don't have to include that in your solution. The Azure portal is useful for one-off deployments of a small number of resources.

4. D. The Azure CLI is available for installation on Windows 10, Mac, and Linux, enabling it to run natively on all three. You can also run the Azure CLI from within the Azure Cloud Shell. Azure PowerShell and the Azure CLI are different tools that provide essentially the same functionality, but you cannot run one inside the other, making option D the only answer that does not fit this scenario.

5. B, C. The Azure Mobile App enables you to run the Azure CLI, and you can also run the CLI within the Azure Cloud Shell, which you access through your browser, making options B and C correct. You cannot run the Azure CLI directly in the Azure portal, but you instead must open the Azure Cloud Shell. You cannot run the Azure CLI from PowerShell.

6. C. The Security Center blade in the Azure portal provides quick access to the Security Center, where you can view alerts and security recommendations. The other options either do not exist as blades or do not provide the easiest means for accessing the Security Center.

Index

A

Account Administrator role, 95, 187
Active Directory (Azure AD),
    84–86, 185–186
ADC (application delivery controller), 64
address translation, 63
Advanced Threat Protection
    (ATP), 91, 186
Advisor, Azure, 103–105, 145, 191
AI. *See* artificial intelligence (AI)
AIP (Azure Information
    Protection), 91, 186
AKS (Azure Kubernetes Service),
    43–44, 183
answers to review questions
    cloud computing, 180–181
    core networking services, 184–185
    core services, 181–184
    pricing, service levels, and
        lifecycle, 190–191
    resources, 192
    security, compliance, privacy, and
        trust, 185–189
    solutions, 189–190
App Service, Azure, 42, 183
application delivery controller (ADC),
    64
Application Gateway, Azure, 64, 66, 184
Application Insights, 100
application layer, as a layer of defense
    in depth, 78
application rules, 80
application security group
    (ASG), 83, 185

architectural components, of core
    services, 26–33, 50
ARM (Azure Resource Manager), 33, 98,
    131, 163, 182, 187, 190
Artifacts, Azure, 130, 190
artificial intelligence (AI)
    about, 126
    Azure Bot Service, 128, 189
    Azure Cognitive Services, 128, 189
    Azure Machine Learning,
        127–128, 189
AS3 (Azure Sphere Security Service), 126
ASG (application security
    group), 83, 185
Assessment Test
    answers to, xliv–xlvii
    questions on, xxxii–xliii
assessments, in Microsoft Cloud
    Adoption Framework for Azure, 99
ATP (Advanced Threat
    Protection), 91, 186
authentication and authorization
    about, 86–87
    Azure Active Directory (Azure AD),
        84–86, 185–186
    conditional access, 87–88
    multifactor authentication
        (MFA), 87, 186
    single sign-on (SSO), 88
Automated Actions, 100
availability, as a benefit of cloud
    computing, 7
availability sets, 40–41
availability zones, 28–29, 30,
    150–151, 182

Azure, becoming certified on, xix–xx

Azure Active Directory (Azure AD),
84–86, 185–186

Azure Advisor, 103–105, 145, 191

Azure App Service, 42, 183

Azure Application Gateway, 64, 66, 184

Azure Artifacts, 130, 190

Azure Blob storage, 44–45

Azure Blueprints
about, 97–98, 187
lifecycle, 98
roles, 99

Azure Boards, 130, 190

Azure Bot Service, 128, 189

Azure China, 109–110, 181, 189

Azure CLI, 161, 163, 192

Azure Cloud Shell, 161–162, 192

Azure Cognitive Services, 128, 189

Azure Cosmos DB, 48–49, 183

Azure Cost Management + Billing,
148–149, 191

Azure Database
for MySQL, 49, 183, 184
for PostgreSQL, 49

Azure Database Migration Service,
49

Azure Dedicated Hosts, 92

Azure DevTest Labs, 131, 190

Azure ExpressRoute, 68–69, 184

Azure Files, 183

Azure Firewall, 78–80, 185

Azure Front Door, 64, 66, 184

Azure Functions, 129, 189, 190

Azure Government, 109, 188

Azure Hybrid Benefit, 147, 191

Azure Information Protection (AIP),
91, 186

Azure IoT Central, 125–126, 189

Azure IoT Hub, 124–125, 189

Azure Key Vault, 90, 186

Azure Kubernetes Service (AKS),
43–44, 183

Azure Load Balancer, 65, 184

Azure Logic Apps, 129–130, 189, 190

Azure Migration Program, 100

Azure Mobile App, 162–163, 192

Azure Monitor
about, 100–102, 188
for Containers, 100
for VMs, 100

Azure Pipelines, 130

Azure portal, 158–160, 192

Azure PowerShell, 160–161, 163, 192

Azure Repos, 130, 190

Azure Reservations, 146, 191

Azure Resource Manager (ARM), 33, 98,
131, 163, 182, 187, 190

Azure REST API, 160

Azure Security Center, 88–90, 186

Azure Sentinel, 92

Azure Service Health, 102–103, 188

Azure Sovereign Regions, 109

Azure Sphere
about, 126, 189
micro-controller units (MCUs), 126

Azure Sphere Security Service (AS3),
126

Azure SQL database, 47–48, 183, 184

Azure Status, 102, 150, 188

Azure Test Plans, 130

Azure Traffic Manager, 64, 66, 184

Azure VPN Gateway, 67–68, 184

B

billing accounts
about, 34–35
for cost efficiency, 146–147

billing scope, 35–36, 50
billing zones, 141
blades, in Azure portal, 159
Blob, Azure, 44–45
Blueprint Contributor role, 99, 188
Blueprint Operator role, 99
Blueprints, Azure
    about, 97–98, 187
    lifecycle, 98
    roles, 99
Boards, Azure, 130, 190
Bot Service, Azure, 128, 189

C

CanNotDelete lock, 97, 187
capital expenditure, 180
CDN (Content Delivery Network),
    69–70, 71, 80–81, 185
China, Azure, 109–110, 181, 189
choosing less expensive regions, 146
CLI, Azure, 161, 163, 192
client-server, 60–61
cloud computing
    about, 2–4, 18
    answers to review questions, 180–181
    benefits of, 4–9, 18, 180
    exam essentials, 18–20
    financial models, 9–10
    hybrid cloud, 17, 18, 180
    models and responsibilities, 10–16,
        18
    private cloud, 17, 18, 180
    public cloud, 16–17, 18, 180
    review questions, 21–23
Cloud Shell, Azure, 161–162, 192
Cloud Solution Provider (CSP), 139
Co-administrator role, 95
Cognitive Services, Azure, 128, 189

compliance. See security, compliance,
    privacy, and trust
compliance and data
    protection standards
    Azure China, 109–110, 189
    Azure Government, 109, 188
    Compliance Manager, 108, 188
    Data Protection Addendum
        (DPA), 107
    industry compliance standards and
        terms, 105–106
    Microsoft Privacy Statement, 106
    Microsoft Trust Center, 107, 188
    Online Service Terms (OST), 107
    Service Trust Portal, 107–108, 188
Compliance Manager, 108, 188
composite service level agreements
    (SLAs), 150, 191
compromised credentials, 91
compute layer, as a layer of defense
    in depth, 78
computing, serverless
    about, 60–61, 128–129
    Azure Functions, 129, 189, 190
    Azure Logic Apps, 129–130, 189, 190
conditional access, 87–88
consumption monitoring, with Azure
    Advisor, 145
consumption-based model, 180
container instances, 42–43, 183
Content Delivery Network (CDN),
    69–70, 71, 80–81, 185
Contributor role, 96, 99, 187
core networking services
    about, 60, 70–71
    answers to review questions, 184–185
    Azure ExpressRoute, 68–69, 184
    Azure VPN Gateway, 67–68, 184
    client-server, 60–61

Content Delivery Network (CDN),
    69–70, 185
Domain Name System (DNS), 61–62
exam essentials, 71
load balancers, 64–66
network addressing, 61
networking concepts, 60–63
review questions, 72–73
routing, 63
serverless computing, 60–61
virtual networks, 63–64
VPN Gateway, 66–69, 184
core services
    about, 26, 37, 50–51
    answers to review questions, 181–184
    architectural components, 26–33, 50
    availability sets, 40–41
    availability zones, 28–29, 30, 182
    Azure App Service, 42, 183
    Azure Blob storage, 44–45
    Azure Cosmos DB, 48–49, 183
    Azure Database for MySQL,
        49, 183, 184
    Azure Database for PostgreSQL, 49
    Azure Database Migration Service, 49
    Azure Kubernetes Service (AKS),
        43–44, 183
    Azure Resource Manager
        (ARM), 33, 182
    Azure SQL database, 47–48, 183, 184
    billing accounts, 34–35
    billing scope, 35–36, 50
    container instances, 42–43, 183
    data services, 47–49, 51
    disk storage, 45–46, 183
    exam essentials, 51–52
    file storage, 46, 183
    geographies, 26–28, 30, 181

Microsoft Marketplace, 50
    regions, 26–28, 30, 181, 182
    resource groups, 31–32, 182
    resources, 31–32, 182
    review questions, 53–57
    SQL Managed Instance, 48
    storage, 44–47, 51
    storage accounts, 46–47, 183
    structured data, 47
    subscriptions, 33–34, 50, 182
    tenants, 37
    unstructured data, 47
    virtual machine scale set, 39–40
    virtual machines (VMs), 38–39
    Windows Virtual Desktop
        (WVD), 44, 183
Cosmos DB, Azure, 48–49, 183
Cost Management + Billing, Azure,
    148–149, 191
costs
    billing for efficiency, 146–147
    estimating, 144–145
    factors affecting, 139–141
    planning and managing, 141–149
CSP (Cloud Solution Provider), 139

D

Dashboards, 100
data layer, as a layer of defense
    in depth, 78
Data Protection Addendum (DPA),
    107
data protection and
    compliance standards
    Azure China, 109–110, 189
    Azure Government, 109, 188
    Compliance Manager, 108, 188

Data Protection Addendum
(DPA), 107
industry compliance standards and
terms, 105–106
Microsoft Privacy Statement, 106
Microsoft Trust Center, 107, 188
Online Service Terms (OST), 107
Service Trust Portal, 107–108, 188
data services, 47–49, 51
data transfer, cost and, 140–141
Database, Azure
for MySQL, 49, 183, 184
for PostgreSQL, 49
Database Migration Service, Azure, 49
DDoS (distributed denial-of-service)
attack, 84, 185
Decision, as an Azure Cognitive
Service, 128
Dedicated Hosts, Azure, 92
defense in depth, 77–78
denial-of-service (DoS), 62
DevOps
about, 130, 190
Azure DevTest Labs, 131, 190
GitHub/GitHub Actions, 130, 190
services, 130
DevTest Labs, Azure, 131, 190
disaster recovery, as a benefit of cloud
computing, 8
disk storage, 45–46, 183
distributed denial-of-service (DDoS)
attack, 84, 185
DNS (Domain Name Service),
61–62, 71
domain dominance, 91
Domain Name Service (DNS), 61–62, 71
DoS (denial-of-service), 62
drag-and-drop questions, xxi

E

EA (Enterprise Agreement), 139
economic benefits, of cloud
computing, 4–5, 180
economy of scale, 180
elasticity, as a benefit of cloud
computing, 5–7
Enterprise Agreement (EA), 139
estimating costs, 144–145
exam essentials
core networking services, 71
core services, 51–52
pricing, service levels, and
lifecycle, 152–153
resources, 175–176
security, compliance, privacy, and
trust, 111–113
solutions, 131–132
exam questions
drag-and-drop, xxi
multiple choice, xx–xxi
select questions, xxi
text replacement questions, xxi
yes/no questions, xxi
ExpressRoute, Azure, 68–69, 71, 184
ExpressRoute Direct, 68, 184

F

FastTrack for Azure, 99–100
fault tolerance, 7–8, 181
file storage, 46, 183
Files, Azure, 183
financial models, of cloud
computing, 9–10
Firewall, Azure, 78–80, 185
firewall, defined, 78

FQDN (fully qualified domain name), 80
Front Door, Azure, 64, 66, 184
fully qualified domain name (FQDN), 80
Functions, Azure, 129, 189, 190

G

GDPR (General Data Protection
    Regulation), 106, 188
general availability, of service
    lifecycles, 151, 191
General Data Protection Regulation
    (GDPR), 106, 188
geographies, 26–28, 30, 181
GitHub/GitHub Actions, 130, 190
governance methodologies
    about, 93
    Azure Blueprints, 97–99
    initiatives, 94, 185, 187
    Microsoft Cloud Adoption
        Framework for Azure,
        99–100, 189
    policies, 93–94, 185, 186–187
    resource locks, 97
    role-based access control (RBAC),
        94–96, 185
Government, Azure, 109, 188

H

hands-on experience, xxii
Health Insurance Portability
    and Accountability Act
    (HIPAA), 105, 188
home lab setup, xxv
hop, network, 83
horizontal scaling, 180

human resources, as a benefit of cloud
    computing, 9
Hybrid Benefit, Azure, 147, 191
hybrid cloud, 17, 18, 180

I

identity and access layer, as a layer of
    defense in depth, 78
identity signals, 87
IEC (International Electrochemical
    Commission), 106
implementing spending limits, 146
industry compliance standards and
    terms, 105–106
Infrastructure-as-a-Service (IaaS), as a
    cloud computing model, 12–13,
    181
initiatives, Azure, 94, 185, 187
International Electrochemical
    Commission (IEC), 106
International Organization for
    Standardization (ISO), 65, 106, 188
Internet of Things (IoT)
    about, 124
    Azure IoT Central, 125–126, 189
    Azure IoT Hub, 124–125, 189
    Azure Sphere, 126, 189
IoT Central, Azure, 125–126, 189
IoT Hub, Azure, 124–125, 189
IPv4/IPv6, 61
ISO (International Organization for
    Standardization), 65, 106, 188

K

Key Vault, Azure, 90, 186

L

Language service, as an Azure Cognitive Service, 128
lateral account movement, 91
layers, load balancing and, 65
lifecycle. *See* pricing, service levels, and lifecycle
Load Balancer, Azure, 65, 184
load balancers, 64–66, 71
locks, 182
Log Analytics, 100
Logic Apps, Azure, 129–130, 189, 190

M

machine learning, 127–128, 189
management software, 126
management tools
    about, 158, 163
    Azure CLI, 161, 192
    Azure Cloud Shell, 161–162, 192
    Azure Mobile App, 162–163, 192
    Azure portal, 158–160, 192
    Azure PowerShell, 160–161, 192
    Azure Resource Manager (ARM) templates, 163
managing
    consumption with Azure Advisor, 145
    costs, 141–149
    resources, 146–147
    subscription limits, 146
    virtual machines (VMs), 146–147, 191
MFA (multifactor authentication), 87, 186
Microsoft AZ-900 Certification Exam
    about, xix

achieving AZ-900 fundamentals certification, xxii–xxiii
    becoming certified, xix–xx
    exam objectives, xxv–xxvi
    types of exam questions, xx–xxi
Microsoft Cloud Adoption Framework for Azure, 99–100, 189
Microsoft Marketplace, 50
Microsoft Privacy Statement, 106
Microsoft Trust Center, 107, 188
Migration Program, Azure, 100
MIIT (Ministry of Industry and Information Technology), 110
minimizing costs, 144–148
Ministry of Industry and Information Technology (MIIT), 110
Mobile App, Azure, 162–163, 192
models
    cloud computing, 18
    for cloud computing, 10–16
Monitor, Azure bout, 100–102, 188
monitoring and reporting options
    Azure Advisor, 103–105
    Azure Monitor, 100–102, 188
    Azure Service Health, 102–103, 188
multifactor authentication (MFA), 87, 186
multiple choice questions, xx–xxi

N

NAT rules, 80
National Institute of Standards and Technology (NIST), 106, 188
network addressing, 61
network hop, 83
network layer, as a layer of defense in depth, 78

network rules, 80
network security
    about, 77
    application security groups, 83, 185
    Azure Firewall, 78–80, 185
    defense in depth, 77–78
    distributed denial-of-service (DDoS)
        protections, 84, 185
    network security groups (NSGs),
        81–82, 185
    user-defined routes (UDRs),
        83–84, 185
    Web Application Firewall (WAF),
        80–81, 185
network security groups (NSGs),
    81–82, 185
network traffic, cost and, 140
networking addressing, 70
networking concepts, 60–63
networking services, core
    about, 60, 70–71
    answers to review questions, 184–185
    Azure ExpressRoute, 68–69, 184
    Azure VPN Gateway, 67–68, 184
    client-server, 60–61
    Content Delivery Network (CDN),
        69–70, 185
    Domain Name System (DNS),
        61–62
    exam essentials, 71
    load balancers, 64–66
    network addressing, 61
    networking concepts, 60–63
    review questions, 72–73
    routing, 63
    serverless computing, 60–61
    virtual networks, 63–64
    VPN Gateway, 66–69, 184

NIST (National Institute of Standards
    and Technology), 106, 188
NSGs (network security groups),
    81–82, 185

O

Online Service Terms (OST), 107
operational expenditures, 180
Owner role, 96, 99, 187

P

pay-as-you-go subscription, 138
perimeter layer, as a layer of defense
    in depth, 78
physical security, as a layer of defense
    in depth, 78
Pipelines, Azure, 130
planning costs, 141–149
Platform-as-a-Service (PaaS), as a cloud
    computing model, 13–15, 180
point-to-site VPN, 68, 184
policies, Azure, 93, 185, 186–187
portal, Azure, 158–160, 192
PowerShell, Azure, 160–161, 163, 192
prepaying, with Azure Reservations,
    146, 191
preview phase, of service
    lifecycles, 151, 191
pricing, service levels, and lifecycle
    about, 138, 152
    answers to review questions, 190–191
    exam essentials, 152–153
    planning and managing
        costs, 141–149
    purchasing services, 138–141
    review questions, 154–156

service level agreements
(SLAs), 149–151
service lifecycles, 151
Pricing Calculator, 143–144, 190, 191
privacy. *See* security, compliance,
privacy, and trust
private cloud, 17, 18, 180
private subnets, 63
protocol attacks, 84
public cloud, 16–17, 18, 180
public subnets, 63
purchasing services, 138–141

Q

questions, answers to review
cloud computing, 180–181
core networking services, 184–185
core services, 181–184
pricing, service levels, and
lifecycle, 190–191
resources, 192
security, compliance, privacy, and
trust, 185–189
solutions, 189–190
questions, exam
drag-and-drop, xxi
multiple choice, xx–xxi
select questions, xxi
text replacement questions, xxi
yes/no questions, xxi
questions, review
core networking services, 72–73
core services, 53–57
pricing, service levels, and
lifecycle, 154–156
resources, 177–178

security, compliance, privacy, and
trust, 114–122
solutions, 133–135
quotas, 146

R

Reader role, 96
ReadOnly lock, 97, 187
reconnaissance attacks, 91
regions, 26–28, 30, 181, 182
registering, for Microsoft AZ-900
Certification Exam, xxii
reporting and monitoring options
Azure Advisor, 103–105
Azure Monitor, 100–102, 188
Azure Service Health, 102–103, 188
Repos, Azure, 130, 190
Reservations, Azure, 146, 191
reserved capacity, 148
resource allocation, 140
resource groups, 31–32, 165–166, 182
Resource Health, 102–103, 188
resource layer attacks, 84
resource locks, 97
resources
about, 31–32, 158, 175, 182
answers to review questions, 192
creating and managing, 163–175
deleting, 174–175
exam essentials, 175–176
management tools, 158–163
managing, 146–147
review questions, 177–178
responsibilities
of cloud computing, 18
cloud computing and, 10–16

REST API, Azure, 160
review questions
    core networking services, 72–73
    core services, 53–57
    pricing, service levels, and
        lifecycle, 154–156
    resources, 177–178
    security, compliance, privacy, and
        trust, 114–122
    solutions, 133–135
review questions, answers to
    cloud computing, 180–181
    core networking services, 184–185
    core services, 181–184
    pricing, service levels, and
        lifecycle, 190–191
    resources, 192
    security, compliance, privacy, and
        trust, 185–189
    solutions, 189–190
role-based access control (RBAC)
    about, 85–86, 94–95, 185, 186
    roles in, 95–96, 187
    using with management
        scopes, 96, 187
roles
    Azure Blueprints, 99
    role assignment for RBAC, 85–86
routing, 63, 70

S

SA (Software Assurance), 147
SaaS (Software-as-a-Service), as a cloud
    computing model, 10–12, 180
sample tests, xxii

scalability, as a benefit of cloud
    computing, 5–7, 180
scope, role assignment for RBAC, 85–86
security, compliance, privacy, and trust
    about, 77, 110
    answers to review questions, 185–189
    application security group (ASG),
        83, 185
    authentication and authorization,
        84–88, 86–87, 185
    Azure Active Directory (Azure AD),
        84–86, 185–186
    Azure Advanced Threat Protection
        (ATP), 91, 186
    Azure Advisor, 103–105
    Azure Blueprint, 97–99, 187
    Azure China, 109–110, 189
    Azure Dedicated Host, 92
    Azure Firewall, 78–80, 185
    Azure Government, 109, 188
    Azure Information Protection
        (AIP), 91, 186
    Azure initiatives, 94, 185, 187
    Azure Key Vault, 90, 186
    Azure Monitor, 100–102, 188
    Azure monitoring and reporting
        options, 100–105
    Azure policies, 93–94, 93–100,
        185, 186–187
    Azure Security Center, 88–90, 186
    Azure Sentinel, 92
    Azure Service Health, 102–103, 188
    compliance and data protection
        standards, 105–110
    Compliance Manager, 108, 188
    conditional access, 87–88

Data Protection Addendum (DPA), 107

defense in depth, 77–78

distributed denial-of-service (DDoS) protection, 84, 185

exam essentials, 111–113

industry compliance standards and terms, 105–106

Microsoft Cloud Adoption Framework for Azure, 99–100, 189

Microsoft Privacy Statement, 106

Microsoft Trust Center, 107, 188

multifactor authentication (MFA), 87, 186

network security, 77–84

network security groups (NSGs), 81–82, 185

Online Service Terms (OST), 107

resource locks, 97

review questions, 114–122

role-based access control (RBAC), 94–96, 185

security tools and features, 88–92

Service Trust Portal, 107–108, 188

single sign-on (SSO), 88

user-defined routes (UDRs), 83–84, 185

Web Application Firewall (WAF), 80–81, 185

security, network

  about, 77

  application security groups, 83, 185

  Azure Firewall, 78–80, 185

  defense in depth, 77–78

distributed denial-of-service (DDoS) protections, 84, 185

network security groups (NSGs), 81–82, 185

user-defined routes (UDRs), 83–84, 185

Web Application Firewall (WAF), 80–81, 185

Security Center, Azure, 88–90, 186

security information and event management (SIEM) systems, 92

security principal, role assignment for RBAC, 85–86

select questions, xxi

Sentinel, Azure, 92

serverless computing

  about, 60–61, 128–129

  Azure Functions, 129, 189, 190

  Azure Logic Apps, 129–130, 189, 190

Service Administrator role, 95

Service Health, Azure, 102–103, 188, 191

service level agreements (SLAs)

  about, 149–150

  availability zones, 150–151

  composite, 150, 191

service levels. *See* pricing, service levels, and lifecycle

Service Trust Portal, 107–108, 188

services

  deleting, 174–175

  DevOps, 130

  purchasing, 138–141

services, core

  about, 26, 37, 50–51

  answers to review questions, 181–184

architectural components, 26–33, 50

availability sets, 40–41

availability zones, 28–29, 30, 182

Azure App Service, 42, 183

Azure Blob storage, 44–45

Azure Cosmos DB, 48–49, 183

Azure Database for MySQL, 49, 183, 184

Azure Database for PostgreSQL, 49

Azure Database Migration Service, 49

Azure Kubernetes Service (AKS), 43–44, 183

Azure Resource Manager (ARM), 33, 182

Azure SQL database, 47–48, 183, 184

billing accounts, 34–35

billing scope, 35–36, 50

container instances, 42–43, 183

data services, 47–49, 51

disk storage, 45–46, 183

exam essentials, 51–52

file storage, 46, 183

geographies, 26–28, 30, 181

Microsoft Marketplace, 50

regions, 26–28, 30, 181, 182

resource groups, 31–32, 182

resources, 31–32, 182

review questions, 53–57

SQL Managed Instance, 48

storage, 44–47, 51

storage accounts, 46–47, 183

structured data, 47

subscriptions, 33–34, 50, 182

tenants, 37

unstructured data, 47

virtual machine scale set, 39–40

virtual machines (VMs), 38–39

Windows Virtual Desktop (WVD), 44, 183

shared responsibility, as a cloud computing model, 15–16

SIEM (security information and event management) systems, 92

single sign-on (SSO), 88

site-to-site VPN, 68, 184

SLAs. *See* service level agreements (SLAs)

Smart Alerts, 100

Software Assurance (SA), 147

Software-as-a-Service (SaaS), as a cloud computing model, 10–12, 180

solutions
  about, 124, 131
  answers to review questions, 189–190
  artificial intelligence (AI), 126–128
  DevOps, 130–131
  exam essentials, 131–132
  Internet of Things (IoT), 124–126
  review questions, 133–135
  serverless computing, 128–130

Sovereign Regions, Azure, 109

Speech, as an Azure Cognitive Service, 128

spending limits, implementing, 146

Sphere, Azure
  about, 126, 189
  micro-controller units (MCUs), 126

spot pricing, 147–148

SQL Databases, Azure, 47–48, 172–174, 183, 184

SQL Managed Instance, 48

SSO (single sign-on), 88

Status, Azure, 102, 150, 188

storage, 44–47, 51

storage accounts, 46–47, 165–169, 183

structured data, 47

studying, xxii

subnets, 63

subscriptions
  about, 33–34, 50, 138–139, 182, 190

creating free, 164

managing limits, 146, 191

Sybex, contacting, xxv

T

tags, 182

TCO (Total Cost of Ownership)
Calculator, 141–142, 190, 191

templates
Azure Resource Manager (ARM), 163
in Microsoft Cloud Adoption Framework for Azure, 99

tenants, 37

Test Plans, Azure, 130

text replacement questions, xxi

time-to-live (TTL) property, 69

tools, management
about, 158, 163
Azure CLI, 161, 192
Azure Cloud Shell, 161–162, 192
Azure Mobile App, 162–163, 192
Azure portal, 158–160, 192
Azure PowerShell, 160–161, 192
Azure Resource Manager (ARM) templates, 163

tools and features, security, 88–92

Total Cost of Ownership (TCO)
Calculator, 141–142, 190, 191

Traffic Manager, Azure, 64, 66, 184

trust. *See* security, compliance, privacy, and trust

TTL (time-to-live) property, 69

U

UDRs (user-defined routes), 83–84, 185

Unified Support, 190

unstructured data, 47

uptime, 140

User Access Administrator role, 96

user-defined routes (UDRs), 83–84, 185

V

virtual machine scale set, 39–40

virtual machines (VMs)
about, 38–39
creating, 169–172
managing, 146–147, 191
spot pricing, 147–148

virtual networks, 63–64

virtual private network (VPN), 71

Vision, as an Azure Cognitive Service, 128

VMs. *See* virtual machines (VMs)

VNet service, 63–64

VNet-to-VNet VPN, 68

volumetric attacks, 84

VPN (virtual private network), 71

VPN Gateway, Azure, 66–69, 184

W

Web Application Firewall (WAF), 80–81, 185

Web Direct, 139

Windows Virtual Desktop (WVD), 44, 183

wireless access points (WAPs), 63

Workbooks, 100

Y

yes/no questions, xxi

Online Test Bank

Register to gain one year of FREE access after activation to the online inter-active test bank to help you study for your MC Azure Fundamentals certification exam—included with your purchase of this book! All of the chapter review questions and the practice tests in this book are included in the online test bank so you can practice in a timed and graded setting.

Register and Access the Online Test Bank

To register your book and get access to the online test bank, follow these steps:

1. Go to bit.ly/SybexTest (this address is case sensitive)!
2. Select your book from the list.
3. Complete the required registration information, including answering the security verification to prove book ownership. You will be emailed a pin code.
4. Follow the directions in the email or go to www.wiley.com/go/sybextestprep.
5. Find your book on that page and click the "Register or Login" link with it. Then enter the pin code you received and click the "Activate PIN" button.
6. On the Create an Account or Login page, enter your username and password, and click Login or, if you don't have an account already, create a new account.
7. At this point, you should be in the test bank site with your new test bank listed at the top of the page. If you do not see it there, please refresh the page or log out and log back in.

SYBEX
A Wiley Brand